LINES OF ENQUIRY
Studies in Latin Poetry

LINES OF ENQUIRY
Studies in Latin Poetry

NIALL RUDD

Professor of Latin in the University of Bristol

CAMBRIDGE UNIVERSITY PRESS

CAMBRIDGE

LONDON · NEW YORK · MELBOURNE

Published by the Syndics of the Cambridge University Press
The Pitt Building, Trumpington Street, Cambridge CB2 1RP
Bentley House, 200 Euston Road, London NW1 2DB
32 East 57th Street, New York, NY 10022, USA
296 Beaconsfield Parade, Middle Park, Melbourne 3206, Australia

Library of Congress catalogue card number: 75–12467

ISBN: 0 521 20993 5

First published 1976

Printed in Great Britain
by W & J Mackay Limited, Chatham

Contents

Preface

Although the book which follows cannot be said to make a formal whole, it is not just a collection of miscellaneous essays. Each chapter starts intentionally from a different position and employs a different method; yet they all converge on the subject of Latin poetry. And so, taken together, they illustrate, however imperfectly, the idea that in the study of literature no single point of view (whether philological, religious, historical, or economic) has any special authority, and that the value of a given technique depends entirely on its fruitfulness.

Apart from this impure, empirical, theory, there is another common factor. While these papers no doubt contain their share of prejudice and error, they do attempt in their different ways to expound some kind of thesis. They work through argument and are therefore open to refutation. And they assume that the old tag *de gustibus non disputandum* is something which a critic utters only when he wishes to break off an argument without coming to blows. In case this sounds too attractively pugnacious I should add that, when other writers are referred to, it means that I value their work, have learned much from it, and wish to put forward a different view only on the particular point at issue. Usually this is not a matter of direct confrontation but of trying to modify or supplement what those scholars have said. This has particular reference to Professors Rogers and Thibault (chapter 1), Austin and Williams (chapter 2), Highet and Anderson (chapter 4), Otis and Skutsch (chapter 5), and Trilling and Delany (chapter 6).

The oldest of the papers (1) is based on seminars given at Yale in 1967, though I have tried to take account of more recent material in preparing this book. A secondary purpose in writing about Ovid and Augustus at that time was to maintain that if one didn't appreciate the historical situation the satirical element would pass unnoticed, and one's understanding of the *Ars Amatoria* as literature would be impaired. That argument was more germane in the 1960s when the doctrine of poetic autonomy was still being swallowed in its undiluted form.

The only reason for writing about Dido is that she remains perennially interesting. The general position taken here is that, although Virgil may have believed that in virtue of its range and inclusiveness the Roman empire marked some kind of culmination in world history, he does not imply in his treatment of Troy and Carthage that those people were in themselves morally or culturally inferior. If by her relationship with Aeneas Dido behaved irresponsibly towards her subjects (and it is not clear that she did), the same is true of Aeneas. And although in Virgil's day a certain respect may still have been accorded to women who remained widows, there is no evidence that remarriage was considered disgraceful. So we have to think very carefully before deciding that Dido's suffering is related to her deserts.

Chapter 3 is the only essay which might claim to bring forward new facts. The interpretation is in places rather speculative but it seems reasonable to frame some sort of hypothesis about how in Persius' case the associative process worked. I should perhaps add that this chapter and chapter 5 are the most specialized sections of the book, and so the reader may take heart or warning according to his interests. In chapter 5 I do not mean to argue that the search for architectural patterns is right or wrong in principle (in fact this is a rather unprincipled book), but only that in any given case certain questions must be answered before we can be sure that such a pattern exists.

The chapter on Juvenal (4) was written during summer school in Harvard in 1972. I have put it in the middle because it looks both ways. The opening section harks back to chapter 1, for it recalls the fact that one may have to cope with a historical problem before apprehending a writer's tone; a later section makes use of translations, thus looking forward to chapter 7.

At certain periods in the history of literature it is possible to discern some central idea which is widely accepted by both poets and critics. Gradually, as a result of deep and complex forces, this idea is swept away and replaced by something almost its opposite. The second idea remains predominant, perhaps for several decades, until it too begins to lose momentum. Finally it becomes possible to see both ideas in perspective and to interpret them as opposite phases of the same preoccupation. In chapter 6 I have tried to sketch this development (which I suppose one would call Hegelian) in connection with the ideas of sincerity and the mask from the nineteenth century to our own day, and to relate this process to the criticism of ancient (mainly Latin) literature. In doing so I am also trying to draw attention to the fact that in their essential forms these ideas were well known to the ancients and were not invented at the time of the renaissance. This may strike some readers as obvious. But when one hears learned men asserting *without the necessary qualifications* that romantic love was discovered by the French in the eleventh century, or that the Italians of the fifteenth century were the first individuals, or that the Spanish invented the picaresque novel in 1554, or that the English around 1600 brought about 'something like a mutation in human nature' by discovering sincerity, then one has a real fear that the ancient world may be slipping out of the consciousness of educated people.

Much of the best criticism of classical literature is to be found in essays on translation. There is a continuous tradition stretching from Dryden's prefaces (to go no further back) to Matthew Arnold, and from him to Ezra Pound and the critics of our own day. This long-standing interest in translation has led to a great variety of theories, which have been very clearly outlined by Theodore Savory.[1] While I should like to think that chapter 7 had benefited from those discussions, it contains very little theorizing. Nor does it do much to explain why a particular translation satisfied the requirements of its period. This interesting question has been taken up by M. R. Ridley[2] and others, but I am not qualified to discuss it, and in any case my purpose is different – namely, to use translations as a means of exploring certain Latin poems. As comparison is a two-way process, this has also involved some comment on the translations, but I have tried to keep such remarks within reasonable limits.

I should like to thank the readers of the Cambridge University Press for several comments and suggestions, one of which has led to the disappearance of an entire chapter. I have also received help from other scholars, in particular Mr D. A. Russell who read a draft of chapter 6. I am grateful to the Loeb Classical Library (Harvard University Press: William Heinemann) for permission to quote from its translations of Dio and Suetonius; to the Clarendon Press for permission to quote from Mr D. A. Russell's translation of Longinus (Oxford 1965); to Mr L. P. Wilkinson for permission to quote his translation of Ovid,

---

[1] T. Savory, *The Art of Translation* (London 1968). A very useful bibliography is that of B. Q. Morgan in *On Translation*, ed. R. A. Brower (Oxford 1966) 271–93.

[2] M. R. Ridley, *Second Thoughts* (London 1965). Ridley is primarily concerned with Homer. On this topic see also H. A. Mason, *To Homer through Pope* (London 1972).

Amores 1.5, which appeared in *Ovid Recalled* (Cambridge 1955); and to Mr A. G. Lee for permission to quote his translation of the same poem, taken from *Ovid's Amores* (John Murray 1968). But my chief debt is to former colleagues at Toronto and Liverpool, who talked to me about literature and other things at various tables and bars over a period of fifteen years. I thank them most warmly.

Abbreviations

AJA	*American Journal of Archaeology*
AJP	*American Journal of Philology*
CP	*Classical Philology*
CQ	*Classical Quarterly*
CR	*Classical Review*
D.L.	Diogenes Laertius
HSCP	*Harvard Studies in Classical Philology*
JRS	*Journal of Roman Studies*
PBSR	*Papers of the British School at Rome*
REL	*Revue des études latines*
Rh. Mus.	*Rheinisches Museum*
TAPA	*Transactions of the American Philological Association*
TLL	*Thesaurus Linguae Latinae*
W	*Remains of Old Latin*, ed. E. H. Warmington, Loeb Classical Library
WS	*Wiener Studien*
YCS	*Yale Classical Studies*

1
HISTORY
Ovid and the Augustan myth

Writing from exile in A.D. 9 Ovid says that two things ruined him – a poem and a blunder:

> perdiderint cum me duo crimina, carmen et error
>
> (*Trist.* 2.207)

The blunder remains mysterious, and I have no new suggestions to offer. Presumably, however, it was quite a serious matter, for when Ovid confessed to his friend Cotta, who was then on the island of Elba, what had taken place, Cotta was very angry.[1] Soon after, Augustus summoned the poet to Rome, reviled him bitterly,[2] and imposed a savage penalty which was never revoked. Ovid says more than once that the blunder was the more serious charge, and on other occasions he speaks as if that had been the decisive factor.[3] So it is hard to agree with those scholars who over the centuries have maintained that the real reason for Augustus' anger was the *Ars Amatoria* and that the blunder was only used as a pretext for getting rid of the poet.[4]

The opposite approach has been more common. Many writers since the renaissance have ignored or underestimated the effect of the poem. To them the *error* was all important, though they disagree about what it may have been. A few have supposed that Ovid came upon something by chance in the imperial palace – theories range from Augustus committing incest to Livia having a bath. Several have conjectured that Ovid became involved in a conspiracy centred on Agrippa Postumus, the emperor's grandson. Most believe that he somehow got mixed up

---

[1] *Pont.* II.3.61–4.   [2] *Trist.* 2.133; *Pont.* II.7.56.

[3] *Pont.* II.9.72–6; III.3.71–6; *Trist.* 2.109–10; IV.10.99–100.

[4] The evidence concerning Ovid's exile, and the various theories that have been held about it, are set forth very fully and clearly by J. C. Thibault in *The Mystery of Ovid's Exile* (California 1964). The older discussion by S. G. Owen in his commentary on *Trist.* 2 (1924) is also well worth reading.

in the affairs of the younger Julia.[5] Vague as it is, the last theory may well be right. All I am concerned to argue is that the *Ars Amatoria* contributed to the poet's fall.

Let us start with a few negative considerations. It is often maintained that the interval between the publication of the *Ars Amatoria* and Ovid's banishment was so long that one event could have had no bearing on the other. It is true that Ovid himself makes a great deal of this in *Trist.* 2.539–46:

> 'Long ago I too sinned in writing poetry of that kind [i.e. amatory verse]. So a misdemeanour which is not new is paying a new penalty...The poems which in my thoughtless youth I believed would bring me no harm have now brought me harm in my old age. The vengeance which you have taken for that little volume of long ago is late and overwhelming. The punishment has come a long time after the act which provoked it.'

That passage is designed to show how unreasonable it was to punish the poet for writing the *Ars Amatoria*, and so it exaggerates the interval in question, making it sound like one of at least twenty years. Several modern scholars, like Owen, Rogers, and Thibault, have accepted Ovid's plea rather too easily. They all speak of a ten-year period. But if the poem was finally published in A.D. 1 and Ovid was exiled towards the end of A.D. 8, we get a period of just over seven years, and that, surely, was not too long.[6] Consider a rather similar point which arose in the case of Oscar Wilde. At the trial of Lord Queensberry at the Old Bailey on 3 April 1895 Sir Edward Clarke in his opening speech for the prosecution referred to what he called 'an extremely curious count at the end of the plea', namely that in July 1890 Mr Wilde published, or caused to be published, with his name upon the title page a certain immoral and indecent work, with the title of The Picture of Dorian Gray, which was intended to be understood by the readers to describe the relations, intimacies, and passions of certain persons guilty of unnatural practices. That, said Sir Edward, was a very gross allegation. The volume could be bought at any bookstall in London. It had Mr Wilde's name on the title page and had been published five years.[7]

---

[5] See Thibault, *The Mystery of Ovid's Exile*, Appendix 1.

[6] The poem may have been published in instalments in the period 1 B.C. to A.D. 1.

[7] Stuart Mason, *Oscar Wilde: Art and Morality* (London 1912) 203–4.

At this point it may occur to us to put a very simple question: if the *Ars Amatoria* had nothing to do with Ovid's downfall, why does he say the opposite on more than one occasion? R. S. Rogers is candid enough to face this problem. His solution is that Ovid knew his blunder was *not* defensible and therefore devoted most of his excuses to the poem, which *was* defensible.[8] If Rogers is right, we have to assume that in the second book of the *Tristia*, which contains nearly six hundred lines, Ovid is like a man arraigned for dangerous driving, who protests at great length and with great ingenuity that he has never picked a pocket in his life.

Another argument which one occasionally hears is that Ovid states explicitly in at least six passages that the *Ars* is a guide to the relations of men and *freed*women; it was not intended for married ladies and therefore could not have had any harmful effect on social morality. Not many readers, I imagine, take these protestations seriously, but it is worth considering for a moment just why they *are* so unconvincing. First of all the Roman public would have approached the *Ars* with expectations already engendered by the *Amores*. In *Amores* ii.1.3f. Ovid serves warning that his poems are not for the strict (*procul hinc, procul este, seueri*). But there is no social distinction implied; and indeed we are asked to believe that the work is especially suitable for engaged couples:

> me legat in sponsi facie non frigida uirgo
> *I hope to be read by the girl who feels a glow at the sight of her fiancé.*

(In connection with the special status of the betrothed one thinks of the two highly respectable old ladies who stood looking at Rodin's statue 'The Kiss'. After a minute's silence one turned to the other and remarked rather dubiously: 'I take it they must be engaged...') In ii.4.47–8 Ovid says: 'Whatever girls are admired by anyone in the entire city – my love has designs on them all.' That comes at the end of a piece which sets out in great detail just how comprehensive the poet's aspirations are. Or take a verse like iii.4.37:

> rusticus est nimium quem laedit adultera coniunx
> *only an oaf is offended by his wife's infidelities.*

Those words occur in a poem committed to the thesis that if a husband refuses to connive at his wife's adultery he is a bad sport, a bore, and no gentleman.

[8] R. S. Rogers, *TAPA* 97 (1966) 377–8.

There are also passages in the *Ars Amatoria* itself which seem to rule out any distinction within the female population. In 1.269–70, for example, we have the following:

> prima tuae menti ueniat fiducia cunctas
> posse capi; capies, tu modo tende plagas.

> *You must first convince yourself that all girls can be caught. You will catch them; all you have to do is spread your nets.*

Shortly after, we are told that it is an adynaton – an actual reversal of nature – for a girl to refuse a presentable man. Are we really supposed to say to ourselves: 'Of course he means every girl *except* the wives of the upper classes'? The fact is, surely, that the nature of the didactic genre demands that the author's precepts should be universally valid. Ovid's lover and his lass are in the same category as the farmer, the fisherman, the hunter, and the other types made familiar by the didactic poetry of Hellenistic Greece. The τέχναι which govern these various occupations are entirely independent of social distinctions.

Last of all, some of Ovid's disclaimers look rather odd when seen in their context. In 1.33–4 we read:

> nos Venerem tutam concessaque furta canemus
> inque meo nullum carmine crimen erit.

> *I will sing of sex which is not illicit and of intrigues which are allowed; in my song there will be no wrong.*

The previous couplet, however, is this:

> este procul, uittae tenues, insigne pudoris,
> quaeque tegis medios instita longa pedes.

> *Keep away, ye fine headbands, badge of purity, and the long flounce that reveals only the toes.*

The headband and flounce were the signs of respectable womanhood, but the formula *este procul*, which recalls the Sibyl's *procul o procul este profani*, suggests that Ovid is celebrating *sacra* or rites of a holy kind from which these ladies must be rigorously excluded. It is they who are in danger of blasphemy, not the poet.[9]

---

[9] 'Écrire en tête d'un ouvrage "Éloignez-vous d'ici, vous qui portez des bandelettes légères, insigne de la pudeur", n'est-ce-pas donner à quelques-unes d'entre elles le désir de s'approcher?...La manière de tromper un mari ressemble beaucoup à celle de tromper un amant.'
G. Boissier, *L'Opposition sous les Césars* (sixth ed. Paris 1909) 124. The whole chapter on Ovid's exile is full of charm and good sense.

4

In 2.152ff. Ovid recommends that love should be fostered by sweet talk; quarrelling should be left to those who are married. 'That is appropriate for wives; quarrels are a wife's dowry – *hoc decet uxores; dos est uxoria lites.* But see to it that a mistress always hears welcome words. It is not by the law's decree that you have ended up in the same bed. In your case love does the duty of law.' Here there is certainly a distinction between Ovidian and conjugal love, but the advantage seems to lie heavily with the former. Marriage means strife – better give it a miss. Would this amusing advice have appealed to the emperor, who was trying so hard to promote matrimony? Would the epigram *dos est uxoria lites* have pleased the Empress Livia, who had dedicated a shrine to Concordia and presented it to her dear husband?[10] And do the phrases *legis iussu* and *munere legis* not look dangerously like defiant references to the *leges Iuliae*? There is no doubt that *amor* is seen as something alien to *lex*.

In 2.557ff. young men are advised not to catch their girlfriends out: 'Let them sin, and as they do so let them think they are fooling you.' Detection only makes matters worse – a point illustrated by the story of Mars and Venus. Presented in ample, if not extravagant, detail, it culminates in the assertion that Vulcan, the injured husband, was a stupid interfering fool; his action only made the guilty pair more determined. Turning to his readers Ovid says: 'You be warned by this; Venus' detection warns you not to set such traps' (593–4). That is really the end of the section and the conclusion is plain enough. But Ovid goes on to say that this kind of detective work should only be practised by husbands, though even they may not think it worth while. And then comes the formal disclaimer: 'You see – I say it again – there is no game here that is not allowed by law. No flounce takes part in my fun' (599–600). Did Ovid really believe that this feeble couplet cancelled out the effect of the previous fifty lines?

Finally, in 3.611ff. Ovid says:

> qua uafer eludi possit ratione maritus
> quaque uigil custos, praeteriturus eram.
> nupta uirum timeat, rata sit custodia nuptae:
> hoc decet, hoc leges duxque pudorque iubent.
> te quoque seruari, modo quam uindicta redemit,
> quis ferat? ut fallas, ad mea sacra ueni.

I was going to pass over the techniques for bamboozling a cunning husband or a vigilant guardian. Let a wife respect her husband, let

10 Ovid. *Fast.* iv.637–8.

5

there be thorough surveillance over a wife; that is proper, that is enjoined by law, decency, and our leader. But that a watch should be kept on you too, who have just been freed by the Praetor's rod – who would stand for that? Come to my service and learn how to practise deception.

Freedwomen, then, are fair game. And they for their part may be expected to use every wile to outwit the men who would restrict them. This carefree attitude, however, was not shared by Augustus. In the *leges Iuliae* he had made it legal for every citizen, except senators, to marry freedwomen. According to Dio (LIV.16.2), ἐπέτρεψε καὶ ἐξελευθέρας τοῖς ἐθέλουσι, πλὴν τῶν βουλευόντων, ἄγεσθαι, ἔννομον τὴν τεκνοποιίαν αὐτῶν εἶναι κελεύσας. We may be fairly sure that when Augustus passed this measure he did not add as a rider that such women would, of course, be at liberty to deceive their husbands and would be exempt from the penalties of adultery.

To sum up: Ovid's disclaimers are unconvincing because we already know the *Amores*, because the effect of his protestations is obliterated by the rest of the material, and because the protestations themselves are nearly always nullified by the context. The *Ars Amatoria*, then, is really all-inclusive – indeed all-embracing – in its message. As Matthew Prior put it:

> Ovid is the surest guide
>   You can name to show the way
> To any woman, maid or bride,
>   Who resolves to go astray.

So far our attention has been focused mainly on Ovid. It is time now to consider the other actor in the drama – viz, the Emperor Augustus. Here we shall be criticizing a different line of reasoning – one which contends that since Augustus was a man of the world with a rather dubious past he could not possibly have been shocked by the *Ars Amatoria* and therefore the poem could not have contributed to Ovid's disgrace.

There is not much evidence concerning Augustus' love-life, but there is too much to present here, and so I shall have to select and summarize. First, many people thought he showed an unbecoming impatience in divorcing Scribonia and marrying Livia just three months before the birth of Livia's son Drusus. When Drusus was born rumour suspected that Augustus (then Octavian) was the father, and the following verse became popular:

τοῖς εὐτυχοῦσι καὶ τρίμηνα παιδία[11]

The fortunate have babies in three months.

Secondly, a year or two before Actium Antony complained about the campaign of vilification which was being directed against him and Cleopatra. He alleged that Octavian for his part was having immoral relationships with Tertulla, Terentilla, Rufilla, and Salvia Titisenia.[12] If this is to be discounted because of Antony's malice, another piece of evidence is suspect for the opposite reason. I refer to the eulogy of Octavian by Nicolaus of Damascus, in which we are told that Octavian had to attend divine service at night because his good looks drove women mad. 'But although they plotted to ensnare him he was never taken captive, partly because his mother shooed them all away and protected him, partly because he was exceptionally sensible for his years.'[13] One can't help feeling that this kind of testimony raises the very suspicions it was designed to quell.

Those passages all refer to the Triumviral period. Suetonius (71) says that later too (*postea quoque*) Augustus had the reputation of being keen on young girls. No doubt he had, and perhaps he deserved it. But when Suetonius adds that his wife and others used to obtain such girls for him from all over the place, our credulity falters. There is something decidedly implausible about Livia in the role of imperial procuress. The same kind of discrimination is called for in dealing with Dio LIV.16.3. There we are told that in 18 B.C. comments were made in the senate about the promiscuity of women and young men; this was alleged to be the reason for their reluctance to marry. Senators urged Augustus to set this right too, making ironical allusions to his intimacy with numerous women (ὅτι πολλαῖς γυναιξὶν ἐχρῆτο). According to Dio the emperor gave a rather weak reply. Again, this account may be taken as further evidence of the emperor's reputation, but it is hard to believe that senators would have dared to go in for that kind of bar-room banter with the Princeps. Finally there was a rumour that Augustus had an affair with Maecenas' wife Terentia.[14] There is

---

[11] Suetonius, *Claud.* 1.1.   [12] Suetonius, *Aug.* 69.

[13] See C. M. Hall, *Smith College Classical Studies* 4 (1923). The passage comes from Nicolaus, chap. 5. In chap. 15 he adds the remarkable fact (θαυμαστόν τι) that at an age when young men are especially licentious Octavian abstained from sex for a whole year. The motive ascribed, however, is perhaps not the highest: it was for the sake of his voice and general physique.

[14] Dio LIV.19.3. Dio is the only source, unless we identify Terentia with the Terentilla mentioned by Antony in the letter cited by Suetonius, *Aug.* 69. In that case we have to believe that the affair lasted at least sixteen years.

nothing inherently incredible in such an idea, but when Dio reports that some people believed that the reason why Augustus set out for Gaul in 16 B.C. was his wish to live quietly with Terentia beyond the reach of gossip, and when he adds that Augustus was so in love with Terentia that he made her enter a beauty contest against Livia, then one sighs for evidence of a more pedestrian kind. Let us suppose, then, that there was something in what Dio and Suetonius say, and that the emperor allowed himself an occasional mistress; that still would not mean that he was willing to overlook the tone and implications of the *Ars Amatoria*, for there was, I would suggest, a tension, and in certain matters a contradiction, between the private and public areas of Augustus' personality.

In the spring of 1869, during the excavations ordered by Napoleon III, a house was discovered on the Palatine under the imperial residence. Because her name was found on one of the pipes this is commonly called the House of Livia, but Lugli, Maiuri, and many others believe that it is in fact the house of Augustus, as described by Suetonius. On the back wall of the tablinum is a painting of Polyphemus wading after Galatea, who is making her escape on the back of a hippocamp. A winged eros stands on Polyphemus' shoulders and guides him with reins. Two nereids are to be seen, one in the centre background and one on the left, while in the foreground Galatea sits sidesaddle on the hippocamp, half draped, with her back to the viewer and looking over her right shoulder at her gigantic but gentle pursuer. The picture on the right wall, though damaged, is better preserved and can be seen in Maiuri's book entitled *Roman Painting*, published in the Skira series. It represents Io in a bluish grey, rather diaphanous, dress, sitting on a rock in the centre foreground. She is observed from the right by a completely humanized Argus; and on the left, coming round the corner of the rock, is the figure of Mercury. In the reproductions printed by Rizzo two tiny horns are sprouting from Io's forehead. Maiuri comments: 'Such romantic tales of the loves of the gods were in high favour, not only with the artists of Rome and Campania, but also with the local élite. Indeed the upper class had a predilection for those amorous adventures of maidens in distress which were the stock in trade of the Alexandrian littérateurs.'[15] Not very much hinges on this,

---

In two passages that are hostile to Terentia (*Epist.* 114.4–6 and *De Prov.* 3.10–11) Seneca says nothing about her alleged adultery with Augustus.

[15] A. Maiuri, *Roman Painting* (English trans. by S. Gilbert) 28. The fullest description and illustration of these paintings will be found in G. E. Rizzo, *Monumenti della pittura antica scoperti in Italia*, sec. III, Roma, Fasc. III.

but if the house *is* that of Augustus the decoration suggests that in private the emperor could enjoy works which were not dedicated with a heavy seriousness to glorifying himself, his family, and his regime.

Augustus' private taste in art was consistent with his private taste as a writer. He once began a tragedy on the subject of Ajax, but failed to complete it; and when his friends asked how Ajax was coming on he replied that the hero had fallen on his sponge (Suet. *Aug.* 85.2). Epigram was more in his line. Pliny the elder mentions verses in Greek, written for the dedication of a picture in Caesar's temple (*NH* 35.91). Another couplet is referred to by Macrobius (II.4.31). Apparently a Greekling had made several attempts to hand Augustus a complimentary epigram as he came down from the Palatine. When the emperor saw him pressing forward again, he quickly scribbled a couplet and sent it to the other man first. Unfortunately the contents are not preserved. Two other trivial verses in Greek *are* preserved; they will be found in Suetonius, *Aug.* 98.4. A more serious composition was a poem in Latin hexameters on Sicily. No doubt it described the history, legends, and sights of the island – including Etna, which Seneca says was a regular topic for poets (*Epist.* 79.5). Suetonius, who mentions this poem (85.2) also refers to an epitaph in Latin verse carved on Drusus' tomb (Suet. *Claud.* 1.5).

More important, perhaps, for our purpose are the abusive verses written in the Triumviral period. Some were directed at Pollio, who wisely refrained from answering back: *at ego taceo; non est enim facile in eum scribere qui potest proscribere* – 'But I'll keep my mouth shut, for it isn't easy to write *against* someone who can write you *off*' (Macrobius II.4.21). Other pieces were aimed at Antony and Fulvia and were so indecent that Martial judged them worthy of praise and preservation. They can be found in the twentieth epigram of Book XI. Much later, when Pliny was justifying his own rather frivolous lines (*uersiculos seueros parum*), he said 'Need I be afraid that a practice which was proper for the divine Augustus and others should be somewhat *im*proper for me?' (*Epist.* 5.3). As we know from *Epist.* 4.14, Pliny's verses were hendecasyllables of a rather risqué kind. 'If some of them', he says, 'seem a little on the naughty side (*petulantiora paulo*), bear in mind that the highly distinguished and respectable men who have written such pieces have not refrained from wanton subject-matter nor even from unvarnished phrases.'

We therefore possess or know of the following pieces: a few improvisations and a dedicatory epigram in Greek, a longer poem in Latin hexameters on Sicily, an epitaph on Drusus (presumably in elegiacs), fescennine verses against Pollio, Fulvia, and Antony, and some *nugae* of a saucy kind (probably in hendecasyllables). Suetonius also mentions a short book of epigrams which the emperor composed in the bath (Suet. *Aug. 85*). When to all this we add some items from his private correspondence and the remarks attributed to him and made about him by others,[16] it is clear that Augustus had sufficient taste and wit to understand what Ovid was doing. In fact he understood it all too well.

The tension in Augustus' mind between public and private can also be seen in his attitude to his own moral legislation. Although he passed laws against adultery one has the impression that he was reluctant to take account of particular cases. During his censorship a young man was brought to trial for committing adultery with a woman whom he had subsequently married. Augustus was embarrassed – perhaps because he had done the same thing himself – and after some hesitation he said in effect: 'Go away and don't let it happen again' (Dio LIV. 16.6). It has often been remarked that while the emperor did his best to promote marriage and so arrest the falling birthrate, his friends Horace and Virgil remained single all their days. And Dio (LVI.10.3) calls attention to the fact that the consuls Papius and Poppaeus who brought in the marriage law of A.D. 9 were 'not only childless, but not even married' – an odd but quite logical distribution of emphasis.

But this tolerance, however limited, was not extended to his own family. 'In bringing up his daughter and grand-daughters', says Suetonius (*Aug. 64.2*), 'he even had them taught spinning and weaving, and he forbade them to say or do anything except openly and such as might be recorded in the household diary.' Augustus, who had many old-fashioned patriarchal views, may have thought that the ordinary Roman family should be reared in this way. But in any case his was not an ordinary Roman family; it was the royal family and the dynasty depended on it. He was therefore quite ruthless in his treatment of Julia, marrying her first to Marcellus (Dio LIII.27.5), then to Agrippa (LIV.6.5), and finally to Tiberius (LIV.31.2, Suet. *Aug. 63*); and compelling the last two men to divorce wives with whom they were happily settled. Not surprisingly this treatment of a spirited young woman led to trouble. In 2 B.C. the rumours of Julia's behaviour could no longer be hushed up and the scandal broke. It was more than a matter of sexual immorality. Of the five *nobiles* mentioned as ringleaders by Velleius (II.100.4–5) the most striking is Iullus Antonius, who as Augustus'

16 See H. Malcovati, *Imperatoris Caesaris Augusti Operum Fragmenta* (Paravia 1962).

nephew stood fourth in relation to the emperor. Leaving out Agrippa Postumus, we have first the grandsons Gaius and Lucius who were both in their teens, then Tiberius who was in disgrace on the island of Rhodes, and then Antonius (who was, of course, Mark Antony's son). So the affair looks like a conspiracy, though we cannot tell what its immediate objectives were. At any rate Augustus handled it under the heading of treason and sacrilege, and inflicted cruel punishments (Tacitus, *Ann.* 3.24). The point I wish to emphasize here is that according to Dio (LV.10.16) many other women were also involved in the scandal. 'But the emperor would not entertain all the suits; instead he set a definite date as a limit and forbade all prying into what had occurred previous to that time. For although in the case of his daughter he would show no mercy. . .he was disposed to spare the rest.' Later (LVI.40.6) Tiberius is made to say of Augustus 'He was relentless in dealing with wantonness on the part of his next of kin, but he treated the offences of others humanely.' An earlier incident is mentioned by Dio (LV.10.11–12) in which knights and women of some social consequence were induced to go on the stage. Although he must have disapproved strongly, Augustus took no notice. So again we have the same point. Anyone who caused a threat to the prestige or security of the regime was likely to suffer. Other offenders escaped more lightly.

This brings us to the obscure affair of the younger Julia's exile.[17] Her husband L. Aemilius Paulus was executed perhaps in A.D. 1 and Julia was banished. She was later restored, but was banished again in A.D. 8. At the same time Augustus withdrew his friendship from D. Junius Silanus, and the latter went into voluntary exile. This, it seems, was the web in which Ovid became entangled. His *error*, whatever it may have been, was the decisive factor in his ruin, but he knew that the *carmen* had been a contributory cause.

Yet he couldn't see why. In the second book of the *Tristia*, looking back on the whole dismal affair, he pleads that the *Ars Amatoria* was not intended for married women; it did not reflect his own morals; and it was not a lampoon. Others had written about frivolities like dice and ball-games without giving offence; generations of poets from Anacreon to Propertius had been preoccupied with love; writers of mimes had presented indecent episodes on the stage; famous painters had depicted romantic or erotic subjects. Why was he the only one to suffer? The sad thing about these arguments is that they were all true – and

---

[17] See Suetonius, *Aug.* 19.1; the scholiast on Juvenal 6.158; Tacitus, *Ann.* 4.71; Suetonius, *Aug.* 65.4; Tacitus, *Ann.* 3.24; R. Syme, *The Roman Revolution* 432, n. 4.

all beside the point. For what angered Augustus in the *Ars Amatoria* was not merely that Ovid had written about sex, but that he had done so in such a way as to make fun of the regime and its policies. The cleverness and urbanity which pervaded the poem made its satire all the more insidiously subversive.

Before going on to consider where the satire lay I should like to take account of one possible criticism, namely that some of the topics which occur in the *Ars* had already been employed by Tibullus and Propertius and might therefore be regarded as traditional to the genre. There is some force in this argument; a great deal of Ovid's material *is* traditional. But when we put similar motifs side by side the Ovidian passage is often found to contain a different tone or emphasis. A few examples must suffice. In 1.6.67–8 Tibullus expresses the hope that Delia will remain pure (i.e. confine her attentions to him) even though she is not entitled to wear the headband and robe of a Roman matron. Ovid assumes that women without the headband and robe (i.e. freedwomen) will be promiscuous. On two occasions (II.32.11–12 and IV.8.75) Propertius speaks of a colonnade as a fashionable rendezvous for young men and girls, but in each case it is the colonnade of Pompey and so, unlike those mentioned by Ovid, it is not directly connected with the imperial house. Or again, at II.6.21–2 Propertius maintains that Romulus himself, by arranging the abduction of the Sabine women, set a precedent for the lax behaviour of later times. This is the germ of a passage in Ovid which will be discussed below. But Propertius deplores the situation he describes and strongly affirms his own fidelity:

> semper amica mihi semper et uxor eris (42)

> *you will always be my girl and my wife too,*

whereas Ovid regards 'swinging Rome' as a source of challenge and excitement.

One cannot always draw such distinctions, but it remains true that the implicitly anti-Augustan motifs in Ovid are part of a major poem with a unified conception, which at any rate purports to advocate the pursuit of *amor* as a way of life. The elegies of Tibullus and Propertius are not pervaded by the same ethos of blithe immorality.

Equally important is the factor of chronology. Augustus was in his thirties and early forties when Propertius and Tibullus were publishing their work; he was seventy when he banished Ovid to Tomis. By that time he was a sick and sad old man. His programme for moral reform had been defied by his own daughter and grand-daughter; his dynastic plans had gone tragically awry; the Pannonian revolt had been raging for over two years;[18] there was a plague in Rome and famine in Italy. Pliny the elder tells us that these and other troubles brought the emperor to the verge of suicide.[19] The year A.D. 8 was a bad time to incur his displeasure.

In chapters 19–21 of the *Res Gestae* Augustus records his proud achievement in transforming the face of Rome.[20] Temples, theatres, porticoes, and aqueducts are mentioned, in addition to his new forum. To these can be added arches, baths, gardens, granaries, warehouses, docks, a mausoleum, and many other projects. Like the *Aeneid* and the Roman Odes, these works contributed to and helped to define the Augustan spirit. But there were certain buildings in which, it is safe to assume, the emperor took a special interest. One was the temple of Apollo on the Palatine, vowed during the war against Sextus Pompeius in 36 B.C. and dedicated in 28. An important feature of this building was the colonnade of the Danaids (the fifty daughters of Danaus who, with one exception, murdered their husbands on the instructions of their father). It is mentioned by Augustus himself in the *Res Gestae*, and also by Propertius, Velleius, Suetonius, and Dio. How does Ovid pay tribute to this magnificent colonnade? Well, in the *Amores* II.2.3ff. he tells us that he saw a pretty girl walking there, and on making the usual proposition he was told to his dismay that her guardian Bagoas made any progress impossible. In the *Ars* the Porticus is referred to three times.[21] In each case it is commended not for its columns of *giallo antico* nor for its impressive statuary,[22] but simply because it provides an excellent hunting-ground for young men on the loose.

Another colonnade offering similar facilities was the Porticus Liviae, which Augustus built on the site of Vedius Pollio's house and dedicated to Livia in 7 B.C. (Vedius Pollio will be remembered as the gentleman who dealt with unsatisfactory servants by feeding them to his lampreys – Dio LIV.23.2.) Livia's portico is mentioned twice in the

---

18 For an account of this see J. J. Wilkes, *Dalmatia* (London 1969) 68–77.
19 Pliny, *NH* 7.149.
20 Apart from the *Res Gestae* (which is printed along with Velleius in the Loeb series), the main works of reference used in what follows are Platner and Ashby, *Topographical Dictionary of Ancient Rome* (London 1929) and F. W. Shipley, 'The Building Activities of the Viri Triumphales from 44 B.C. to A.D. 14' in *Memoirs of the American Academy in Rome* 9 (1931).
21 *AA* 1.73–4; 1.492; 3.389. The first reference is specific, the other two general.
22 See Propertius II.31.3–4; Ovid, *Trist.* III.1.59–62; the scholiast on Persius 2.56.

Ars.[23] It surrounded the Aedes Concordiae which was dedicated to her husband.

Yet another colonnade was the Porticus Argonautarum, built by Agrippa in 25 B.C. to commemorate the victories of Naulochus and Actium. Ovid refers to it in a lofty periphrasis as the monument constructed by 'The son-in-law whose head is wreathed with naval glory' – *navalique gener cinctus honore caput* (3.392). This recalls Virgil's sonorous line *tempora navali fulgent rostrata corona* (*Aen*. 8.684). In Virgil Agrippa is portrayed on the shield of Aeneas and takes his place in the mighty pageant of Roman history. In Ovid he earns mention for providing a congenial setting in which a girl can find a lover.

Lastly there was the Porticus Octaviae.[24] This replaced the colonnade of Q. Caecilius Metellus some time after 27 B.C. It was a magnificent marble building containing many famous works of art, of which one was a seated statue of Cornelia, mother of the Gracchi.[25] We can imagine the great lady glaring down in horrified disapproval at the goings-on described by Ovid.

If we add the theatre of Marcellus, which is referred to in the same sort of spirit,[26] we now have works associated with Augustus' father, his wife, his sister, his son-in-law, his nephew, and his patron deity. He must have been in some sense emotionally involved in these buildings. And apart from personal considerations the buildings served a national purpose. It does not matter which exact purpose we choose to emphasize. Were they to honour the gods, to beautify the capital, to dignify the Roman *imperium*, to glorify the ruling house, to impress foreign visitors, or to please the *plebs*? It doesn't greatly matter, I say, because the power and prestige were inseparable. If the prestige was damaged the power suffered too.

The places just referred to were all in Rome, but there were also attractions elsewhere. The coastal town of Baiae, for instance, was notorious for its luxury and dissipation. It was the scene of Clodia's activities – or at least some of them (Cicero, *Pro Cael*. 47–9). Propertius was understandably concerned when Cynthia lingered there (I.11.27–30):

23 *AA* 1.71–2; 3.391.
24 For the Porticus Octaviae see, in addition to Platner and Ashby,
   M. J. Boyd, *PBSR* 21 (1953) 152–9.
25 Cornelia's statue is mentioned by Pliny, *NH* 34.31.
26 *AA* 3.394. Marcellus is also the *natus* mentioned in 1.69; the building
   referred to there is probably the library erected in his honour by Octavia.
   See Plutarch, *Marcellus* 30; Platner and Ashby, *Topographical Dictionary of
   Ancient Rome*, 427.

tu modo quam primum corruptas desere Baias:
    multis ista dabunt litora discidium,
litora quae fuerant castis inimica puellis:
    a pereant Baiae, crimen amoris, aquae!

*Get away from the corruption of Baiae as soon as possible. That
stretch of coast will cause many a couple to break up. It has always
been a danger-spot for good girls. To hell with Baiae and its
waters! They give love a bad name.*

Seneca wrote a moral epistle (51) on the iniquity of the place, speaking
of 'the drunks wandering along the beach, the yachting parties, the
lakes loud with the songs of musicians, and all the other sins which
luxury not only commits but actually flaunts, when it has been released,
as it were, from the restraints of law'. Augustus delivered a stiff reprimand to Lucius Vinicius, a polite young gentleman, who had acted with
insufficient decency (*parum modeste*) in coming to call on Julia in
Baiae. Martial, as usual, put it most compactly. Of a wife who visited
Baiae he said: *Penelope uenit, abit Helene* (1.62.6) – 'she was a Penelope
when she arrived, a Helen when she left'. It was precisely this reputation which led Ovid to recommend the place to predatory young men
(1.253–8). In citing this passage I am not arguing that in itself the
reference would have given offence. But with dozens of others it helped
to constitute an ethos which Augustus was bound to regard as the
negation of everything his government stood for.

We now move on to something with which the emperor was more
directly concerned. In 2 B.C. – i.e. a couple of years before the appearance of the *Ars Amatoria* – Augustus staged an epic extravaganza below
the Janiculum to celebrate the dedication of the temple of Mars Ultor.
This was a representation of the battle of Salamis, in which 3,000 men
took part, not counting rowers. It was a colossal show, and the emperor was proud of it.[27] Ovid gave it two lines, and then added another
four to comment on the limitless opportunities it provided for seduction (1.171–6).

Shortly after this, young Gaius, the emperor's grandson, set out on
his Parthian campaign, from which he was never to return. The occasion called for a passage in high, ceremonious style with allusions to
Hercules, Bacchus, Mars, and Augustus himself (1.177–204). The
pageant in itself can hardly have had any satirical purpose. It was intended rather as a compliment to the royal house; at the same time it
enabled Ovid to vary his erotic theme with a digression in the form of

---

[27] *Res Gestae* 23; Dio LV. 10.7; Velleius II. 100.2.

an elaborate encomium. Nevertheless, within the plan of the poem all the sabre-clashing rhetoric is justified only in so far as it leads to a picture of the future triumph (213–16); and the triumph, in its turn, is mentioned solely because it provided an excellent chance of picking up a girl in the crowd (217–28). So once again an important public event involving the emperor and his family has been placed in a frivolous and slightly disreputable framework.

While on the subject of soldiering we should mention a passage in the second book (2.233ff.). It begins:

> militiae species amor est: discedite, segnes;
> non sunt haec timidis signa tuenda uiris

> *Love is a kind of campaign. The lazy had better keep out of it. This is no standard for the faint-hearted to guard.*

Here we have an echo of the brilliant conceit worked out in *Amores* I.9: *militat omnis amans* – 'every lover is on active service'. In particular the phrase *discedite segnes* recalls the lines (31–2):

> ergo desidiam quicumque uocabat amorem,
> desinat

> *so if anyone was inclined to call love sloth he should stop,*

and (46)

> qui nolet fieri desidiosus amet

> *anyone who wants to shake off sloth should go in for love.*

As Brooks Otis remarked many years ago,[28] the patriotic Roman would have regarded the amatory career as a form of *desidia*. Ovid claims to rebut such criticism by insisting that the lover's preoccupation makes *desidia* impossible; indeed the best cure for sloth is to become involved in an affair.

In the Augustan scheme of things strenuous military effort was needed to ensure the safety of the frontiers, but peace and harmony were the watchwords within the state. The Aedes Concordiae, the temple of Concordia Augusta, the Ara Pacis, coins with the images of Victory and Peace, statues to Concordia and Pax, famous lines from the poets, the emperor's own proud declarations in the *Res Gestae* – the list could easily be extended.[29] But if we try to add items from the *Ars*

---

[28] Brooks Otis, *TAPA* 69 (1938) 200.
[29] See L. R. Taylor, *The Divinity of the Roman Emperor* (APA Monograph 1931), index under *Concordia* and *Pax*.

Amatoria we shall be in rather a quandary. After recounting an unfortunate quarrel with his girl-friend Ovid says:

> proelia cum Parthis, cum culta pax sit amica
> et iocus et causas quicquid amoris habet (2.175f.)

> *let there be battles with the Parthians, but with a smart girl-friend there should be peace and fun and whatever serves to promote love –*

a sentiment which fails, somehow, to reflect imperial policy. Later (2.459–64) we find this characteristically brilliant passage:

> oscula da flenti, Veneris da gaudia flenti:
>   pax erit; hoc uno soluitur ira modo.
> cum bene saeuierit, cum certa uidebitur hostis,
>   tum pete concubitus foedera: mitis erit.
> illic depositis habitat Concordia telis,
>   illo, crede mihi, Gratia nata loco est.

> *kiss her when she's crying, give her sexual pleasure when she's crying: peace will ensue; that is the one way of soothing anger. When she's really furious, when she seems an implacable enemy, lie down together and negotiate a treaty: then she'll be gentle. That is where weapons are laid aside and Harmony dwells. Believe me, that is the place where Reconciliation was born.*

That was not quite what Virgil had in mind when he claimed that one of the glories of Roman rule was *paci imponere morem*.

Another idea, closely associated with the Augustan peace, was that of *fides*. In the *Carmen Saeculare* (57–9) Horace wrote:

> iam Fides et Pax et Honos Pudorque
> priscus et neglecta redire Virtus
> audet

> *Now Good Faith, Peace, Honour, ancient Modesty, and neglected Virtue dare to return.*

In his great prophecy in Book 1 of the *Aeneid* (292–4) Jupiter says:

> aspera tum positis mitescent saecula bellis:
> cana Fides et Vesta, Remo cum fratre Quirinus
> iura dabunt

> *then wars will cease and the rough ages grow mild. Grey-haired*

17

Faith and Vesta and Quirinus with his brother Remus will hold sway.

Fides is grey-haired because she was one of the oldest personifications of an abstract idea. Her temple on the Capitol was founded about 250 B.C. and her cult was older still. Some people believed that her worship went back to the age of Numa. As good faith was, in Cicero's words, the *fundamentum iustitiae* it figured prominently in Augustus' moral revival. But in the game of *amor* as described by Ovid credibility is largely a matter of clever tactics. In one passage (1.740) we are even told that *fides*, like friendship, is an empty term:

> nomen amicitia est, nomen inane fides.

Of the other virtues mentioned by Horace in the lines just quoted, *Honos* plays no part in the *Ars Amatoria* and *Pudor* is only justified when it can be overcome.[30]

A passage which amusingly illustrates the poet's attitude to both purity and militarism occurs in the first book (1.101–34). The theatre, says Ovid, is one of the best places for finding a girl; in fact it has always been a menace to chastity ever since the days of Romulus; he established a precedent by using it as a trap for the Sabine women. After telling the story with his usual dexterity, Ovid concludes (131–2):

> Romule, militibus scisti dare commoda solus:
> haec mihi si dederis commoda, miles ero

> *Romulus, you're the only man who has ever known how to reward his troops. Give that reward to me and even I will join up.*

Those lines also have another kind of resonance. There is good evidence that in his early days Octavian was keen to take the name of Romulus as second founder of the city.[31] This was eventually ruled out because of associations with monarchy and fratricide, but, as Augustus, the emperor was connected with Romulus in various ways.[32] He was supposed to have seen twelve vultures when taking his first augury; he restored the temple of Quirinus and had the augury of Romulus and Remus depicted on the pediment; the soothsayer Tarutius calculated that his horoscope was identical with that of Romulus; in *Odes* III.3

---

30 See, e.g., *AA* 1.607–8: *fuge rustice longe | hinc Pudor* – 'away with countrified prudishness'.

31 Dio LIII.16.7. The idea was discussed in the senate (Suetonius, *Aug.* 7.2; Florus II.34.66).

32 What follows is based on K. Scott, *TAPA* 56 (1925) 82–105. See also R. J. Getty, *CP* 45 (1950) 1–12.

Horace asserted that Augustus would gain immortality in the same manner as Romulus; when Augustus died, there was an officially fostered rumour that he had been seen ascending to heaven like Romulus; on Augustus' coinage, on the gemma Augustea, and on the altar of the Lares Augusti in the Uffizi the presence of the *lituus* is designed to connect him with Romulus. In view of all this it is a pity that the founder of Rome should have figured in the *Ars Amatoria* solely as the organizer of a mass rape.

That passage about the Sabine women tells us something else as well. The spectators sat on grassy tiers wearing garlands of ill-assorted leaves on their untidy hair. The stage was without art; the applause uncouth. The women themselves are not described, but we know from *Amores* 1.8.39 that they were grubby (*immundae*) and from the *Medicamina Faciei* that they were unkempt and had red faces (12–13). One thinks also of the Umbrian wife in Book 3 of the *Ars* (303–4) who is *rubicunda* and takes long galumphing strides. To the amused sophisticate the early Romans had a lot to learn about *cultus*.

Such an attitude stood in sharp contrast to the official, patriotic, view of the Roman past. Early in the second century B.C. Ennius had proclaimed:

> moribus antiquis res stat Romana uirisque (W.467)

> *it is on customs and men of the good old type that the Roman state depends.*

When Ovid was still a boy Virgil wrote in his second Georgic (532ff.):

> hanc olim ueteres uitam coluere Sabini,
> hanc Remus et frater; sic fortis Etruria creuit
> scilicet et rerum facta est pulcherrima Roma,
> septemque una sibi muro circumdedit arces.

> *Such was the life once lived by the Sabines of old, and by Remus and his brother; this surely was how Etruria grew strong and how Rome became the fairest thing in creation and surrounded her seven hills with a single wall.*

Those lines come at the end of one of the finest passages in Roman literature. Instinct with love and reverence for the past, they reaffirm the sources of Roman greatness and in doing so body forth the deepest feelings of both poet and emperor.

Ovid had more to say on the topic of ancient versus modern Rome in 3.121ff.

prisca iuuent alios; ego me nunc denique natum
gratulor: haec aetas moribus apta meis.

*Let others take pleasure in the olden days. I am delighted to have
been born just at this time. This is an age which suits my character.*

The age suits him, he goes on to say, not because of its gold and marble
but because civilization has arrived and the old country ways have
vanished. There is a rather similar sentiment in Horace, where a
character says: 'you praise the conditions and morals of the people of
yore, and yet if a god suddenly urged you to go back you would
strenuously refuse'. In other words the man who yearns for the good
old days is a self-deceiver, if not a hypocrite. Horace's lines are from a
satire (*Sat.* ii.7.23–4). And that is the point I am making about the
Ars Amatoria. Such an attitude had its dangers. *Prisca iuuent alios* – all
very well, but the admirers of antiquity included Augustus himself.

In the passage of Virgil quoted above the health and contentment of
earlier generations were connected with their work on the land. But
with the civil wars agriculture declined (*Georg.* 1.506–8):

non ullus aratro
dignus honos, squalent abductis arua colonis
et curuae rigidum falces conflantur in ensem

*The plough does not receive proper respect, the farmers have been
taken away and their fields are overgrown, and the curved sickle is
forged into a tough sword.*

It has been estimated that 'in the twenty years after Caesar crossed the
Rubicon some 200,000 Italians were often under arms'.[33] So it is not
surprising that the land belonging to independent farmers fell into
neglect. Maecenas' speech in Dio lii.27 points out that farming and
other peaceful pursuits will flourish only if men are not called up for
service abroad. It is also clear that agriculture was not always readily
resumed on the army's return. Many farmers were evicted for choosing
the wrong side, and the veterans who took their place were not always
successful. All this encouraged people to drift to the capital – a process
which had already been going on for a long time.

While he recognized the seriousness of this national problem Virgil
can hardly have imagined that his poem would have much in the way
of a practical effect. The *Georgics* are concerned with small independent
farmers (whether owners or tenants) and have nothing to say about

[33] P. A. Brunt, *JRS* 52 (1962) 75.

the large grazing-lands worked by slave labour. Even within this narrow context their advice is often rather incomplete. As L. P. Wilkinson says: 'What would the prospective farmer make of Virgil's inventory of requisites for growing crops? 1. Ploughshare, 2. heavy timber of curved plough, 3. slow-rolling wains of the Eleusinian mother, 4. sledges and drags, 5. mattocks, 6. rough wicker utensils of Celeus, arbutus baskets, and Iacchus' mystic winnowing fan (*Georg.* 1.162–6).'[34] The contrast with agricultural writers like Cato, Varro, and Columella need not be elaborated. One cannot imagine, then, that as a result of Virgil's selective and idealized picture many readers took up agriculture themselves. (Heitland has some realistic remarks about this in his *Agricola*.) Some may perhaps have invested more heavily in the land. But the main effect of the *Georgics* was to influence the way people *thought* about the land. In this respect they advanced and enriched Augustus' patriotic revival. Later on a similar function was performed by Horace in odes 5 and 15 of Book IV and also in the *Carmen Saeculare*, which speaks of

> fertilis frugum pecorisque Tellus (29)
>
> *Tellus fertile in crops and herds*

and of

> beata pleno
> Copia cornu (59–60)
>
> *blessed Plenty with her full horn.*

Tellus (Earth) with children and cornucopia was shown on the cuirass of the Prima Porta Augustus, on the gemma Augustea, and most notably on the east wall of the Ara Pacis. The cornucopia also figures on the Altar of Carthage, on a silver cup from Boscoreale, and on a bas relief from Sorrento.[35] Horace refers to it in some happy lines of *Epist.* I.12:

---

[34] L. P. Wilkinson, *Greece and Rome* 19 (1950) 20.

[35] For illustration and documentation see E. Strong, *Roman Sculpture* (London 1907) vol. 1, plates 3, 8, 27, and 30. and pp. 42–6, 84, 88, 93; and L. R. Taylor, *The Divinity of the Roman Emperor*, 169, 179, 197ff., 226. I have spoken of Tellus on the *Ara Pacis*. G. K. Galinsky has argued in *AJA* 70 (1966) 223–43 that the figure is not Tellus but Venus, and S. Weinstock has maintained in *JRS* 50 (1960) 44–58 that the altar in question is not the *Ara Pacis*. J. M. C. Toynbee believes that it is the *Ara Pacis* but that the figure is that of Italia; her articles are in *Proc. Brit. Acad.* 39 (1953) 67–95 and *JRS* 51 (1961) 153–6. I am not qualified to take part in these controversies, and fortunately they do not affect the substance of my argument.

aurea fruges
Italiae pleno defudit Copia cornu.

*Golden Plenty has poured forth her fruits upon Italy from a full
horn.*

How is all this relevant to the *Ars Amatoria*? Well, it can be shown,
I think, that at several points Ovid exploits this edifying conception of
agriculture in his own characteristic way. The bull's neck submits to
the yoke: Amor will submit to Ovid (1.19ff.); in time oxen come to
the plough, the ploughshare is worn down, so persevere and you will
conquer Penelope herself (1.471ff.); by compliance the curved branch
is bent away from the tree, it breaks if you apply your strength, so
remember to comply with your mistress' whims (2.177ff.); at first
love is sensitive to shortcomings, but years bring tolerance; while the
young grafted branch is growing in the green bark it will fall off if a
breeze shakes it; in time it will grow tough and stand up to the wind
(2.649ff.); when you're sure you'll be missed, then you can relax your
attentions; a field allowed to rest repays trust and a dry soil drinks in
the water from the sky (2.351ff.). Love, then, like farming requires
patience, care, and insight. The main difference is that one is a serious
and the other a frivolous pursuit. As Wilkinson says in another place:
'The *Ars* is not a parody' (by which he means it is not a parody of any
specific work). 'Yet its dealing at length and systematically with such
a subject in a form associated with serious instruction inevitably
generates a pleasing atmosphere of burlesque.'[36] It need only be added
that this atmosphere of burlesque might not have pleased those who
were eager to make the land and its work part of a national ideo-
logy.[37] By this I do not mean that the humorous analogies with agriculture (which occur elsewhere in elegy, e.g. in Tibullus II.6.21ff.,
Propertius II.3.47f. and II.34.47f.) would have given offence in themselves. My point is rather that they form part of a general pattern in

---

[36] L. P. Wilkinson, *Ovid Recalled* (Cambridge 1955) 120.
[37] A number of didactic formulae common to Ovid and Virgil are noted by
E. J. Kenney in *Ovidiana* (Paris 1958) 201–9. He also quotes other
formulae common to Ovid and Lucretius. As most of these formulae also
occur in the *Satires* and *Epistles* of Horace this supports the view that the
Ars is a burlesque of didactic poetry in general, including of course the
Georgics. In *TAPA* 95 (1964) Mrs E. W. Leach examines various
parallels in theme and imagery which occur in the *Georgics* and the *Ars*.
In her last footnote (n. 15, p. 154) she agrees that Ovid's parody is not
confined to the *Georgics*. One observes, for example, that a passage
containing an agricultural simile may also contain references to
medicine, navigation, soldiering, and the law.

which respectable things are made light of. Other elements in the pattern are more likely to have caused annoyance *per se*.

Although, as I have just said, specific parody is not an important feature of the *Ars*, there are examples. In one of the most solemn scenes of Virgil's great Augustan epic Aeneas receives instructions from the Sibyl about his journey to Hades. The way down, she explains, is easy enough:

> sed reuocare gradum superasque euadere ad auras,
> hoc opus, hic labor est. (6.128–9)

> *But to retrace one's steps and reach the air above, that is the task,*
> *that is the trouble.*

In the *Ars* Ovid gives instruction about another kind of pilgrimage which also has its difficulties. Since girls are by nature greedy, the most testing challenge is to obtain their favours without first having to give a present:

> hoc opus, hic labor est, primo sine munere iungi. (1.453)

This allusion to Aeneas brings us to the supposedly divine ancestry of the Julii.[38] The fiction that the family were descended from Venus through Aeneas' son Iulus began to be exploited for political purposes towards the end of the second century B.C. About 125 Sextus Iulius Caesar issued coins with Venus Genetrix on them, and the same theme was continued by Lucius Iulius Caesar twenty years later. Another member of the family wrote about the origins of Rome and the Aeneadae. Plutarch has a passage which links Marius' wife Julia, who was Caesar's aunt, with Venus; and at her funeral in 68 B.C. Caesar made this claim quite explicitly in his oration. Again, on the instructions of Caesar, Venus Victrix was the watchword at Pharsalus and Munda; and the same goddess was represented on Caesar's ring. At Pharsalus Caesar vowed a temple in her honour, though in the end it was dedicated to Venus Genetrix, mother of the Julian house and of the Roman people. This temple, standing in the Forum Iulium and made of solid marble, contained a cult statue by Arcesilaus, the greatest sculptor of his age. Venus also figured on Caesar's coinage, and after his death she appeared on a number of monuments with Diuus Iulius – the Altar of Carthage is a good example. Velleius soberly assures us that the legend was accepted by all ancient investigators (II.41.1).

[38] See S. Weinstock, *Divus Iulius* (Oxford 1971) 15–18, and K. Scott, *CP* 36 (1941) 257–72.

Ovid uses the legend in his own way. Early in the *Ars* (1.60) he announces:

> mater in Aeneae constitit urbe sui

> *the mother of Aeneas has come to stay in the city of her son –*

a thought which would have been welcomed by Augustus had it not been for the context. Rome, we are told, is sufficient for all amatory needs: 'many as are the stars in the sky, so many are the girls living in your own Rome.' And then:

> mater in Aeneae constitit urbe sui.

One recalls that Socrates found it unnecessary to go outside Athens, for the city provided all that was needful for a life of virtue.

In 3.397ff. Ovid has a witty version of what might be called the 'light under a bushel' topos:

> quod latet ignotum est; ignoti nulla cupido:
> fructus abest, facies cum bona teste caret.

> *The hidden is unknown; the unknown is never desired. There is no gain when a good-looking face goes unobserved.*

The words *ignoti* and *caret* suggest that there may be an allusion to Horace's famous stanza in *Odes* IV.9.25–8:

> uixere fortes ante Agamemnona
> multi, sed omnes illacrimabiles
> urgentur ignotique longa
> nocte carent quia uate sacro.

> *Many brave men lived before Agamemnon, but they all lie unwept and unburied in the long night because they have no sacred bard.*

This is confirmed by v. 403:

> quid petitur sacris, nisi tantum fama, poetis?[39]

> *What is sought by sacred poets except fame alone?*

Now in the previous couplet (i.e. 401–2) we have:

> si Venerem Cous nusquam posuisset Apelles,
> mersa sub aequoreis illa lateret aquis.

> *If Apelles of Cos had never painted Venus, she would still be sunk invisible beneath the watery wave.*

---

[39] Cf. v. 400 and vv. 413ff.

24

An amusing touch, but Ovid can hardly have forgotten that Apelles' Anadyomene (the prototype of Botticelli's masterpiece) was the very picture that Augustus had placed in the shrine of Julius Caesar.[40]

These examples will show that when Ovid mentions a serious aspect of Venus or her cult he gives it a facetious twist. On other occasions, when there is a choice between a serious and a frivolous treatment, he normally chooses the latter. Lucretius, for instance, had shown how the relationship of Mars and Venus could be allegorized into something gravely impressive (*De Rerum Natura* 1.31–40). Ovid turns the episode into a piece of cocktail gossip (2.561ff.): Mars was hopelessly smitten, and Venus, who was no old-fashioned prude, was willing to comply. Together the guilty pair used to laugh at Venus' husband, poor clumsy Vulcan. Venus had even perfected an imitation of him. The Sun, however, discovered the affair and was ill-advised enough to inform the husband – ill-advised because he could have used his knowledge for a little gentle blackmail (Venus would have paid the price). As it was, Vulcan set a trap for the lovers, and provided the other divinities with some Homeric amusement. But it did him no good whatever, because the couple simply continued their liaison without concealment.

Even after his banishment, when he is supposed to be writing an apologia, Ovid still cannot leave the joke alone. If, he says in *Tristia* 2.295, a girl enters the temple of mighty Mars, she will find Venus standing close to the Avenger (i.e. the statues of Venus and Mars are close together), while her husband is outside the door. It is perhaps worth remembering that, less than ten years before, Augustus had dedicated an altar to Vulcan[41] and that there was an ancient festival in his honour.

While Augustus could be linked with Venus through his ancestors, it was possible to connect him in other ways with Jupiter.[42] In Horace, *Odes* i.12, we have an example of association: 'O father and guardian of the human race, O son of Saturn, to thee the Fates have entrusted the charge of mighty Caesar; mayest thou reign with Caesar next in power' – *tu secundo* | *Caesare regnes*. In other odes we find instances of analogy; e.g. because Jupiter thunders we believe he rules in heaven; Augustus will be deemed a god on earth when he has subdued the Britons and Parthians (iii.5.1–4). Finally there is identification. This is very rare in Horace – there is an ironical instance in *Epist.* i.19.43–5,

---

[40] Pliny, *NH* 35.91.   [41] *CIL* vi.457.

[42] See K. Scott, *TAPA* 61 (1930) 52–8; M. M. Ward, *Studi e materiali di storia delle religioni* 9 (1933) 203–24.

where someone makes an unfriendly complaint that Horace is reserving his poems for the ear of Jupiter (i.e. Augustus) alone. But there are a couple of serious examples in the work of Ovid,[43] and the idea is common enough in art and inscriptions. Augustus was called Zeus Eleutherios in Egypt and Zeus Olympios on Lesbos. The Blacas cameo shows him with sceptre and aegis; on the gemma Augustea he is enthroned as Jupiter with the sceptre in his raised left hand and an eagle at his feet. In Naples there is a statue of Augustus with a sceptre in his right hand and a thunderbolt in his left. So too in poetry, and on coins, inscriptions and cameos, Livia is represented as Juno.

In Ovid the king of gods and men appears once as the seducer of Io (1.78); he is obliquely referred to in connection with Semele, Leda, and Europa (3.251–2), and he is commended for his initiative in 1.713–14:

> Iuppiter ad ueteres supplex heroidas ibat;
> corrupit magnum nulla puella Iouem.

> *Jupiter always went and made his requests to the heroines of old;
> no girl ever seduced mighty Jove.*

That is, he always took the first step. In 3.653–4, after recommending that awkward guardians should be bribed, Ovid adds that gifts prevail over men and gods:

> placatur donis Iuppiter ipse datis

> *Jupiter himself is won over by the giving of gifts.*

Finally, we have this interesting passage in 1.633–8:

> Iuppiter ex alto periuria ridet amantum,
> et iubet Aeolios inrita ferre Notos.
> per Styga Iunoni falsum iurare solebat
> Iuppiter: exemplo nunc fauet ipse suo.
> expedit esse deos et, ut expedit, esse putemus;
> dentur in antiquos tura merumque focos.

> *Jupiter from on high smiles at the false oaths of lovers and bids the winds of Aeolus carry them away unfulfilled. Jupiter would often swear untruthfully to Juno by the Styx;[44] now he treats with indulgence the precedent he has set. It is convenient that there should be gods, and as it is convenient let's assume there are, and let incense and wine be offered on the hearth in the old way.*

43 Ovid, *Fast.* 1.650; cf. 1.607–8 and *Pont.* ii.2.63f.
44 In Homer, *Iliad* 15.36–8, an oath sworn by heaven, earth, and the Styx is the most solemn of all oaths.

Very gay, of course, but was it not also rather dangerous? Might not this treatment of Jupiter (and *fides*) have been taken to imply an attitude of irreverence towards the emperor, who was trying so hard to shore up the Roman moral system by providing it with divine sanctions? To say that a passage of this kind was simply a piece of mythology, like an episode from the *Metamorphoses*, would not have been a convincing defence. Granted the *Metamorphoses* may not have been regarded with disfavour (though many scholars think they were), but that great work was above all an imaginative presentation of traditional material. It was not intended to have any direct bearing on everyday life. In the lines quoted above, however, Jupiter's behaviour is cited as a justification of the poet's immoral advice ('Don't be afraid to make promises; that's how girls are betrayed'). It was all a joke, of course. But Ovid did not make the joke more acceptable by adding that in any case the gods were just a useful fiction.

With Apollo we come to the deity most closely connected with Augustus and, his programme.[45] Veiovis, an old god of the underworld, had been worshipped by the Julii; he eventually became identified with Apollo because Apollo was the god of death. There were other, more important, reasons for the emperor's homage. It was Apollo who had helped Rome's Trojan ancestors against the Greeks; Apollo was the son of Jupiter, and Octavian was the son of Julius, who in his own lifetime had assumed some of the attributes of Jupiter. At a party in the early thirties, where the guests appeared as gods and goddesses, Octavian is said to have dressed as Apollo.[46] Later, as the god of sanity and order, Apollo was a powerful psychological ally against the new Dionysus, who was revelling in oriental depravity with his consort Isis/Cleopatra. By a stroke of luck there happened to be an ancient temple of Apollo on a headland overlooking the sea at Actium. The god bent his bow and the enemy were scattered. In return Octavian enlarged the temple at Actium and built a special shrine on the spot where his tent had stood. In 28 B.C. he dedicated the famous temple of Apollo on the Palatine hill, a building which had been vowed after the defeat of Sextus Pompeius in 36. No doubt the god was only mildly surprised to find that one of his statues bore the features of the emperor.[47] After the constitutional settlement of 27 B.C. the cult of Apollo

45 For Augustus' association with Apollo see L. R. Taylor, *The Divinity of the Roman Emperor*, index under Apollo.
46 Suetonius, *Aug.* 70. The details are very obscure; see K. Scott, *Memoirs of the American Academy in Rome* 11 (1933).
47 Ps. Acron on Horace, *Epist.* 1.3.16–18; Servius on Virgil, *Ecl.* 4.10.

continued to be fostered, though the idea of assimilation seems to have been officially abandoned.[48] Then, in 12 B.C., when Augustus became Pontifex Maximus, a new series of coins appeared with Augustus on one side and Apollo and Diana on the other. The Sibylline books were transferred from the temple of Capitoline Jupiter to Apollo's temple on the Palatine – an act which brought them into direct association with the imperial house. The bas relief from Sorrento, which has a representation of Apollo with the Sibyl at his feet, is also assigned to this period.

The poets were pleased to bear witness to the divine relationship. In *Georg.* 3.36 Virgil promised that Apollo's statue would stand in the temple which he planned for the future Augustus. Apollo's role in the *Aeneid* is well known; he may be said to preside over the sixth book either in his own person or through the Sibyl, his prophetess; and he appears again on Aeneas' shield at the culmination of Book 8. Horace paid his tribute, most notably in the *Carmen Saeculare* and in *Odes* IV.6, while Propertius contributed a long encomium in the sixth elegy of Book IV. These are merely the most familiar passages; it would be easy to cite others.[49]

What does Ovid say about Apollo in the *Ars Amatoria*? He begins with engaging frankness by assuring Apollo that he is not going to tell a lot of lies about divine inspiration:

> usus opus mouet hoc: uati parete perito (1.29)
>
> *It is experience that inspires this work; pay heed to the bard who is an expert.*

Later on, in Book 2, after a quasi-Lucretian passage about the role of Venus in the life of early man, Ovid goes on to say:

> haec ego cum canerem, subito manifestus Apollo
> mouit inauratae pollice fila lyrae (2.493f.)
>
> *As I was singing these words, suddenly Apollo appeared and swept the strings of his golden lyre with his thumb.*

To readers of Virgil (*Ecl.* 6.3), Horace (*Odes* IV.15.1), and Propertius (III.3.13) this epiphany will suggest that some kind of diminuendo is about to follow. And that is what eventually happens: Ovid is reminded that eloquent people ought not to declaim in the middle of their con-

---

[48] This view is advocated by P. Lambrechts in *La Nouvelle Clio* 5 (1953) 65–82.
[49] See E. H. Haight, *AJP* 39 (1918) 341–66.

versation and that the frenzied poet should not give readings of his verses. He takes the hint and the next section begins: 'I am summoned to matters nearer at hand' – *ad propiora uocor* (511). But there is more to the passage than this. Apollo appears in full view with a laurel branch in his hand and a laurel wreath on his brow, carrying a golden lyre. Addressing Ovid as *lasciui praeceptor Amoris*– 'teacher of wanton love' – he bids him summon his pupils to the shrine at Delphi, which has inscribed over its entrance the famous injunction 'Know thyself'. But what form does this immemorial wisdom take in Ovid?

> qui sibi notus erit solus sapienter amabit

> *Only the man who knows himself will make an expert lover.*

Whoever has a handsome face should contrive to be seen as much as possible; if you have an attractive skin recline with your shoulder visible; a pleasant conversationalist should not remain silent; *qui canit arte, canat* – 'if you sing nicely, sing'; then, as a final stroke, *qui bibit arte, bibat* – 'if you drink nicely, drink'. After enjoying these lines it may occur to us to wonder whether Augustus would have been pleased to find his own god acting as sponsor for a manual of seduction, and whether he would have laughed good-heartedly at seeing Apollo made a victim of this urbane effrontery. There are a few other touches too, some of which have been mentioned before. In 2.239ff. Apollo's service to Admetus is explained in terms of homosexual devotion;[50] in Book 3 his hairstyle is recommended as a model for certain types of female beauty (142); his temple is mentioned as a happy hunting-ground for rakes (389); finally Ovid assures us that the oracle of Apollo will not tell any greater truth than he has told in his poetry (789). And what truths has he just been revealing? They are, if you please, the various positions of sexual intercourse.

I have tried to summarize how by his foreign policy, his building programme, his moral legislation, his hopes for agriculture, and his encouragement of the arts Augustus sought to create and perpetuate a myth – a myth concerning Rome's past, the occupations and personalities which had made her great, the values which she stood for, and her place and role in world affairs. I call it a myth because many of the elements in it were half true or fictitious or even fantastic; and yet, as myths do, it exercised an immense power over people's imagination, and in virtue of this power contrived, in a sense, to validate itself.

---

50 This version of the story was employed by Callimachus and Tibullus. It was used by the Church Fathers in their attacks on the pagan religion. See K. F. Smith on Tibullus II.3.11–32.

With his civilized intelligence Ovid saw the myth for what it was, and used it as an instrument of burlesque. This is *not* to say that his primary intention was to satirize the Augustan regime or to poke fun at traditional values. Such an interpretation of the *Ars* would be absurdly unbalanced. But since the official policy was puritanical Ovid could not write about the love-game in his amusing and cynical way without incurring the disapproval of Augustus. The basic conception of the *Ars* therefore involved a risk; and indeed the risk was part of its attraction. As for details, one suspects that Ovid was mischievously alive to most of the points mentioned above, though perhaps not all. In some passages, too, e.g. the lines about the mock naval battle (1.171–6) and Gaius' departure for the east (1.177ff.), the allusion to the regime may also have been intended as a compliment. (There is no real contradiction here; it all depends on whether the element of respect manages to survive its context, as it does in, say, the comparison of Octavian to a nervous horse in Horace, *Sat.* ii.1.19–20.) But whatever the poet's intentions may have been in any given case, it is clear the poem was something of a gamble. It is hard to say how fully Ovid appreciated the dangers. In the *Remedia Amoris* (361ff.) he tells us that some people had taken exception to the *Ars* because of its lubricity:

> nuper enim nostros quidam carpsere libellos,
> quorum censura Musa proterua mea est.

His reply, however, is to sweep these objections aside with a gesture of airy confidence:

> 'So long as I give pleasure in this way, so long as my work is sung throughout the world, let one or two people attack it if they wish. Envy runs down the genius of mighty Homer; whoever you are, Zoilus, it is from him that you get your fame.'[51]

So all the complaints are due to envy and to ignorance about the nature of elegiac verse. There is a note of hybris here which again reminds us disturbingly of Oscar Wilde. Hermann Fränkel may be partly right in saying that 'Ovid...was evidently unable to comprehend the objection because his own nature was devoid of that particular sensitivity. He was naive and ignorant in this respect rather than bold.'[52] One should also take account, however, of the position which he enjoyed in society.

---

[51] Zoilus, who lived in third-century Alexandria, is chosen as typifying the carping critic.

[52] H. Fränkel, *Ovid: a Poet between Two Worlds* (California 1956) 71.

The immense acclaim which greeted his poetry – an acclaim attested by sources as diverse as the elder Seneca and Pompeian inscriptions[53] – must have blinded him to the grim realities of political life. Surrounded by adulation, he assumed that wit and artistry put him beyond the reach of power.

But Augustus, alas, was not amused. For seven years he took no action, and we should do him the credit of believing that, had it not been for the latter incident, the poet of naughtiness would have remained unharmed. Once the *error* took place, however, the emperor's anger was fanned by the memory of those impudent verses which undermined his own and his family's dignity and which used that portentous myth as material for flippant amusement. No appeals could move him, and the most urbane of poets was banished from the civilized world. And so in a sense the myth won; but its victory was not permanent. Later generations, no longer living under the good Augustus, have savoured the wit of the *Ars Amatoria*, and have cherished the poem as one of the most attractive monuments of a great, imposing, civilization, in which lightness and elegance were all too rarely achieved.

[53] Seneca, *Contr.* 3.7; *CIL* iv.1895, 1928. Ovid's own testimony is given in *Trist.* 2.115–20, iv.10.121–8. See L. P. Wilkinson, *Ovid Recalled*, 366ff.

2

IDEA
Dido's *Culpa*

It has long been acknowledged that the story of Dido in Books 1 and 4 of the *Aeneid* has some of the elements associated with tragedy. These elements have been listed by A. S. Pease on pp. 8–11 of his massive commentary and discussed at greater length by DeWitt, Maguinness, Quinn, and others.[1] We therefore enquire from time to time what tragic view the episode embodies. In a lecture to the Virgil Society in 1951 Professor R. G. Austin described the death of Dido with his usual blend of sympathy and scholarship, adding as a comment: 'The Queen of the Gods...had ended her sport at last. You will remember Hardy's words at the end of *Tess*: they have their place here.' Hardy's words come, of course, in the last paragraph of the book, just after Tess has been executed for murder: ' "Justice" was done, and the President of the Immortals (in Aeschylean phrase) had ended his sport with Tess.' In his introduction to the same novel Hardy cites as a precedent for this remark Gloucester's well-known words in the fourth act of *King Lear*:

> As flies to wanton boys are we to the gods;
> They kill us for their sport.

The two quotations are connected by the idea of divine sport. Men and women suffer and die to provide amusement for the gods. On the plainest interpretation both Gloucester and Hardy are claiming that the gods take a malevolent pleasure in destroying human lives. Even if we modify the idea of deliberate cruelty implied in this conception, we are still left with the notion of caprice. The gods' behaviour does not indicate any rational purpose.

---

[1] N. W. De Witt, *Class. Journ.* 2 (1907) 283–8; W. S. Maguinness in his presidential address to the Virgil Society, 1955; K. Quinn, *Virgil's Aeneid: A Critical Description* (London 1968) 323–39.

Stated in these terms the idea can hardly be applied to the action of the *Aeneid*; for there, we are told, Jupiter does have a rational purpose. He is shaping the events of history so as to bring about the foundation and development of Rome's imperial power. Austin, to be sure, was talking about Juno, not Jupiter. Yet Juno too had her purpose:

> hoc regnum dea gentibus esse,
> si qua fata sinant, iam tum tenditque fouetque
>
> (1.17–18)

> *That this city [i.e. Carthage] should rule the world, if in any way the fates allowed it – this was even then the goddess's aim and cherished plan.*

And so it would hardly be fair to see Dido as Juno's plaything. This difficulty was, one imagines, observed by Austin himself when he came to write the introduction to his commentary on Book 4. For although he incorporated a certain amount from the earlier lecture and again called attention to Hardy's tragic insight, he did not reproduce the reference to *Tess of the D'Urbervilles*. I shall come back later to Gloucester's comment in *Lear*, because in spite of what has just been said it seems to embody an important truth about the *Aeneid*. For the moment, however, I would suggest that another well-known quotation from the same play is a more accurate reflection of what Virgilian critics have tended to feel. I mean the words of Edgar in Act V, when he addresses the dying Edmund:

> The gods are just, and of our pleasant vices
> Make instruments to plague us.

This notion has been more attractive than the other for two reasons: first, because in the civilized periods of European history men have been reluctant to believe in a god that used his power in a wholly arbitrary way, bringing ruin and misery without just cause; and secondly, because this theory makes it seem possible to reconcile divine providence with the freedom of human will. Although many factors in Dido's life, such as race, rank, and sex, have been assigned to her by fate, she remains responsible for her own decisions and acts. That, as I say, is an attractive idea, and I used to think it might be true. I now suspect that it is a misleading oversimplification.

> The gods are just, and of our pleasant vices
> Make instruments to plague us.

What, then, was Dido's vice? Or, to use the more polite term, what was her 'moral flaw'? Before we try to answer this it is well to be sure about what kind of thing we are looking for. A moral flaw is a disposition or tendency to act reprehensibly in a certain way in response to certain conditions. Hence it is a flaw in a man's character if he is prone to anger, avarice, gluttony, jealousy, lechery, pride and sloth – to name only the more familiar vices. So what was Dido's moral flaw? I must admit I am quite unable to say. Was she, perhaps, inordinately susceptible to men? This can hardly be so. Since her husband's death she had had no dealings with any men, and this (we are assured) was not from a lack of opportunity. In Anna's words:

> aegram nulli quondam flexere mariti,
> non Libyae, non ante Tyro; despectus Iarbas
> ductoresque alii, quos Africa terra triumphis
> diues alit.

> (4.35-8)

> *Sick at heart as you were, no suitors in the past prevailed upon you, not in Libya, not earlier in Tyre; Iarbas was scornfully rejected and also other chieftains reared in Africa, that land rich in triumphs.*

Nor, again, is there anything in the text of Book 1 to suggest that she was given to acts of wild impetuosity. On the contrary, we are given an impression of steadiness and dignity. So although it makes sense, if very incomplete sense, to say that Macbeth's ambition or Othello's jealousy was a flaw which led to disaster, Dido's tragedy cannot, it seems, be discussed in these terms.

If we look more closely at Pease's introduction we may possibly see how the mistake arose. On p. 9 he says 'Hero and heroine have each a distinct blemish in character, Dido's being her unfaithfulness to her vows to Sychaeus, that of Aeneas his temporary neglect of his divine mission...' But surely this is rather a confused way of thinking. Dido broke her vows to Sychaeus, yes. But that was an act – an act entailed by entering into a relationship with Aeneas. But an act can never be a blemish of character. The two things belong to different logical categories. It is interesting to find a similar mistake in C. M. Bowra's *From Virgil to Milton*. After speaking of 'great women whose character is their doom', Bowra goes on to say (p. 49) that 'Dido, like Turnus, has a tragic fault. She has taken a vow to be faithful to the spirit of her dead husband Sychaeus, but she breaks it when she unites herself to Aeneas.' The word 'fault' tends to conceal the confusion of categories, but it is there none the less.

If we go further and enquire what led Pease to look for a blemish in Dido's character, we shall probably find the answer on p. 39 of his introduction: 'Yet admirable as Dido's character in many respects is, it illustrates – and was surely intended to illustrate – that flaw or error which Aristotle recognized as necessary for a tragic hero or heroine.' This raises the old question about the meaning of *hamartia* in Aristotle's *Poetics* (13, 1453 a 10). Pease says 'flaw or error', but these are two different things, and there is only one word in Aristotle. 'Flaw' has been the more popular interpretation since the appearance of Butcher's essay on Aristotle's theory of poetry and fine art,[2] but 'error', 'mistake', or 'misapprehension' is more probably what Aristotle meant. The matter is discussed in some detail by D. W. Lucas in the fourth appendix of his commentary on the *Poetics*,[3] and that is his conclusion. Even if we are tempted to compromise and to look for some intermediate concept which will include both an ethical and an intellectual element,[4] we must still (I believe) reject the simple notion of a moral flaw.

Nevertheless, it may yet be possible to hold that Dido's suffering was a punishment for her sinful relationship with Aeneas. This view would enable us to retain the idea of divine justice, emending Shakespeare to read:

> The gods are just, and of our pleasant sins
> Make instruments to plague us.

Someone better versed that I am in the history of Virgilian scholarship could no doubt show that this opinion has been held for centuries. It can be found in its most extreme form in Servius (though we cannot be sure that he is giving his own view). On the first line of Book 4 he comments *uidetur et post amissam castitatem etiam iustus interitus* – 'After the loss of her chastity even her death appears to be just.' In the nineteen-twenties H. W. Prescott put the same point in a slightly different way: 'Dido deserved her death; she broke her solemn oath to Sychaeus.'[5] It may be apposite here to quote an observation by A. C. Bradley: 'We might not object to the statement that Lear deserved to suffer for his folly, selfishness, and tyranny; but to assert that he

---

[2] S. H. Butcher, *Aristotle's Theory of Poetry and Fine Art*, fourth edition (London, 1911).

[3] D. W. Lucas, *Aristotle, Poetics* (Oxford 1968).

[4] See, e.g., G. M. A. Grube, *Aristotle on Poetry and Style* (New York 1958) xxiv–xxv, and G. M. Kirkwood, *AJP* 92 (1971) 711–15.

[5] H. W. Prescott, *The Development of Virgil's Art* (Chicago 1927 repr. 1963) 290.

deserved to suffer what he *did* suffer is to do violence not merely to language but to any healthy moral sense.'[6]

I doubt if many readers of Virgil share Prescott's opinion, but it does raise a question of methodology which is sometimes overlooked, namely 'Is Virgil's judgment of Dido invariably identical with Dido's judgment of herself?' Brooks Otis believes it is. On p. 78 of his *Virgil* he writes: 'Dido...reflects Virgil's own morality. In fact Dido's speeches...convey...a generalized analysis of the total moral-historical situation as both she and Virgil see it.' Well, that may often be true, but consider the following case. Towards the end of Book 4, after pondering and rejecting various courses of action, the heroine cries:

> quin morere ut merita es, ferroque auerte dolorem
>
> (547)
>
> *No! Die, as you deserve, and with steel put an end to your pain.*

Are we therefore to conclude that Virgil also thought she deserved to die? Luckily one does not have to argue from probability; the poet has been quite explicit. In vv. 693ff. Iris is sent down to release Dido from her agony because she has not yet been formally assigned to death. And why has she not be en assigned to death?

> quia nec fato merita nec morte peribat
>
> (696)
>
> *Because it was not by fate's decree nor by a deserved death that she was dying.*

So the queen did not deserve to die, and Virgil's verdict is not the same as Dido's own.

But did she deserve to suffer? And if so, why? Let us take first the contention that, in Otis' words, '[Dido] violates her duty to Carthage.'[7] What effect does the liaison have on Carthage as a whole? We are not told very much about this. In the period just before the 'marriage', work in the city comes to a halt, military exercises cease, and people are (one assumes) beginning to talk (86–9, 91, 170). After the 'marriage' has been consummated Fama (Rumour) redoubles its activities, putting about the report that Dido and Aeneas are spending the entire winter in sensual pleasure:

> regnorum immemores turpique cupidine captos
>
> (194)

---

[6] A. C. Bradley, *Shakespearian Tragedy* (London repr. 1949) 32.
[7] Brooks Otis in *Virgil* ed. D. R. Dudley (London 1969) 57.

36

Forgetful of their kingdoms, prisoners of foul lust.

But Fama, as Virgil says, tells lies and half-truths as well as facts (190). It is not clear that Dido *is* forgetful of her kingdom, though it could certainly be argued that Aeneas is forgetful of the kingdom which he is supposed to found in the future.[8] At any rate some caution is advisable in view of the line which sums up Fama's reports:

> haec passim dea foeda uirum diffundit in ora
>
> (195)

These were the tales which the filthy goddess spread abroad on men's lips.

If we give weight to such evidence, we must also bear in mind that when Mercury comes to remind Aeneas of his mission he finds him, not in the queen's boudoir, but on the building sites of Carthage *fundantem arces et tecta nouantem* (260) – 'laying the foundations of towers and building new dwellings'. This busy activity is further emphasized in Mercury's reprimand:

> tu nunc Karthaginis altae
> fundamenta locas pulchramque uxorius urbem
> exstruis?
>
> (265-7)

Are you now laying the foundations of lofty Carthage and building a fine city in devotion to your wife?

Some scholars are reluctant to admit this as evidence of Dido's renewed activity, because Dido herself is not immediately present. But dramatically Dido cannot be present, because Mercury's words are for the ears of Aeneas alone. In any case it is clear that work has been resumed, and so the stoppage mentioned earlier must be regarded as temporary.

Caution is again required when we come to assess certain things said by Dido and her sister. In v. 321 Dido claims that because of her liaison with Aeneas the Tyrians are now hostile to her (*infensi Tyrii*). But this is part of a tremendous rhetorical appeal to Aeneas, and allowance must be made for exaggeration.[9] So too, when Dido in v. 468 sees herself

---

[8] See v. 267. When Rumour, reinforced by the prayers of Iarbas, reaches Jupiter, he turns his eyes towards the lovers. They are now said to be *oblitos famae melioris* (221), which is not the same thing as *regnorum immemores*.

[9] From Jupiter's words in v. 235 it might seem that the Carthaginians were bitterly hostile to Aeneas: *qua spe inimica in gente moratur?* But

looking for the Tyrians in a desolate land, we must remember that this is the dream of a desperately unhappy woman overwhelmed by grief and shame. The balance has to be corrected the other way when Anna cries:

> extinxti te meque, soror, populumque patresque
> Sidonios urbemque tuam

(682–3)

You have destroyed yourself and me, my sister, and the senate and people of Sidon, and your own city.

That too is the rhetoric of distraught affection. It implies that the survival of the state was utterly dependent on the queen. In literal fact, of course, it wasn't. Carthage was still to enjoy centuries of prosperity. What we can say for sure is that the city was at first stunned by the news of Dido's suicide and then broke into wild lamentation (666–71). From this it is fairly clear that at the deepest level Dido had not lost the hearts of her people.

Taking all these points together it is fair to conclude that at some point the Carthaginians began to disapprove of Dido's union with Aeneas, and that this weighed heavily on her conscience after she had been deserted. Nevertheless, we also have to remember that at an earlier stage of the relationship Dido had good reason to believe that an alliance with the Trojans would help rather than harm her city. Although she had other, different, scruples about falling in love with Aeneas, it never for a moment occurred to her that she was failing in her duty to Carthage. The political arguments advanced by Anna in vv. 39–49 were not questioned at the time: Carthage was surrounded by hostile peoples, there was danger of pursuit from Tyre itself; but with a Trojan alliance the state of Carthage had immense prospects of power and glory. Professor Otis says in his *Virgil*: 'It is made quite plain that Anna is wrong to undermine Dido's...resolve' (78). Well, it may be plain to someone who knows the outcome, but it certainly wasn't plain to Anna, or to her sister. One sometimes forgets that as early as 1.572ff. Dido offered the Trojans an equal share in her kingdom. In other words, without any prompting from Anna and before she even *saw* Aeneas, Dido thought it desirable for the Trojans to stay. So did Juno, who certainly had Carthage's interests at heart.

> Jupiter may be speaking in his full knowledge of destiny. It is perhaps significant that when Mercury conveys the message to Aeneas the point is not mentioned. Instead the question is changed to: *qua spe Libycis teris otia terris?* (271).

So although we may grant that there was some political failure on Dido's part – even if only a failure of tact – this ought not to be judged too harshly. More important, that failure was in no way a *cause* of her desertion and humiliation. It was rather a consequence of her passionate attachment to Aeneas. Hence her political failure cannot be regarded as part of her initial guilt.

When scholars speak of Dido's guilt they are, of course, referring primarily to her breach of faith with her dead husband Sychaeus. T. R. Glover, whose treatment of this episode is still among the best, chides the queen very gently for 'sacrificing her sense of right to her inclination'.[10] Earlier he says: 'To resolve to win the love of Aeneas is no wrong thought or action, but to attempt it against her conscience is the first step towards shame.'[11] The point is put more forcefully by K. Quinn: 'She could have resisted passion more successfully: she could have known, or learnt, to put duty or *pudor* before infatuation; and after yielding to infatuation she could have been honest enough with herself not to pretend she had marriage within her grasp.'[12] Brooks Otis is even more severe: 'Dido now realises her plight and her guilt (*En quid ago?* 534f.), her helplessness and the criminal folly of her deed.'[13] This represents an impressive body of testimony, but before we reach a final conclusion (if indeed finality is ever possible in such a matter) let us look once more at the relevant passages.

At the end of Book 1 Venus instructs Cupid to assume the form of Ascanius and inflame Dido's heart with love. Cupid must therefore gradually efface [her feelings of obligation to] Sychaeus – *paulatim abolere Sychaeum* (720), and occupy her long inactive affections with a living love. No censure so far – simply a statement of fact. At the banquet the queen drinks deep draughts of love (749), and by the time Aeneas has finished his tale she is wholly infatuated. Speaking to Anna at the beginning of Book 4, she says in effect: 'Had I not resolved to have done with marriage after Sychaeus' death I could perhaps have yielded to this one *culpa*' (15–19). The logic of this deserves comment. Strictly speaking, if Dido had not resolved to remain single then presumably she could have contemplated marrying Aeneas without any misgivings and there would have been no question of *culpa*. In fact she *has* made such a resolution and so marriage with Aeneas *would* involve *culpa*. These two ideas are compressed into one. The phrase *succumbere*

---

[10] T. R. Glover, *Virgil* (London 1912) 203.   [11] *Ibid.* 190.

[12] K. Quinn, *Virgil's Aeneid*, 325.

[13] Brooks Otis, *Virgil: A Study in Civilized Poetry* (Oxford 1964) 84. Cf. 'Dido's moral lapse is deliberate' etc. p. 77.

culpae is hard to translate. One cannot properly be said to surrender to a 'frailty', 'weakness', or 'lapse', and yet in this particular line 'sin' is too heavily condemnatory. Perhaps 'surrender to this one temptation' would come nearest to the meaning, though *culpa* normally does not mean temptation.

At any rate it is clear from what follows that at this point Dido is claiming that her modesty and her sense of loyalty to Sychaeus prevent her from forming an attachment to Aeneas. She reaffirms her oath, saying in effect 'May I die before I do violence to *pudor* (shame, modesty, self-respect), and may Sychaeus keep my love with him in the grave' (24–30). So the first suggestion that a new marriage would be in some way reprehensible comes from Dido herself. Then follows the speech of Anna, who, we are told, 'fanned into flame the queen's heart already kindled with love, gave hope to her wavering mind, and undid her *pudor*' – *soluitque pudorem* (54–5). The repeated image of fire in v. 54 may well imply destructiveness, and here I would agree with Brooks Otis (78). But that doesn't prove that Virgil is censuring Anna for giving such advice or Dido for taking it. Virgil can imply that the passion is destructive because he knows the outcome. This knowledge (which we share with the poet after our first reading of the book) lends a sad irony to the next phrase, because giving hope to someone in doubt is normally a kind thing to do; Anna was not to know that such hope was doomed. Finally, the undoing or unfastening of *pudor* (a quasi-sexual phrase) is in itself a neutral idea. It is a task which may be faced not only by a seducer but also by a first or even a second husband. Suppose that Aeneas had been free to settle in Carthage, would there have been anything wrong on Dido's part in allowing herself to have hopes of marrying him? That is a question we shall have to discuss.

With the symbolic marriage in the cave a further stage is reached.

> Ille dies primus leti primusque malorum
> causa fuit; neque enim specie famaue mouetur
> nec iam furtiuum Dido meditatur amorem:
> coniugium uocat, hoc praetexit nomine culpam.
>
> (169–72)

That day first was the cause of death and woe. For Dido ceases to be moved by appearances or by what people say. Nor does she engage any longer in a clandestine love-affair. She calls it marriage; with this name she provides a respectable covering for her wrong behaviour.

Virgil does not think it necessary to tell us how many Carthaginians were against the union in principle (and how strong their feelings were) and how many were simply indignant that there had been no official celebration. All we know is that people disapproved of what Dido was doing. So too, we aren't told whether Dido hopes they will accept the position in time, or whether she is defiant or merely indifferent. All we know is that she goes ahead. She calls the union marriage (and, with whatever justification, she has convinced herself that it *is* marriage[14]), but the wording of v. 172 cautions the reader against accepting this view, and we find later that Aeneas explicitly rejects it (338-9). The important word for us is *culpam*. In view of the case developed so far one wonders whether it might mean simply 'what she regarded as her guilt', but this won't do. For here *culpa* is distinguished from *coniugium*, and the word *nomen* implies that the relationship isn't really a *coniugium* at all. The phrase therefore cannot represent Dido's view of what is happening. When Dido was still in two minds, she believed that *coniugium* with Aeneas would *be a culpa*. Now that she has, as she believes, married him, an appropriate comment would be 'She marries him and suppresses her feelings of guilt at having done so.' But that is not what Virgil says. We must therefore assume that he is not describing her feelings but condemning her conduct. Nevertheless it is worth noting that this is the only line in which Virgil makes such a definite judgement. And even here he does not decide for us how serious in moral terms her guilt is. The *results*, of course, are disastrous, but how wicked is the queen herself? We are not yet in a position to say.

It is natural – and significant – that we hear no more of Dido's own sense of guilt until she realizes that Aeneas is about to leave her. Then it all comes flooding back. 'It was on your account', she cries to Anna, 'that my *pudor* was destroyed and my previous good name, which was my only path to immortal glory' (321-3). Later, after all her pleas have failed, we learn for the first time that Dido has kept in her palace a marble shrine in memory of Sychaeus (457-9). She is now so overwrought that at night-time she hears her dead husband's voice calling to her from the shrine; other sounds and visions also terrify her. She resolves to die and begins to make preparations. We then have a splendid soliloquy, ending with the lines:

> Non licuit thalami expertem sine crimine uitam
> degere more ferae, talis nec tangere curas;

[14] The passages which establish this are conveniently listed by Gordon Williams in *Tradition and Originality in Roman Poetry* (Oxford 1968) 381.

non seruata fides cineri promissa Sychaeo.

(550–2)

*I was not allowed to remain unmarried, passing my life without
blame like a creature of the wilds, immune from such unhappy love.
The promise made to the ashes of Sychaeus has not been kept.*

Here again the assertion that Dido is to blame for being unfaithful
comes from the queen herself. Finally, when she sees the Trojans
actually departing she launches into another powerful speech in which
she says:

infelix Dido, nunc te facta impia tangunt?　　(596)

*Luckless Dido, is it now that your godless deeds are coming home
to you?*

Facta impia – that is the last and most bitter of all her reproaches
against herself. Once more we must ask whether Virgil means us to
judge the queen as harshly as she judges herself.

At this point we should consider the ideal of what Tertullian calls
uniuiratus.[15] How important was it that a woman should have only one
husband in her lifetime? In very early days certain religious ceremonies
could only be conducted by *uniuirae*. Servius on 4.19 mentions the
crowning of Fortuna Muliebris, Livy speaks of sacrifices to Pudicitia,
Varro says that in marriage ceremonies the *pronuba*, or matron of
honour, had to be a woman who had married only once,[16] and Valerius
Maximus (II.1.3) refers to special honours reserved for *uniuirae*. Let
us look more closely at two of these passages. The first is Livy, x.23.5.
In the year 296 B.C. the senate decreed two days of supplications to
avert numerous portents which had occurred. During the celebrations
a quarrel broke out among the matrons in the shrine of Pudicitia
Patricia. It seems that a patrician woman called Verginia had been excluded from the rite on the grounds that she had married a commoner.
Verginia retaliated by setting up a shrine in her own house. Calling the
plebeian matrons in she said 'I dedicate this altar to Pudicitia Plebeia.'
The plebeian altar, like the other, was tended by matrons of proven
modesty who had been married to one man alone. Then, perhaps a
little sadly, Livy adds: 'Afterwards the cult was degraded by ritually

---

15 The status of the *uniuira* is mentioned in Pease's long note on v. 29. The
relevance of this to *Aeneid* 4 is explored by Gordon Williams in *JRS*
48 (1958) 23–5. I am much indebted to Williams' discussion, though I
reach rather different conclusions.
16 Servius on *Aen.* 4.166.

disqualified women, not matrons only but women of every station, and it finally passed into oblivion'.(10)

The context of the passage of Valerius Maximus is also interesting. It occurs in Book II, in the third section of the chapter headed *De Institutis Antiquis*. One such custom was that whereby women sat at meals while the men reclined. This custom was extended to religious observances, in which Jupiter lay on a couch while Juno and Minerva sat on chairs. Valerius adds: 'In our age this kind of austerity is retained on the Capitol more assiduously than in our homes, no doubt because it is more vital that goddesses should be kept in order than women.' Then comes the section beginning *quae uno contentae matrimonio fuerant corona pudicitiae honorabantur* – notice the tenses. Section four tells us that the first divorce took place five hundred years after the foundation of Rome, i.e. about 250 B.C., if the text is emended on the basis of Aulus Gellius.[17] Finally section five says that the use of wine was once unknown to Roman women – *uini usus olim Romanis feminis ignotus fuit*. The sober Valerius explains: 'No doubt it was for fear that they might lapse into some kind of disgraceful conduct, because after Liber, the father of intemperance, the first step is usually to illicit sex.' These passages indicate that the *religious* importance of *uniuiratus* was by 25 B.C. very much a thing of the past.

No doubt it still survived as a social ideal, though how widespread and how deeply cherished it was is hard to assess. Some of the evidence that has been used in discussing the problem is less helpful than it seems. In Plautus, *Mostellaria* 190, a courtesan is listening to her maid, who says *matronae non meretricium est unum inseruire uirum* – 'It's for a married lady not for a courtesan to devote herself to one man.' In Terence's *Eunuchus* 122 Parmeno says to the courtesan Thais: *neque tu uno eras contenta neque solus dedit* – 'You weren't content with one man nor did just one of them reward you.' Here marriage to one man is opposed to the life of a prostitute.

In Plautus, *Mercator* 824–5, the old slave-woman Syra complains about the double standard whereby wives are divorced for infidelity though husbands aren't:

> nam uxor contenta est, quae bona est, uno uiro:
> qui minus uir una uxore contentus siet?

> *A wife, if she's good, is content with one man. Why shouldn't a man be content with one wife?*

---

[17] There is a penetrating discussion of this divorce by A. Watson in *Revue d'Histoire du droit* 33 (1965) 38–50 – a reference which I owe to Mr R. Seager.

In poem 68.135 Catullus complains, as if he were an aggrieved husband, that his mistress is not content with him alone: *uno non est contenta Catullo*. In these two passages a permanent relationship with one man is contrasted with infidelity.

Horace provides yet another type of contrast (*Odes* I.13.17–20):

> felices ter et amplius
> quos irrupta tenet copula nec malis
> diuulsus querimoniis
> suprema citius soluet amor die.

> *Thrice happy and more are those who are held together by an un-broken bond, whose love is not wrenched apart by bitter quarrelling, and who stay united until the final day.*

Here a permanent relationship with one man means a marriage not broken by divorce. Turia's husband makes a similar point when he writes in her epitaph: *rara sunt tam diuturna matrimonia finita morte non diuertio interrupta* – 'Rare are marriages that last so long, ter-minated by death not dissolved by divorce.'[18] None of these cases, therefore, provides the type of contrast which would be relevant to Dido – viz, that between a widow who marries again and one who does not.

The same point must be borne in mind when we consider the numer-ous epitaphs containing phrases like *solo contenta marito, uno contenta marito, uni deuota marito* etc.[19] Granted such phrases include the idea that the dead woman was never previously married to anyone else, but surely the important assertion is that she was never divorced. This is sometimes brought out elsewhere in the epitaph. In *Carm. Epigr. 652*, for example, we have the words:

> contemptisque aliis me dicto iure secuta es

> *and rejecting others you loyally followed me.*

When Cornelia pronounces her own encomium in Propertius IV.11, the poet makes her say: *in lapide hoc uni nupta fuisse legar* (36) – 'on this stone you will read that I was married to one husband'. Perhaps she *is* claiming that she wasn't married to anyone else before she married Paulus, but her primary purpose is surely to state that she was never divorced. This is supported by the sentence immediately following,

---

18 *Laudatio Turiae CIL* vi.1527, 27. See M. Durry, *Éloge Funèbre* (Paris 1950) 9.
19 See *Carm. Epigr.* 455, 643.5, 736.4.

which says (in paraphrase) 'I call my dead ancestors to witness that I never caused the Censor's rule to be relaxed and that my hearth never blushed for any sin of mine.' Similarly, when she says to her daughter 'see to it that, like me, you remain attached to a single husband' – *teneas unum uirum* – the intention uppermost in her mind is to warn the girl against divorce.[20]

Some further information can be gathered from Seneca's remarks on marriage in his *De Matrimonio*, bits of which are embodied by St Jerome in his work *Aduersus Iouinianum* (Migne, vol. 23.222ff.).[21] On p. 286 Jerome begins a section on wives who refused to survive after their husbands' deaths. This includes a summary of Timaeus' account of Dido's suicide (see below) and an approving reference to the Indian custom of suttee. On p. 287 he goes on to mention certain Roman widows who resolved not to remarry. This he finds admirable, but the reasons given by the ladies themselves range from 'For me my husband is always alive' to 'I don't see any man who wants me more than my money.' One notices, too, that the words were spoken in reply to someone who thought the decision either odd or ill-advised. Annia, for instance, was urged by a kinsman to marry again, because she was still young and attractive. The younger Porcia is supposed to have asserted *felix et pudica matrona nunquam praeterquam semel nubit* ('a happy and respectable wife marries only once'), but she said it when she heard someone praising a woman of good character (*quaedam bene morata*) who had married again. This would suggest that the women mentioned by Seneca were rather exceptional. Seneca himself clearly thought that for a woman second marriages were wrong, but one wonders how typical this censorious outlook was. For later sections of Jerome (pp. 291ff.) show that Seneca also took a rather jaundiced view of *first* marriages. The marital troubles of Cicero, Socrates, Sulla, Pompey, and Cato the Censor are all referred to, and we are reminded of notorious women like Pasiphaë, Clytemnestra, Eriphyla, and Helen. The fact is that to the Stoic sage women were a nuisance; they interfered with his autonomy. So in as much as Seneca aspired to that ideal he felt at liberty to take an anti-feminist line. In another essay, entitled *How to cope with misfortune*, he addresses a man who is mourning the death of a good wife: 'How do you know she'd have *remained* good? Nothing is so fickle and unreliable as the female disposition. We all know of marriages that have broken up and of quarrels even more ugly

---

20 See D. R. Shackleton Bailey's note on Propertius iv.11.68 in *Propertiana* (Cambridge 1956) 265.

21 Printed in Seneca, *Supplementum*, ed. F. Haase (Lipsiae 1902) 26–32.

than divorce between incompatible partners.'[22] These words of comfort indicate that like St Paul, his fictitious correspondent, Seneca considered marriage only marginally preferable to combustion. The fact that he himself married twice and was apparently very happy (at least with his second wife) merely illustrates that here, as in other areas, there was an enormous gap between the great man's preaching and his practice.

Let us concede, then, that a certain amount of old-fashioned, rather sentimental, respect was still paid to women who had never been divorced and who, when widowed, chose not to remarry. Nevertheless, in the last century of the republic both divorce and remarriage were extremely common. This was especially true among the families of the aristocracy, in which marriage had an important political function. Augustus himself was Scribonia's third husband, and the Empress Livia, the most respected lady of the age, was not an *uniuira*, in spite of the polite fiction entertained by Horace in *Odes* iii.14.5. When Augustus drafted his social legislation remarriage took on a new importance. We don't know how prominently it figured in the abandoned programme of 28 B.C., but certainly the Lex Iulia of 18 B.C. penalized widows if they *didn't* remarry. If, then, we put the question in the form most relevant to our enquiry, viz 'Was it regarded as a disgrace for a widow to remarry?' the answer must surely be No. In Book 3 of the *Aeneid* the character of Andromache, who has been married to Hector, Pyrrhus, and Helenus, is treated with tenderness and respect. In Lucan's epic the same is true of Cornelia. Although she reproaches herself for bringing trouble to two husbands (Crassus and Pompey), no one else thinks her in any way blameworthy. As she leaves Lesbos the people grieve openly:

tanto deuinxit amore
hos pudor, hos probitas castique modestia uultus   (8.115–6)

So great was the affection with which she held them by her decency and goodness and by her pure and modest looks.

We have been discussing how deeply the Romans of the period from, say, 70 to 20 B.C. disapproved of widows' remarrying. It may, of course, be argued that the character of Dido is constructed on a much older model; that she holds before her the ideal of the early Roman *matrona*; and that the values of Virgil's day are not strictly relevant. It is quite true that Dido does prize the ideal of *uniuiratus*, but that is only part of

---

[22] *De Remediis Fortuitorum*, in the *Supplementum ed. cit.* 54.

a complex situation; for she is not in fact in the same position as an early Roman *matrona*. She is the queen of a young, forward-looking community; and so, over and above her latent maternal feelings, she has a duty to produce an heir for the royal family. The citizens of republican Rome had no immediate parallel in their own experience. But a somewhat analogous situation arose when the Emperor Augustus planned to continue his dynasty through the marriage of his daughter Julia. These plans were, as we know, tragically frustrated. Her first husband, Marcellus, died in 23 B.C. at the age of nineteen. She was then married to Agrippa and finally to Tiberius. If Augustus had any respect for the ideal of *uniuiratus*, such feelings were set aside without compunction when the interests of the state so demanded.

Dido also had reasons of state, which, as Virgil well knew, were inseparable from her own longings. With characteristic subtlety he arranges for the love of the childless queen to be awakened in the first place by Cupid in the form of Aeneas' son Ascanius. This is one of the many points in which Virgil departs from the story of Jason and Medea as told by Apollonius; more will be said about it below. Anna then adds fuel to the fire: 'You are dearer to your sister than the light of life. Are you going to pine away through the whole of your youth in loneliness and sorrow, and not know the sweetness of children and the joys of love – *nec dulcis natos Veneris nec praemia noris?*' (33). In his note on this line Servius Danielis carefully points out that intercourse precedes birth, and he supplies a technical term for Virgil's change of order. Buscaroli remarks that the second expression is coloured by the purity of the first.[23] Pease understands Anna to mean 'neither parental nor (even) conjugal joys'. But could it not be that Anna's discreet nuance reflects Dido's emotional priorities? Soon after, we are told that when Aeneas is not with her Dido takes Ascanius on her knee (84–5). Later, when Aeneas decides to leave she appeals to him to pity her dying house – *miserere domus labentis* (318). It is not certain (though quite probable) that this includes the notion that without an heir the royal family will become extinct. But the thought of an heir emerges unmistakably in vv. 327–30:

> saltem si qua mihi de te suscepta fuisset
> ante fugam suboles, si quis mihi paruulus aula
> luderet Aeneas, qui te tamen ore referret,
> non equidem omnino capta ac deserta uiderer.

> *At least, if before you hurried away I had borne a child of yours,*

23 C. Buscaroli, *Il libro di Didone* (Milano–Roma 1932) 65.

if I had a little Aeneas playing in the palace whose face would remind me of you in spite of everything, I would not feel so utterly ruined and desolate.

Consider a leader from an old royal house, whose marriage has been broken by death; one who, when warned by a dream, escaped the enemy's sword and led a band of followers to found a new city in exile; one who through many vicissitudes on land and sea has been distinguished for piety. Such a leader is Dido. It has, indeed, often been pointed out that in many respects she is Aeneas' *alter ego*. But there is one parallel which does not seem to be commonly mentioned. As Troy is burning Aeneas feels again and again the pull of the old heroic ideal – to die gloriously for one's country.[24] In the end he is persuaded to make his escape from Troy and to survive for the sake of his people's future, but he is more than once assailed by feelings of guilt and regret:

> o terque quaterque beati,
> quis ante ora patrum Troiae sub moenibus altis
> contigit oppetere!

(1.94–6)

Thrice and four times blessed are you who had the good fortune to die before your fathers' eyes under the high walls of Troy!

So too, one might reasonably say that Dido reveres the old ideal of *uniuiratus* and cannot abandon it without remorse. Granted the balance of emotions is different in the two cases, but the dilemma is surely analogous. If, therefore, we are determined to judge the morality of Dido's behaviour, it seems unfair to present it simply as a conflict between love and duty. On one side was her love for Sychaeus, her duty to his memory, and the force of the oath which she had sworn. On the other her love for Aeneas, her desire for children, and her hopes for the future of her people.

Before leaving the question of Dido's loyalty to her dead husband let us consider for a moment what function Sychaeus performs within the epic. In the account preserved by the third-century Sicilian historian Timaeus the Libyan king was determined to marry Dido. She was unwilling, but was pressed by her people to agree. Finally, pretending she was going to conduct a ritual which would release her from her oath to her husband, she built a pyre by the palace wall, lit it, and leaped into the blaze. Substantially the same version is given by Justin,

---

24 See, e.g., Homer, *Iliad* 22.73; Horace, *Odes* iii. 2.13; Virgil, *Aen.* 2.431–4.

writing in the third century A.D. According to him, Dido built the pyre on the pretext of appeasing the spirit of her dead husband. Aeneas is not mentioned in either account. This may serve to remind us that the story of Dido and Sychaeus has no necessary connection with the story of Dido and Aeneas. Dido could, after all, have been captivated and then deserted by Aeneas even if she had not sworn to remain a widow or even if she had never previously been married.

Virgil, of course, uses the Sychaeus story with masterly skill. Thanks to Sychaeus, Dido's character is given an extra dimension in time. We are told how as a girl in Tyre she loved him and grieved at his death – perhaps with an added bitterness in that he was murdered by her own brother.[25] It is Sychaeus who constitutes the cause of her inner struggle – a struggle which gives her moral stature even though she has no chance of winning it. A psychological critic might further argue that Dido's feelings as a woman were the more powerful because they had been so long suppressed, and that the morbid and excessive nature of her passion was directly related to the torments of her guilty conscience.

Yet even if all these points are conceded it remains true that what brings disaster is not Dido's guilt but her love of Aeneas. Everything comes back to that. Thus if we set aside the notion of a moral flaw and choose the other, more Aristotelian, idea of an error or mistake, we may find the error, as Quinn does, in her failure to realize that the relationship did not mean the same to Aeneas as it did to her; or we may point to the fact that Dido has heard and overlooked all the prophecies given to Aeneas by the Penates and Celaeno and Helenus about his Italian destiny; in either case the mistake was an immediate consequence of her love.

When we look more closely at the nature of this love we face a final question which is bound to affect our total view of the tragedy. As a way of leading into the point let us think for a moment about Dido's death. Her motives for killing herself may be stated in various forms, but most readers would probably agree that she does so because she has been betrayed and humiliated. The only way she can retrieve her dignity is by taking her own life. But while the act of suicide reflects her proud heroic temper, it is still the result of a rational decision. Venus did not compel her to die, nor did Juno. As Virgil says, she died not as a result of fate's decree but before her time (*ante diem*). She could have chosen otherwise.[26]

25 *Aen*. 4.21.
26 See the note of R. D. Williams on *Aen*. 4.696–7. The phrase *subitoque*

The same, however, is not true of her falling in love with Aeneas. This is a point of central importance. Antigone buries her brother in the full knowledge of the consequences. Agamemnon, in agony of mind, chooses to kill his daughter so that the Greek fleet may sail for Troy. But Dido never chooses to fall in love with Aeneas. It may, of course, be objected that no one ever chooses to fall in love; but normally a romantic relationship, however ardent, can be fostered or discouraged. People do consider whether or not to become more deeply involved. But Virgil makes it quite clear, I think, that this privilege was never given to Dido. When her conversation with Anna takes place at the beginning of Book 4, it is already too late. 'The queen has long been injured with a deep love; she nourishes the wound with her life-blood, and is consumed by the fire which she keeps concealed.' To state the argument in a determinist form one might refer to the intervention of Venus, later abetted by Juno, and maintain that the goddesses' combined will was too strong for any mortal to withstand. A more libertarian reader might prefer to say that the divine action in the *Aeneid* should not be understood as a *cause* of human behaviour but rather as a parallel phenomenon lending weight and universality to the drama below. Yet it doesn't really matter which view one takes, because wherever Dido's passion originates (from without or within) it is portrayed as a force which by its very nature overpowers resistance.

Let us recall how it began. Venus substitutes Cupid for Ascanius with the deliberate intention of making Dido fall madly in love:

> At Cytherea nouas artis, noua pectore uersat
> consilia, ut faciem mutatus et ora Cupido
> pro dulci Ascanio ueniat, donisque furentem
> incendat reginam atque ossibus implicet ignem
>
> (1.657–60)

> *But the Cytherean devises new wiles and new schemes within her heart: Cupid, with his appearance and face altered, is to come instead of Ascanius, by his gifts he is to inflame the queen to madness and wind fire around her bones.*

She explains the plan to her son:

> quocirca capere ante dolis et cingere flamma
> reginam meditor
>
> (1.673–4)

accensa furore, however, is rather difficult. How far it is consistent with our interpretation depends on what phase of Dido's *furor* is referred to.

And so I intend to forestall [Juno], taking the queen by a trick and encircling her with flame.

She will steal Ascanius away to prevent him from discovering her trick (*dolos*). Cupid is to assume his appearance:

> tu faciem illius noctem non amplius unam
> falle dolo
>
> (1.683–4)

You by a trick are to counterfeit his appearance for just one night.

[When Dido takes you on her lap and kisses you]

> occultum inspires ignem fallasque ueneno   (1.688)

You are to breathe into her an invisible fire and secretly administer poison.

These lines all emphasize Venus' trickery. The essence of a trick is, of course, its unexpectedness. The victim must be unaware of what is happening until it is too late. In due course Dido takes Cupid on her knee and fondles him, 'little knowing how mighty a god is sitting there and what misery he brings her' –

> inscia Dido
> insidat quantus miserae deus.   (1.718–19)

In other words, the fatal passion comes on Dido unawares. Her resistance is undermined before she can collect herself.

Another important word in vv. 657–60 (quoted above) is *furentem*. Cupid is to inflame the queen to *madness*. In Book 4 there are many variations on the theme of madness, but the only madness that concerns us here is that which afflicts Dido before Aeneas decides to leave; for this is the madness of Eros. Later, other emotions become mingled with it. We first hear of Dido's *furor* in Book 4 when she and Anna are conducting sacrifices to the deities of marriage with the intention of obtaining their good will and in particular of releasing the queen from her oath of loyalty to Sychaeus. It looks as if the priests of Carthage tried to give an encouraging interpretation of the ritual, but whatever they said was utterly irrelevant:

> heu uatum ignarae mentes! quid uota furentem,
> quid delubra iuuant? est mollis flamma medullas
> interea et tacitum uiuit sub pectore uulnus.
> uritur infelix Dido totaque uagatur

urbe furens, qualis coniecta cerua sagitta,
quam procul incautam nemora inter Cresia fixit
pastor agens telis liquitque uolatile ferrum
nescius.   (65–72)

*Alas for the ignorance of the priests' minds! What use are prayers,
what use are shrines to one who is in a frenzy? All the time the
flame devours her soft marrow, and the wound remains silently
alive beneath her breast. The wretched Dido is on fire and paces
through every part of the city in a frenzy, like a deer after the
shooting of an arrow, a deer which, all unwary, amid the woods of
Crete has been pierced from afar by a shepherd's hunting-weapon;
he has left the flying steel behind him, unaware of what has
happened.*

This is a very significant passage. The word *incautam* reminds us once
again that Dido was caught unawares; the repetition *furentem . . .furens*
emphasizes the irrational nature of her love; and its raging intensity is
brought out by the images of fire and wounding.

The motif of fire is introduced by Venus as early as 1.660, where she
instructs Cupid to inflame the queen and wind fire round her bones. It
reappears in 1.673 and 688 (also quoted above). We are told of Cupid's
burning face – *flagrantis uultus* (710), and of Dido's love which grows
more intense as she gazes at him – *ardescit tuendo* (713). The fire is
still raging in the second line of Book 4 – *caeco carpitur igni*. The motif
recurs again and again throughout the book, eventually finding its
consummation in the flames of Dido's funeral pyre, which are visible
to the departing Trojans from far out at sea (5.1–7). The motifs of
hunting, wounding, poison and illness are slightly less prominent, yet
each has its own significance. The hunt, for instance, is prefigured by
the epiphany of Venus in Book 1, where she is dressed as a huntress
(318ff.); Dido goes forth to hunt in 4.136ff.; but all the time she
herself is the stricken quarry. The motif of the wound follows a similar
course to that of fire; for Dido's wound of love becomes eventually the
wound inflicted on her own body.

All these images reinforce one another. The violence of madness,
fire and wounding conveys the overwhelming power of Dido's passion, which sweeps aside all scruples however honourable. One of the
few scholars to stress this point is W. A. Camps, who says: 'the
obsessive love that seizes her is a demonic force, not an impulse which
her will could have overcome'.[27] The pity we feel as we see her in the

[27] W. A. Camps, *An Introduction to Virgil's Aeneid* (Oxford 1969) 34.

grip of this terrible power turns to horror as we watch her total dis-
integration. But even when she is screaming for vengeance and calling
down a curse of eternal enmity, it hardly occurs to us to condemn her.
For whatever her deserts may have been (and I have argued that it is
not easy to make a clear case against her) she did not deserve to suffer
so cruelly.

And so we return to the quotation from *Lear* which we discussed at
the beginning:

> As flies to wanton boys are we to the gods;
> They kill us for their sport.

We thought it unwise to accept this as a motto for the *Aeneid* because
it implied that the gods acted merely from caprice. We have to believe,
I take it, that in Virgil's view there *was* a divine purpose discernible in
history. He did not hold such a view in his early days as an Epicurean,
and to the end of his life he may well have had serious doubts, but it is
hard to see how he could have brought his great epic to the verge of
completion if this faith had not on the whole remained dominant in his
mind. Nevertheless, he was too honest not to acknowledge that the
process of history, whether divinely controlled or not, had always
worked and continued to work without any regard for the merits of
individual people, or even for the merits of nations. One recalls the
feelings of Aeneas when he saw Dido for the last time:

> nec minus Aeneas, casu percussus iniquo,
> prosequitur lacrimis longe et miseratur euntem   (6.475–6)

> *Yet none the less, Aeneas, stunned by the unfairness of her fate,*
> *follows her with tears from afar and pities her as she departs.*

Casu percussus iniquo. That is a feeling which thinking men have experienced in every age. Their response may be said to constitute the
history of theology – and of atheism.

3

IMITATION
Association of ideas in Persius

Readers of Persius have always recognized that he owed a special debt to Horace. In the appendix to his edition of 1605 Casaubon noted most of the important allusions, and later editors like Conington and Villeneuve made excellent use of this material when commenting on individual points. In recent times attention has come to focus more upon the way in which the allusions are made. In the first section of his Berlin dissertation (1940) Kugler showed how in a number of cases Persius gave a literal meaning to a Horatian metaphor.[1] Then in *Philologus* 1955 Henss distinguished ten ways in which Persius varied his Horatian material – e.g. by altering plural to singular, putting species for genus, and switching from active to passive voice. Here is an example of his procedure:

> Horace, *Epist.* i.16.64: *in* triuiis *fixum* cum se demittit ob
> assem
> Persius 5.111: *in*que luto *fixum* possis transcendere
> nummum

'Both poets want to show in this picture a miser in a particularly degrading situation: picking up a cheap coin which is stuck in the mud of the street. Horace says "stuck in the street", meaning "in the mud of the street". The idea of sticky mud is demanded by the word *fixum*. Persius allows "street" to be understood, substituting for it the *lutum*, which is now made explicit.'[2]

This is an illustration of what Henss calls *Auflösung der Prägnanz* – making implications explicit. Henss' paper, which is admirably per-

---

[1] W. Kugler, *Des Persius Wille zur sprachlichen Gestaltung in seiner Wirkung auf Ausdruck und Komposition* (Diss. Berlin 1940).
[2] D. Henss, *Philologus* 99 (1955) 292.

54

ceptive and lucid, is concerned above all with classification. Various types of allusion are set out before us and we are invited to distinguish between them. The object of this essay, however, is rather different. Instead of comparing words and phrases on their own we shall be examining lines or groups of lines from the two writers. This may produce a few incidental results. It may reveal one or two verbal correspondences which do not seem to have been observed before; it may suggest that occasionally, where commentators have cited three or four parallels from Horace, only one is relevant; and it may help to define a source of Persius' obscurity by showing that at times the phrasing and vocabulary natural to one sequence of thought (namely that of Horace) have been transferred to another where they are less at home. But our main object is to enquire why Persius thought of a particular Horatian passage at a particular moment. And this, as the title suggests, is a question of association.

In English studies the most celebrated work on the association of ideas is probably *The Road to Xanadu* by Livingston Lowes.[3] With the aid of Coleridge's notebooks Lowes was able to discover what the poet had been reading at the time when he composed *The Rime of the Ancient Mariner* and *Kubla Khan*. This enabled him to show how certain phrases, which had been jotted down in an apparently haphazard fashion, reappeared transfigured and harmonized in those famous poems. Since *The Road to Xanadu* many smaller studies have been undertaken with broadly the same technique and the same general intention. An example fairly close to the present essay in scope would be B. I. Evans' paper on what was in Keats' mind when he wrote *On first looking into Chapman's Homer*.[4] But whereas Evans was relating a single sonnet of Keats to half a dozen earlier works (especially passages from *Odyssey* 5, from Bonnycastle's discourses on astronomy, and from Robertson's history of America) we shall be relating several passages of Persius to a work by a single author, namely the hexameter poems, or *Sermones*, of Horace. No doubt this difference in critical method reflects a difference in the modes of reminiscence employed by Keats and Persius, and ultimately in the quality of their imagination. We shall return to this question later on. But our main concern will be to examine a number of specific instances in Persius.

1.8–11 Rome's critical and moral standards are frivolous:

> nam Romae quis non – a, si fas dicere – sed fas
> tum cum ad canitiem et nostrum istud uiuere triste

---

[3] J. Livingston Lowes, *The Road to Xanadu* (Boston 1927).
[4] B. I. Evans, *Essays and Studies* 16 (1930) 26–52.

aspexi ac nucibus facimus quaecumque relictis,
cum sapimus patruos

*For in Rome who does not – ah, if only I might say it – but I may
when I look at our venerable hair and our stern manner and all
we've been doing since we gave up marbles and assumed the
wisdom of disapproving uncles.*

Rome, as Persius begins to say in v. 8 and finally does say in v. 121,
is a city of asses. The satirist feels justified in making this charge when
he looks at his fellow-citizens' bogus gravity and stern demeanour.
After noting these points Persius (I would suggest) searched for a
third variation on the same theme and hit on the idea of austere wisdom.
This put him in mind of Horace, *Epist.* II.2.141–2:

nimirum sapere est abiectis utile nugis,
et tempestiuum pueris concedere ludum.

*Without doubt it is advisable to cast aside idle amusements and to
learn wisdom, leaving to children the play that suits their age.*

From *abiectis...nugis* Persius manufactured *nucibus...relictis*, a phrase
which represented a gain and a loss, for *nucibus* (literally 'nuts') is more
vivid than *nugis*, but *relictis* is weaker than *abiectis*. Horace had contrasted wisdom with youthful frivolity. Persius followed him, but added
a further touch by bringing in the figure which typified elderly disapproval, viz the uncle. And so Horace's *sapere* was converted into *cum
sapimus patruos*. Ramsay in the Loeb translation brings out the full
meaning by saying 'put on the wise airs of uncles'. It is possible, of
course, to imagine these ideas occurring to Persius in a different
sequence. But in any case it seems fair to maintain that the association
included Horace's *sapere* in addition to his *abiectis nugis*.

1.28–31 Persius has been disclaiming any desire for popularity. The
interlocutor is sceptical:

'at pulchrum est digito monstrari et dicier "hic est."
ten cirratorum centum dictata fuisse
pro nihilo pendes?' ecce inter pocula quaerunt
Romulidae saturi quid dia poemata narrent.

*'But it's nice to be pointed out and for people to say "That's him!"
Do you think it of no importance to have become a set book for a
hundred long-haired schoolboys?' Look – over their wine the well-
fed sons of Romulus are enquiring what* dia poemata *have to say.*

The first phrase refers to Odes iv.3.22, where at the height of his glory Horace thanks the Muse: 'The fact that I am pointed out by passersby (*quod monstror digito praetereuntium*) as the minstrel of the Roman lyre is all your doing.' The last part of Persius' line presents the same situation more sharply visualized. Persius then thinks of another Horatian passage – this time satirical – which has to do with fame. The serious poet, says Horace, should be content with a few readers:

> an tua demens
> uilibus in ludis *dictari* carmina malis? (*Sat.* i.10.74–5)

> *Or would you be mad enough to prefer your poems to become dictation-pieces in shabby schools?*

Persius replaces the school by the boys and, instead of the poems, the author himself is dictated. After that the sequence becomes less smooth. '*Ecce*', says Pretor, 'denotes an abrupt transition.' No doubt it does, in as much as a class of schoolboys is very different from a group of well-to-do Romans at dinner. Yet there is no break in the main line of Persius' argument, for he is still talking about fame. In answer to the question 'Are you indifferent to the glory of becoming a school text?' Persius remarks sardonically in vv. 30–40 'When a poem is recited after dinner and wins applause I suppose the poet's ashes are gratified.'[5] The poet in question is dead. In view of all this there is something to be said for translating *dia* (31) not as 'divine', 'erhabene', or 'egregia' but as 'immortal'. Such a rendering would be fairly close to the meaning of *dia* as it occurs in *Valeri sentenia dia* (Lucilius, W.1240) and *sententia dia Catonis* (Horace, *Sat.* i.2.32), and it would give the whole passage a little more cohesion. This idea derives some support from what follows.

1.41–3 'You are being too scornful', says the interlocutor, 'No one really despises fame.'

> an erit qui uelle recuset
> os populi meruisse et cedro digna locutus
> linquere nec scombros metuentia carmina nec tus?

> *Would anyone deny that he wanted to earn [a place on] the nation's lips, to speak words deserving cedar [oil], and to leave behind poems which have nothing to fear from mackerel or frankincense?*

---

[5] An apposite parallel would be the line by Calvus: *forsitan hoc etiam gaudeat ipsa cinis* (W. Morel, *Frag. Poet. Lat.* (Stuttgart 1963), p. 86).

'To have earned the nation's lips' is not too hard, being a combination of *laudem meruisse* and such expressions as *in ora uenire*. Editors rightly quote Ennius' phrase *uolito uiuus per ora uirum* ('I flit alive on men's lips'). 'Having said things worthy of cedar' means 'having said things worthy of preservation', for cedar oil was used to preserve books. The phrase recalls not only Horace's *carmina...linenda cedro* (*AP* 332) but also Virgil's *Phoebo digna locuti* (*Aen.* 6.662). 'To leave behind poems fearing neither mackerel nor frankincense' could hardly be understood without a knowledge of Catullus and Horace. In 95.8 Catullus proclaims that Volusius' annals will provide many loose jackets for mackerel. That is, the sheets will be used for cooking fish.[6] In *Epist.* II.1.269–70 Horace speaks of frankincense, perfume, and pepper being wrapped in worthless paper. So much is common knowledge. All I wish to do here is to indicate the thread which draws these ideas together – the fact that *uolito uiuus per ora uirum* is Ennius' claim to immortality, that in *Aen.* 6.662 Virgil is speaking of the *pii uates* who live for ever in the abodes of the blessed, that in Catullus 95.7 we have just been told that Volusius' annals will die – *Paduam morientur ad ipsam* – and that the closing lines of Horace's epistle describe a funeral in which the incompetent poet is carried to oblivion along with the man whom he has attempted to celebrate. And so behind lips, cedar, mackerel, and frankincense lie the basic ideas of extinction and survival. But those unifying ideas would be rather hard to find if we failed to catch the allusions.

In answer to the question in 41–3 Persius admits he is not averse to praise (44–7); but he insists that exclamations of *euge!* 'bravo!' and *belle!* 'lovely!' are often too easily evoked. Here he is thinking of a passage in Horace's *Ars Poetica* (428), where a listener cries *pulchre! bene! recte!* 'Delightful! Fine! Excellent!' But Horace's enthusiastic listener has already received some kind of favour from the rich poet whom he is applauding, and this makes his praise useless. 'If', says Horace, 'you have given (*donaris*) anything or intend to give (*donare uoles*) anything to anyone, don't invite him to listen to your verses' (426–7). By way of illustration Horace selects three types of favour: the rich poet can provide a nice dinner, or stand surety for the poor man, or get him out of some legal entanglement. 'I will be surprised', adds Horace, 'if after doing these services he manages to distinguish between an insincere and a genuine friend.'

noscere mendacem uerumque...amicum (425)

---

[6] See D. F. S. Thomson, *Phoenix* 18 (1964) 30–6.

Now in 30–40 Persius has been talking about rich men at dinner. With the aid of Horace's first example he takes up that scene again. Horace had said:

> unctum qui recte *ponere* possit (422)

> *who can serve a rich dinner in the proper way.*

Persius, addressing a rich poet, says:

> calidum scis *ponere* sumen (53)

> *you know how to serve hot sow's udders.*

(The change from the general *unctum* to the particular *sumen* is typical.) A second favour is described in v. 54; then the rich man is supposed to say to his friend:

> uerum...amo, *uerum* mihi dicite de me (55)

> *I'm a lover of truth; tell me the truth about myself.*

qui pote? (How can he?) says Persius. All this goes back to vv. 424–5 of the *Ars Poetica*, but Horace's general observation has been dramatized. One other point is worth noting. Horace, as we saw, mentioned three types of service performed by the rich man. Only one suited Persius; but he wished to find a second. So he recalled another, totally different, passage of Horace which dealt with the same situation, viz *Epist.* 1.19.37–8. There, asserting that he didn't go looking for acclamation, Horace had said:

> non ego uentosae plebis suffragia uenor
> impensis cenarum et *tritae* munere uestis

> *I don't hunt for the approval of the variable public by paying for other's people's dinners and giving away a threadbare cloak.*

Persius had already used the idea of a free dinner; he now took over the present of old clothes, adding an appropriately shivering recipient:

> scis comitem horridulum *trita donare* lacerna

> *You know how to give a threadbare cloak to a shivering companion.*

It is perhaps more likely that *donare* came directly from *AP* 426 than from *munere*, but of course one cannot tell.

1.61–5 Persius is still ridiculing the aristocratic poetasters:

uos, o patricius *sanguis*, quos uiuere fas est
occipiti caeco, posticae occurrite sannae.

    'quis populi sermo est?' quis enim nisi carmina molli
nunc demum numero fluere, ut per leue seueros
effundat iunctura *unguis*?

*O ye blue-blooded patricians, who live by heaven's will with a
blind wall in the back of your skull, run and confront the jeering
grimace at your back door.*

    *'What does the public say?' What else, except that now at last
poems flow along with a soft rhythm so that the join sends critical
nails skidding over a smooth surface?*

Under *caecus* III.A Lewis and Short give several passages where the
word means 'windowless'. This fact, in conjunction with *posticae* and
occurrite, suggests that in v. 62 Persius is operating with the metaphor
of a house. In regard to the previous line we have to remember that
Persius has been speaking of nobles (*proceres* in v. 52) who dictate
poems while reclining on their expensive couches. It seems that he
now wanted to round off the section by urging such men to practise a
little self-criticism. When he searched for a phrase like 'Ye blue-
blooded gentlemen' he thought of Horace's expression in *AP* 291ff.

uos, o

Pompilius *sanguis*, carmen reprehendite quod non
multa dies et multa litura coercuit atque
praesectum deciens non castigauit ad *unguem*.

*Ye descendants of Numa's line, condemn every poem which many
a day and many an erasure have not held back and corrected ten
times over to meet the test of the carefully cut nail.*[7]

But he refused to take over the phrase unchanged, partly because the
process of *aemulatio* demanded some alteration in one's model, partly
because Horace's *o Pompilius sanguis* had a specific reference to the
Pisones, who claimed descent from Numa Pompilius. And so he wrote
o patricius sanguis. After completing his exhortation Persius opened a
new section with the question 'What does the public say?' But the

---

[7] The exact meaning of *praesectum* is unclear. It can hardly mean 'cut
short'; but 'sharpened to a point' would also be inappropriate. By
'carefully cut' I mean a nail which is not rough, jagged, or pointed, but is
long enough to serve the purpose required. Whether *praesectum* can have
this sense is open to question, but the other proposed reading, *perfectum*,
is insipid. See the discussion in C. O. Brink's edition of the *Ars Poetica*,
and also Nisbet–Hubbard's note on *Odes*. 1.6.18.

same passage of Horace remained near the surface of his mind, and he drew on it again to describe the test of the critical nail. It is characteristic that whereas Horace merely implies the careful joinery Persius makes the idea explicit by using *iunctura*, a term taken from stone-cutting and carpentry. It is also reasonable, I think, to regard Persius' *seueros* as a transformation of Horace's *castigauit*.

One observes how Persius handled the idea of smooth versification in circumstances which were almost the exact opposite of Horace's. Horace believed that Latin writers had significant themes and the power to render them into memorable poetry. What they needed was patience and self-criticism. They hated the business of revision, and as a result their work lacked finish. The writers attacked by Persius had neither significant themes nor poetic power (no doubt the two things were related). What they did have was a smooth technique which enabled them to say things that didn't matter in a very fluent style. In the poets of Horace's day smoothness was a desideratum. In the contemporaries of Persius it was a single asset, which in the absence of others appeared highly dubious. So although the two satirists started from widely different positions they converged on the same point.

1.104–6 Scoffing at fashionable poetry, Persius says:

> summa delumbe saliua
> hoc natat in labris et in udo est Maenas et Attis
> nec pluteum caedit nec demorsos sapit *unguis*

This emasculated stuff, this Maenad and Attis, floats on the spit, always on the tip of the tongue, ready to come drooling out. It doesn't pummel the back-rest or taste of bitten nails.

Another passage about nails. As everyone agrees, there is an allusion here to Horace, *Sat.* 1.10.71, where it is said that if Lucilius were alive today he would have to meet higher standards of workmanship; in making his verse he would often scratch his head and

> uiuos et roderet *unguis*

gnaw his nails to the quick.

The train of thought in Persius is that poems like the Maenad and Attis involve no effort or discipline. The idea of effort in making a finished work of art recalled Horace's phrase about bitten nails. But Persius made the usual types of change. Instead of a man gnawing his nails to the quick we now have a poem that 'does not suggest bitten nails'. But we have more than that, for *sapit* carries with it the idea of taste from all those 'oral' images – *saliua, labris, in udo*, and *demorsos*. This drivel does not *savour* of bitten nails. Having thought of Horace's bitten nails Persius now searched for some other sign of the creative artist's exasperation. He found it, I believe, in *Sat.* ii.3.7–8, where we are told that Horace pounds on the wall in his efforts to make poetry:

> immeritusque laborat
> ...paries

> *The unoffending wall suffers.*

This picture found its way into Persius' satire as

> nec pluteum caedit

> *It does not pummel the back-rest.*

That is, in being composed, such poetry does not cause the writer to pummel the back-rest of his couch. If we are right about this, it was the visual image, not the words, that supplied the association.

In spite of the Latin order I have assumed that the bitten nails came into Persius' mind before the pummelled back-rest, because (*a*) the image of bitten nails is closely related to the lips and drivel of the previous lines, (*b*) it is virtually the same as its Horatian model, and (*c*) it has exactly the same function as the Horatian expression – i.e. it describes the agonized frustration of someone who is trying to prune and condense what he has already written. Points (*a*) and (*b*) do not apply to the back-rest, and the function is different from that of its model. Horace's wall is battered because the poet can't get under way; the frustration comes before the creative process has begun. In Persius the back-rest is pummelled (or rather *ought* to be pummelled) in the process of revision.

1.127–30 Persius is now talking of those whom he doesn't wish to have as readers:

> non hic qui in crepidas Graiorum ludere gestit
> sordidus et lusco qui possit dicere 'lusce',
> sese aliquem credens Italo quod honore supinus
> fregerit heminas Arreti aedilis iniquas

> *Not the lout who enjoys jeering at the Greek style of sandals and is low enough to shout 'Hey one-eye!' at a one-eyed man, and who thinks he is somebody just because as aedile at Arezzo he has smashed a few short measures with full municipal pomp.*

Persius has just said that he wishes to be read by those who admire Aristophanes and the old comedy. He now adds that he does not want the attentions of the vulgar type who scoffs at Greek sandals, mocks at a one-eyed man, and is conceited because he has held office in a country town. It is easy to follow Persius' train of thought from those who admire Greek comedy to those who jeer at the Greeks. The sandal or slipper was chosen as a particular object of ridicule.[8] The rest of the sequence, however, from Greek sandals to a one-eyed man to a country magistrate is far from obvious. The common factor, I would suggest, is what we might call a provincial mentality. The fellow who scoffs at the Greeks cannot apprehend the values of an international culture. After mentioning him Persius looks for another example of rudeness and this time hits on a figure who is geographically as well as intellectually provincial – the aedile of a country town. But even as he is framing the description he thinks as usual of the man's Horatian counterpart. This leads him to the pompous magistrate who welcomed Horace and Maecenas at Fundi (*Sat.* 1.5.34–6) and whose name happened to be Aufidius Luscus – Mr One-Eye. When, therefore, he wants to find some kind of behaviour which will reveal a provincial mentality Persius chooses an insult directed at a one-eyed man.[9] Why, finally, does he locate the magistrate in Arretium? Partly, no doubt, because he knew the town himself, but partly too, perhaps, because it was Maecenas' birthplace. The whole process was probably quite unconscious, but (if our hypothesis is right) it did follow a kind of sequence – not of logic but of association.

1.131–3

> nec qui abaco numeros et secto in puluere metas
> scit risisse uafer, multum gaudere paratus
> si cynico *barbam* petulans nonaria *uellat*

> *Nor the witty fellow who sniggers when he sees numbers and cones traced in the sand [of the abacus], and is vastly amused if a saucy Nones-girl tweaks a philosopher's beard.*

Here we have two further examples of philistine jeering. The scoffer's first target is mathematics – an activity doubly suspect, being both intellectual and Greek. After the mathematician, who does not appear

---

[8] The idea that Greek sandals are a mark of affectation is found in Cicero, *Rab. Post.* 27; Livy XXIX.19.12; and Suetonius, *Tib.* 13.

[9] Some scholars, e.g. H. Bardon, *REL* 14 (1936) 342, have taken this as a reference to Nero's attack on Claudius Pollio, which according to Suetonius, *Dom.* 1 was entitled *Luscio*. But Nero was a philhellene, Persius' scoffer was not.

in person, we come to the philosopher or preacher, who does. Horace too had a passage in which a preacher was insulted, viz *Sat.* 1.3.133–4:

> *uellunt* tibi *barbam*
> lasciui pueri

> *Cheeky boys tweak your beard.*

Horace's preacher was a Stoic, but Persius substituted a Cynic. He may have done this deliberately, in order to avoid portraying a fellow-Stoic being subjected to indignities, but it is perhaps more likely that he made the change without having any philosophical distinctions in mind. In Horace too the margin between Stoic and Cynic is often blurred. In the passage just referred to, the beleaguered Stoic shows his anger by barking – *rumperis et latras* (136). The combination of *barbam* and *latras* would have been enough to give rise to Persius' Cynic. There is a difference of intention between the two passages. Horace is more concerned to ridicule the Stoic than to censure the cheeky youngsters. Persius, however, is not ridiculing the Cynic (or if so, only incidentally). He is expressing his contempt for the person who thinks impertinent behaviour is funny. And to make the impertinent behaviour more vulgar and less excusable he replaces the cheeky boys with an adult.

I have followed those scholars who take *nonaria* to mean a Nones-girl.[10] In *Camillus* 33 Plutarch recounts how on the Nones of July serving-girls elaborately decked-out go around chaffing and joking with the men they meet. This practice is traced back to a colourful episode in early Roman history. Serving-girls were sent to the Latins dressed up as free-born brides. During the night they removed the swords from the sleeping enemy. Then their leader signalled from a fig-tree and the Romans dashed out and overran the camp. So Persius' *nonaria* is probably not, as the scholiast thought, simply another word for prostitute. Nevertheless, to judge from Plutarch's description, the phrase *petulans nonaria* had sexual overtones which were certainly not present in Horace's *lasciui pueri*. The *nonaria* was not 'a respectable girl'. It is possible, though naturally unprovable, that the adjective *lasciui* played some part in the transformation.

3.27–9 Here Persius is being cautioned against complacency:

> an deceat pulmonem *rumpere* uentis

---

[10] As far as I know this was first suggested by F. Morice in *CR* 4 (1890) 230. For a discussion of the *Nonae Caprotinae* see S. Weinstock's article in Pauly–Wissowa.

stemmate quod Tusco ramum millesime ducis
censoremue tuum uel quod trabeate salutas?

*Would it be decent to burst your lungs with wind just because you
are the thousandth in a line which traces its origin to Tuscan
stock, or because you parade before your Censor in full regalia?*

Our interest centres on that hyperbolical phrase *pulmonem rumpere
uentis*. It looks as if it might be a transformation of something in
Horace, so we ask if anyone in the *Sermones* puffs his lungs up to bursting point, and this leads us to the story of the mother frog who nearly
bursts herself in her efforts to rival a calf. The passage in question is
Sat. II.3.314ff., especially 318–20:

> cum magis atque
> se magis inflaret, 'non, si te *ruperis*,' inquit
> 'par eris.'

*As she puffed herself up and up her son said 'Not even if you burst
yourself will you be as big.'*

The parallel was spotted by the watchful Villeneuve, though not, I
believe, by any of the other editors. Villeneuve, however, did not go on
to enquire whether there was anything in the general sequence of
Persius' argument which might have led him to those lines. The poet's
companion is being made to say in effect 'Why show excessive pride
just because you come from an old Tuscan family and belong to the
equestrian order?' It seems that with this general idea in view Persius
let his mind play over the *Sermones*, and it came to rest on the passage
where Horace is accused of ridiculous pretentiousness on account of his
efforts to rival Maecenas, who was, of course, an *eques* from an old
Tuscan family. Persius then thought of the fable which was supposed to
serve as a warning to Horace, namely the fable of the frog who literally
inflated herself to bursting point. When Persius took over the idea and
applied it to a human being it was bound to become a metaphor, and a
rather exaggerated metaphor at that. This was entirely in keeping with
Persius' style and procedure.

3.35–8 A passage about remorse:

> magne pater diuum, saeuos punire *tyrannos*
> haut alia ratione uelis, cum dira libido
> mouerit ingenium feruenti tincta ueneno:
> *uirtutem uideant intabescantque relicta.*

Mighty father of the gods, may it please thee to punish cruel tyrants in this way and no other when their nature is moved by terrible lust dipped in fiery poison: may they look upon goodness and waste away at having spurned her.

Persius wants to say that no pain is so severe as the pangs of a guilty conscience. Searching for an apposite illustration he thinks of the infamous tyrants. They must surely deserve the agonies of remorse as a punishment for the pains they have inflicted on others. The germinal passage was Horace, *Epist.* 1.2.58–9:

> *Siculi* non inuenere *tyranni*
> maius tormentum.

The Sicilian tyrants never devised a greater torture.

Greater than what? The missing word is *inuidia,* and the previous line reads:

> inuidus alterius macrescit rebus opimis

The envious man grows thin at the sight of someone else's riches.

This put the idea of 'wasting with envy' into Persius' mind, and a train of thought was set in motion which led to Ovid's striking description of Envy in *Met.* 2, particularly vv. 780–1:

> intabesc*itque uidendo*
> successus hominum.

[Envy] wastes away at the sight of men's successes.[11]

Finally, with envy still in mind, Persius thought of *Sat.* ii.3.13:

> inuidiam placare paras *uirtute relicta*?

Do you hope to placate resentment by abandoning goodness?

These reminiscences, in whatever order they occurred, combined to produce what is perhaps the most famous line in Persius:

> uirtutem uideant intabescantque relicta

For the first time wasting is caused by guilt instead of envy, and the result is very powerful. Milton remembered it in *Paradise Lost* 4.846ff.:

> Abashed the Devil stood,
> And felt how awful goodness is, and saw

---

[11] *Tabescat* is used of envy in Horace, *Sat.* 1.1.111.

Virtue in her shape how lovely; saw and pin'd
His loss.

3.39–42 The same theme is continued:

> anne magis *Siculi* gemuerunt aera iuuenci
> et magis auratis *pendens* laquearibus *ensis*
> purpureas subter *ceruices* terruit, 'imus,
> imus praecipites' quam si sibi dicat...?

> *Were the roars which came from the bronze bull of Sicily more*
> *frightful, and did the sword hanging from the gilded ceiling*
> *terrify the purple neck below more than if one should say to one-*
> *self, 'I am falling, falling headlong'?*

In *Epist.* 1.2.58, as quoted above, Horace had spoken of the *Siculi tyranni*
without referring explicitly to either Phalaris or Dionysius. In v. 35
Persius simply writes *saeuos tyrannos*, but he clearly has the two
Sicilians in mind, for in v. 39 he alludes to Phalaris, transferring the
adjective 'Sicilian' to the bronze bull; and in vv. 40–1 he refers to the
sword of Damocles, which naturally implies a reference to Dionysius.
Editors have noticed that the description in vv. 40–1 is an elaboration
of *Odes* III.1.17–18:

> destrictus *ensis* cui super impia
> *ceruice pendet*

> *The man over whose impious neck the drawn sword hangs.*

So much is clear. There is no obvious reason, however, why the guilty
man should cry *imus, imus praecipites*. Could it be that the nightmare is
an unconscious extension of the preceding picture? From Damocles'
fear (sword about to fall from overhead) Persius moves to the guilty
man's fear (I am falling headlong). If that was the sequence of ideas in
the poet's mind the words in the poem have rather more coherence.

3.73–6 Concentrate on the things that really matter:

> disce nec inuideas quod multa fidelia *putet*
> in locuplete penu, defensis pinguibus *Vmbris*,
> et piper et pernae, *Marsi* monumenta clientis,
> maenaque quod prima nondum defecerit *orca*.

> *Learn this and never mind about the numerous jars that lie rotting*
> *in a rich larder thanks to the acquittal of fat Umbrians, the pepper*
> *and hams (tokens of gratitude from a Marsian client), and the*
> *sardine which is still left in the first barrel.*

Among the rich lawyer's clients fat Umbrians are appropriate enough, whether or not their presence owes anything to the *pinguis Vmber* in Catullus 39.11. The presence of the Marsian in the next line is another matter. We hardly expect it, for unlike the Umbrians the Marsi were known for their hardy simplicity, and the pepper and ham mentioned in v. 75 are gifts of a rather cheap kind. It may be that once again we should seek an explanation in the mental processes of the poet, though I admit that the hypothesis advanced below may seem rather fanciful. We start from the fact that when Persius wrote about the smelly jar in v. 73 he almost certainly had at the back of his mind the Byzantine jar in Horace, *Sat.* II.4.66 which smells of fish pickle: *Byzantia putuit orca.* The verb then (I would suggest) led Persius to its cognate *putet* in *Sat.* II.2.42. It is fair to observe that this is the only occurrence of *putet* in Horace. The subject is a boar – a boar which tastes rotten to the jaded gormandizer: *putet aper.* There is also only one Umbrian in Horace, and he is also a boar—*Vmber...curuat aper lances* ('The Umbrian boar makes the large dish bend'). This occurs in vv. 40–1 of *Sat.* II.4 – the gastronomic poem which contains the jar. Might it not be, then, that this swinish train of thought led the poet to yet another boar – the Marsian boar of *Odes* I.1.28: *seu rupit teretes Marsus aper plagas* ('or if a Marsian boar has broken the fine nets')? If so, that would account for the Marsian client with his gifts of ham. Finally (and here we are once again on firm ground), although in v. 73 Persius substituted *fidelia* for Horace's *orca*, the unusual word *orca* was still close at hand, and he called on it four lines later.

3.100–2 These dreadful lines are part of one of the most memorable passages in Persius. A glutton has disregarded his doctor's advice, and now pays the penalty:

> sed *tremor* inter uina subit calidumque trientem
> excutit e *manibus*, dentes crepuere retecti,
> *uncta* cadunt laxis tunc pulmentaria labris.

> *As he drinks his wine a fit of the shakes comes over him, knocking the warm tumbler from his hands; his bared teeth chatter; then greasy savouries tumble from his loose lips.*

The editors rightly refer us to Horace, *Epist.* I.16.23:

> donec *manibus tremor* incidat *unctis*

> *until your greasy hands are seized with a trembling.*

On close inspection, however, the whole passage of Persius is seen to be an elaboration of three lines of the epistle, where Horace says in effect 'Just because people kept saying you were sound and healthy you would not, I trust, hide a fever at dinner time and pretend not to feel it, until your hands began to tremble when you were actually at table.' In expanding the original, Persius has contrasted the stupid invalid with the friend who sees the truth and comments on it. In Horace's hypothetical situation the invalid has various people on his side encouraging him to ignore the truth. Secondly Persius has concentrated on the unpleasant physical details suggested by the context. Thirdly he has made the scene more dramatic by writing four lines of introductory dialogue, and also by using a more startling style. Thus a trembling not only comes over Persius' invalid but actually knocks the tumbler from his hands. Finally, in his expanded version Persius has included one or two further Horatian reminiscences. When the friend warns the invalid that he looks ill, the latter says:

> ne sis mihi tutor.
>
> iam pridem hunc sepeli; tu restas.

> *Don't you be my guardian. I buried him years ago; it's your turn next.*

In *Sat.* 1.9.26–7 Horace asks the pest whether he has any relatives waiting to greet him. 'No', says the pest:

> 'omnis composui'. felices! nunc ego resto

> *I've buried them all.' Lucky for them! It's my turn next.*

That allusion seems certain, but there may be another. If the editors are right in relating *ne sis mihi tutor* (96) to Horace, *Sat.* II.3.88:

> ne sis patruus mihi

> *don't play the uncle with me,*

this might supply a link in the chain of thought between v. 96 and v. 97. For Horace's words come from a will in which the deceased gave orders for his burial. The idea of burial might then have led Persius to *omnis composui* in the ninth satire.[12]

5.19–21 Persius disapproves of the bombastic language of tragedy:

> non equidem hoc studeo, pullatis ut mihi nugis
> pagina turgescat dare pondus idonea fumo.
> secrete loquimur.

---

[12] The phrase in Horace, *Sat.* II.3.88 comes between *sepulcro* (84) and *saxo* (90) both of which refer to gravestones.

> *I am not eager to make my page swell with black-robed frivolities in an effort to lend weight to smoke. I speak privately.*

On reading *dare pondus fumo* one thinks naturally of Horace, *Epist.* 1.19.42: *nugis addere pondus* ('to lend weight to frivolities'). But why should Persius have thought of that passage? Are the contexts in any way related? It turns out that they are, for both poets are in different ways rejecting the theatre. In the lines immediately preceding these Persius' companion has been deprecating the themes and style of tragedy. 'Leave all that kind of thing alone', he says, 'and concentrate on ordinary life.' In vv. 19–20 Persius accepts this advice: he will avoid the tragic style which is often a mere cloak for frivolities (*nugis*). Then, aided perhaps by the word *nugis*, he thinks of Horace's disarming lines:

> spissis indigna theatris
> scripta pudet recitare et *nugis* addere *pondus*.

> *I am ashamed to recite my poems in crowded theatres (they don't deserve such a setting) and to make something weighty out of mere frivolities.*

The phrase *nugis addere pondus* appeals to him, but he will not take it over without alteration, and in any case he may already have decided to keep his own *pullatis nugis*. And so he substitutes *fumo* for *nugis*, choosing as so often a word with a more precise visual image. We now come to *secrete loquimur* in v. 21. It is a cardinal sentence which allows the thought to swing round from style to ethics. Persius says that he does not affect a theatrical *style*; he speaks privately, revealing his *moral* nature to Cornutus. By now the Horatian passage has receded, but perhaps it is not wholly out of sight, for there too we have a transition from public to private. On hearing the lines just quoted, Horace's opponent cries: 'You're being sarcastic. You're keeping all your work for the ears of the almighty!' The idea of intimacy behind *Iouis auribus ista seruas* is not so very different from that implied in *secrete loquimur*. It is significant, however, that in Persius the confidant is a Stoic philosopher, not the Roman emperor.

5.56 Men have various pursuits. One devotes his time to making money:

> hic satur *irriguo* mauult turgescere *somno*

> *another prefers to eat a large meal and then swell with* irriguo somno,

another enjoys outdoor sports, another gambles, another is soft about women. The words *irriguo somno* are most often explained as 'refreshing sleep', and reference is made to Lucretius 4.907:

> somnus per membra quietem
> irriget

and to *Aeneid* 1.691:

> at Venus Ascanio placidam per membra quietem
> irrigat.

But 'refreshing' would normally imply previous physical exertion, which is not appropriate here. Nor would Persius have admitted that a slothful glutton needed or deserved refreshing sleep. Also it is hard to imagine that drinking has been omitted from this list of pleasures. For these reasons it is better to take *irriguus* as 'well-soaked' and to find the source of *irriguo somno* in Horace, *Sat.* ii.1.8–9:

> transnanto Tiberim *somno* quibus est opus alto,
> *irriguum*que mero sub noctem corpus habento
> *Let those who are in need of deep sleep swim three times across the Tiber and have their bodies well soaked in wine at night-fall.*

Persius has therefore condensed 'deep sleep and a body well soaked in wine' into 'well-soaked sleep'. An imaginative and successful stroke of wit.[13]

5.58–9 Indulgence brings its own penalty. When it comes, men regret their misspent youth:

[13] It may be that in 5.52–3 Persius has already drawn on Horace, *Sat.* ii.1. The lines of Persius read:

> *mille* hominum species et rerum discolor usus;
> uelle suum cuique est, nec uoto *uiuitur* uno.

> *Humanity has a thousand forms; life-styles are variegated: each man has his own wish, and there is more than one desire in life.*

This reflection on human diversity looks like an elaboration of *Sat.* ii.1.27–8:

> quot capitum *uiuunt* totidem studiorum *milia*.

> *For a thousand men alive there are a thousand pursuits.*

If this is right, then Persius switched from the list of pursuits in Horace, *Sat.* ii.1.24ff. to the list of faults in i.4.25ff. For Persius' next line:

> *mercibus hic Italis mutat sub sole recenti*

is certainly based on *Sat.* i.4.29:

> *hic mutat merces surgente a sole* etc.

71

> cum lapidosa *cheragra*
> fregerit *articulos ueteris* ramalia *fagi*

When stony arthritis has broken their fingers, turning them into the boughs of an old beech.

Persius has just mentioned the compulsive gambler (*hunc alea decoquit* in v. 57). This recalled the cripple Volanerius in Horace, *Sat.* II.7.15ff., who employed a man to pick up the dice:

> postquam illi iusta *cheragra*
> contudit *articulos*

when arthritis with good reason had crushed his fingers.

Persius discarded the *iusta*, perhaps because it conveyed no picture to the mind's eye. He then thought of another reference to gout in *Epist.* I.1.31:

> nodosa corpus...prohibere *cheragra*

to save your body from knotty gout.

The adjective *nodosa* was much more vivid than *iusta*, but the rules of *aemulatio* did not allow mere copying. Persius had to go one better – to think of something even harder than a knot of wood. He finally settled on *lapidosa* ('stony'). For the verb Horace had used *contudit* ('crushed'). So Persius said *fregerit* ('broken'). It is impossible to say whether *fregerit* occasioned or accompanied *ueteris ramalia fagi*. The important point is that (perhaps with Horace's *nodosa* still in mind) Persius saw the metaphorical possibilities of *articulos*.[14] Broken fingers gave rise to broken branches, which recalled Virgil's phrase:

> ueteres, iam *fracta* cacumina, *fagos*

old beeches, now just broken tops (*Ecl.* 9.9)

This was taken over as *fregerit* . . . *ueteris* ramalia *fagi*.
5.91–2 The satirist asks for a dispassionate hearing:

> disce, sed ira cadat naso rugosaque sanna,
> *dum* ueteres auias tibi de pulmone reuello.

Listen, but drop the anger from your nose and that wrinkled grimace, while I pull the old auiae *out of your lungs.*

---

14 For *articulus*, as applied to both trees and men, see Pliny the Elder, *NH* 17.224.

Since v. 73 the satire has been concerned with freedom. In vv. 88–90 the adversary says, in effect, 'Now that I have been legally emancipated am I not free?' Persius prepares to reply in the lines quoted above, which could be summarized as 'Restrain your anger while I get rid of your misconceptions.' A similar situation occurs in Horace, *Sat.* II.7, where Davus says that Horace is no freer than *he* is – perhaps less. Seeing his master's furious expression he quickly adds (43–5):

>   aufer
> me uultu terrere; manum stomachumque teneto,
> dum quae Crispini docuit me ianitor edo.

The gist of these lines is 'Restrain your anger while I tell you some important truths.' In each case the lines are a prelude to a Stoic sermon on moral freedom. What we have, then, is another case of transformation. The first of Persius' lines is fairly straightforward. It renders Horace's *aufer me uultu terrere* in more precisely visual terms. As Jahn points out, anger is thought of as being situated in the nose or nostrils, and so Persius can say *ira cadat naso* when he means 'Take that angry look off your face.' Anger, contempt, and disgust were all expressed by screwing up the face in a way which involved wrinkling the nose. The contortion thus produced was called a *sanna*. Therefore, when Persius says 'Drop your wrinkled *sanna*', he is in part repeating and in part extending the previous phrase.

We come now to the *dum* clause, which in form was suggested by the lines from the seventh satire. The content, however, is rather different, and it looks as if Persius has switched to another Horatian passage, also involving a slave, namely the address to the bailiff in *Epist.* I.14.4–5 :[15]

> certemus spinas animone ego fortius an tu
> euellas agro

> *Let's see if I can pull the thorns more resolutely from my heart
> than you from your field.*

As well as providing the source of Persius' line this also supplies the key to its meaning. To translate *auias* as 'grannies' is only partly right and it makes the image needlessly far-fetched. In view of the phrase from the epistle and of Lucilius' expression *stat sentibus pectus* (W. 239) – 'Your heart is full of brambles' – we must look for some connection between grannies and the vegetable world. The link is

---

[15] That the bailiff is a slave is clear from vv. 40–1.

provided by Lewis and Short's dictionary: *auia*, a plant = senecio or erigeron, groundsel.[16] We must therefore translate *ueteres auias* as 'old granny-weeds' or some such phrase. We cannot be sure about what led Persius to *auias*, but it is worth remembering that he had just written *rugosaque sanna*, and within that interesting imagination it is quite conceivable that the wrinkles of anger gave rise to the wrinkles of old age.

Henss maintained that Persius, like Horace, was talking about passions (*Leidenschaften*).[17] But consider the sequence of argument. The foolish and sinful man believes he is free simply because his legal position is not that of a slave: 'I have the power to live as I choose. Am I not freer than Brutus?' 'That is a false inference', says the Stoic. 'I grant the rest, but strike out "power" and "choose".' 'When the Praetor has pronounced me free have I not the power to do as I choose, within the limits of the law?' 'No, and I'll tell you why, but take that angry look off your face *dum ueteres auias tibi de pulmone reuello.*' It is surely an argument about ideas, conducted in Stoic terms, not about passions. Moreover, *anus* and *anilis* ('old woman' and 'old womanish'), which are analogous to *auiae*, are commonly used in connection with foolish ideas, but are not appropriate to passions. Therefore, old granny-weeds are foolish ideas about the nature of freedom. One final point. Whereas *pectus* ('chest') was frequently used like *animus* in the sense of 'mind', *pulmo* ('lung') was not. As far as I know this was another of Persius' innovations.

5.100–5 It will be convenient to divide this into smaller sections.

5.100–1 Persius has just maintained that ignorance disqualifies people from action. He illustrates this by saying:

> diluis elleborum, certo conpescere puncto
> nescius examen?

> *Do you mix hellebore if you don't know how to check the tongue of the balance at the correct point?*

This recalls Horace, *Epist.* II.1.114–15:

> habrotonum aegro
> non audet nisi qui didicit dare

---

[16] *Auia* is identified with senecio, erigeron, or groundsel by Ernout–Meillet and others. Walde–Hofmann disagree. But in any case the botanical description is of minor importance. The existence of the plant *auia* is attested by Columella VI.14.6 and 3.

[17] Henss, *Philologus* 99 (1955) 291.

You don't risk giving hellebore to a patient unless you have learned how.

The two ideas are identical, but for the general word *dare* Persius has substituted the more technical *diluis*; and instead of referring to the knowledge of dispensing in general (*didicit*) he has specified one particular skill, namely that of weighing out doses.

In the first part of *Epist.* II.1.114 Horace had written:

nauem agere ignarus nauis timet

The man who knows nothing about ships is afraid to steer one.

In Persius this becomes:

nauem si poscat sibi peronatus arator
luciferi rudis, exclamet Melicerta perisse
frontem de rebus.

If a ploughman in clodhopping boots who couldn't recognize the morning star asked to be put in charge of a ship, Melicerta would cry out that shame had perished from the world.

The ploughman in his clodhopping boots who can't even recognize the morning star has taken the place of Horace's general concept of the landlubber. Persius' effect is more elaborately ridiculous, but Horace's epigrammatic neatness and rapidity have been lost.

For the source of Persius' apodosis ('Melicerta would cry out that shame had perished from the world') we are directed by the editors to some earlier lines from the same Horatian epistle (vv. 80–1):

clament periisse pudorum
cuncti paene patres

Almost all the elders would cry out that modesty was dead.

What *we* have to do is to ask why Persius switched from one passage to the other. In vv. 114–17 of the epistle Horace ruefully complains that although navigation, medicine, and craftsmanship are left to experts, everyone undertakes to write poetry regardless of skill. Earlier, in 76ff., he contends that the literary taste of his day is quite uncritical. Poems are judged by their age instead of their art. If anyone cast doubt on the structural soundness of a play by Atta, the elders would cry out in protest. The two passages are therefore similar inasmuch as each deplores the absence of proper professional standards. It was this resemblance which allowed Persius to pass from one to the other.

What actually led him across was the need to find some phrase which would convey a protest against stupid conceit. The fact that he found such a phrase in *clament periisse pudorem* shows that he was guided by the general similarity of context plus the energy of the phrase itself. He did not recall, or if he did recall he didn't care, that in Horace the exclamation was directed by the uncritical against the critical. Persius himself used it the other way round.

> tibi *recto* uiuere *talo*
> ars dedit?

Has art shown you how to live an upright life?

This follows directly on the lines already discussed. As medicine is the art of healing and navigation is the art of sailing, so philosophy is the art of living. The way in which Persius argues about life is modelled on Horace's arguments about poetry. To trace this correspondence further we must quote the full text of *Epist.* II.1.79–81:

> recte necne crocum floresque perambulet Attae
> fabula si dubitem, clament *periisse* pudorem
> cuncti paene patres.

> *If I questioned whether a play of Atta's kept its feet as it walked through the saffron and flowers, pretty well all the elders would cry out that modesty was dead.*

Persius' mind glances over this passage and thinks at once of a similar phrase to *recte perambulet* – one which occurs in vv. 175–6 of the very same epistle and contains the well known censure of Plautus:

> gestit enim nummum in loculos demittere, post hoc
> securus cadat an *recto* stet fabula *talo*.

> *For he is eager to drop a coin into his purse; after that he doesn't care whether or not his play stands up properly.*

Persius transfers the final phrase from art to life as *recto uiuere talo*.

In *Sat.* 5 Persius is arguing that real freedom is a matter of moral discipline. At v. 104 he begins a series of questions. Do you live right? Can you distinguish true from false? Are your desires moderate? Can you step across a coin stuck in the mud? When you can truly say *haec mea sunt, teneo*, then consider yourself *liber* and *sapiens*. We might have expected simply 'If you can do these things then consider yourself *liber* and *sapiens*.' Instead Persius has employed a formula which asserts ownership: 'These things are mine; I'm keeping them.' As we saw at the beginning, the coin in the mud comes from Horace, *Epist.* 1.16.64. Its relevance is due to the fact that Horace was there talking about freedom:

> qui melior seruo, qui liberior sit auarus,
> in triuiis *fixum* cum se demittit ob assem,
> non uideo.

> *I fail to see how the miser is better or more free than a slave when he stoops at the cross-roads for the sake of a penny which is stuck there.*

Now a little earlier in the same epistle Horace was discussing praise: when a man is called *sapiens* and *emendatus* can he legitimately acknowledge such titles? The interlocutor says: 'I enjoy being called a good and wise man as much as you do.' Ah yes, says Horace, but these are names, conferred upon you by the public. It can just as easily take them back again: *'pone, meum est' inquit* (35) 'Put that down, it's mine', it says. In a dispute over ownership the counter-claim would, of course, be *haec mea sunt, teneo*: 'these things are mine; I'm keeping them.'

It is certain that at a number of places in this satire Persius had the sixteenth epistle in mind. Yet *Sat.* II.7 was a more important source, and it may be that *haec mea sunt, teneo* was prompted by a passage in that poem (83–9). Davus asks:

> quisnam igitur *liber? sapiens*, sibi qui...

> *Who then is free? The wise man, who...*

After giving a list of the sage's virtues Davus says very sternly:

> potesne
> ex his ut proprium quid noscere?

> *Can you recognize any of these qualities as your own?*

The catalogue of virtues, which is parallel to Persius' list of questions, and the combination of *liber* and *sapiens*, which recurs in Persius v. 114, may tip the balance in favour of the seventh satire. But one cannot be sure. Persius may well have been thinking of both passages.

5.115–18 If you possess those qualities count yourself free:

> sin tu, cum fueris nostrae paulo ante farinae,
> pelliculam ueterem retines et fronte politus
> *astutam* uapido seruas in pectore *uolpem*,
> quae dederam supra relego.

77

> *But if you, who a moment ago were one of our batch,*[18] *retain your old ⟦false⟧ skin, and wear a glossy exterior while keeping a cunning fox in your unhealthy heart, then I draw back the concession I made above.*

There does not seem to be any reference to a snake shedding its skin. Nor does it seem relevant to cite *in propria non pelle quiessem* (Horace, *Sat.* 1.6.22). It is more likely that the idea came in the first place from a phrase in the sixteenth epistle (45):

introrsum turpem, speciosum pelle decora

ugly underneath, made good-looking by a handsome skin.[19]

This immediately sparked off a reminiscence of a similar expression in *Sat.* II. 1.64–5:

detrahere et pellem, nitidus qua quisque per ora
cederet, introrsum turpis

to pull off the glossy skin in which everyone was parading before the public gaze in spite of being ugly underneath.

This supplied Persius with the idea of surface gloss, which he rendered by *fronte politus*. Finally his mind travelled to *Sat.* II.3.186:

astuta ingenuum uulpes imitata leonem

a cunning fox imitating a noble lion.

This provided the *astuta uulpes*. What brought the three passages together in Persius' mind? Presumably the basic idea of a squalid masquerade, which was common to all of them. There was also another link of a more specific kind which becomes apparent if we set out the ideas as follows: (1) something ugly (*turpis*) underneath an attractive skin, (2) cunning fox underneath skin of noble (*ingenuus*) lion. *Ingenuus* is the opposite of *turpis* in its social and moral aspect.

5.124–31 Finally, a most complex passage, in which Persius is arguing that the only true freedom is moral freedom. Again, it will be best to take this piecemeal.

5.124–5

'liber ego.' unde datum hoc sumis, tot subdite rebus?
an dominum ignoras nisi quem uindicta relaxat?

---

[18] A metaphor from baking.
[19] This phrase certainly lies behind Persius 4.14: *summa nequiquam pelle decorus* – 'wearing a handsome outer skin all to no purpose'.

'I'm free' [says the adversary]. What gives you the right to make this assertion, you who are subject to so many things? Are you unaware of any master except the one whom the Praetor's rod lifts from your back?

The passage as a whole is based on Horace, *Sat.* II.7. The adversary's *liber ego* is a reminiscence of *liber, liber sum* in Sat. II.7.92. In each case the other speaker contradicts the assertion by saying in effect 'How *can* you be free when you are mastered by so many passions?' Horace writes:

> urget enim *dominus* mentem non lenis et acris
> subiectat lasso stimulos uersatque negantem

> *For a master far from gentle drives on your will, jabbing the sharp spurs into your weary flanks and pulling round your reluctant head.*

But Persius does not draw on these lines. Instead his attention shifts to an earlier passage in the same poem, also about a *dominus*, viz vv. 75–7, where Davus says to Horace:

> tune mihi *dominus*, rerum imperiis hominumque
> *tot* tantisque *minor* quem ter *uindicta* quaterque
> imposita haud umquam misera formidine priuet?

> *Are you my master, you who are subject to so many imperious orders from men and affairs, who will never be freed from wretched fear no matter how often you are touched by the Praetor's rod?*

Horace's *tot tantisque imperiis minor* becomes in Persius *tot subdite rebus*, and there is a similar point about the Praetor's rod (*uindicta*) and its failure to liberate a man from moral servitude.

5.126

> 'i, puer, et strigiles *Crispini* ad balnea defer.'

> *Off you go, lad, and take Crispinus' strigils to the baths.*

Davus' discourse on freedom in *Sat.* II.7 is based on material supplied by Crispinus' hall porter – *Crispini ianitor* (45). Therefore when Persius thinks of a slave it is not unnatural for him to think of the slave belonging to Crispinus. But to understand why the slave is sent to the baths we have to switch to an earlier passage, viz *Sat.* I.3.137–9, where Crispinus accompanies a fellow-Stoic to the bath-house:

        dum tu quadrante lauatum
rex ibis neque te quisquam stipator ineptum
praeter Crispinum sectabitur

*while you in royal state go for a sixpenny bath unaccompanied by
any follower except that ass Crispinus.*

This, incidentally, makes it clear that in Persius Crispinus is neither
the owner of the baths nor the bath attendant. Grammatically *Crispini*
goes with *strigiles*, not with *balnea*, and the man's existence in this context is purely literary.[20]

5.127–8

si increpuit, 'cessas nugator?', seruitium acre
te nihil inpellit

*If he shouts 'Well, you good-for-nothing loafer?' slavery doesn't
jab you into action [i.e. you are not a slave].*

This takes us back again to *Sat.* ii.7, for *cessas nugator* is a metamor-
phosis of *nequam et cessator* (*Sat.* ii.7.100). That in itself is not too
difficult, but what kind of situation is Persius asking us to imagine?
True, a man is giving peremptory orders to a slave, but the slave is not
the man addressed by Persius. That becomes clear when we reach v.
128. So it looks as if the sense is: 'You hear orders being shouted in
the street, but as you're not a slave you don't find yourself breaking into
a run.'

    The goad of lust is a strong simple metaphor. It is used by Horace in
Sat. ii.7.47–8.

             acris ubi me
natura intendit

when the sharp point of my nature goads me on.

Persius takes over the idea of a goad in vv. 127–8 as quoted above, but
makes it the goad not of lust but of slavery, thus turning literal slavery
into a metaphorical master. This is awkward in itself and is made more
awkward still by the negative form of the sentence. The point is repeated in Persius' next clause:

[20] It is possible, but hardly necessary, to see another stepping-stone in
    Sat. ii.7.109–10:

        an hic peccat, sub noctem qui puer uuam
    furtiua mutat strigili?

    *Is this slave guilty, who at nightfall exchanges the strigil he has stolen for
    grapes?*

> nec quicquam extrinsecus intrat
> quod *neruos* agitet

> *nor does anything enter from outside to jerk your sinews.*

This also means, of course, 'legally and socially you are not controlled by any master', but the awkwardness is greatly reduced because, unlike *seruitium*, the vague subject can quite easily be equated with authority. The question does not arise in the corresponding passage of the seventh satire:

> duceris ut *neruis* alienis mobile lignum   (82)

> *You are jerked about like a puppet moved by other people's strings.*

Here the man is a puppet manipulated by his own passions. One notices how Persius has kept Horace's *nerui* but altered the sense.
  5.129–31

>   sed si intus et in iecore aegro
> nascuntur domini, *qui tu inpunitior* exis
> atque hic quem ad strigiles scutica et metus egit erilis?

> *But if inside, in your unhealthy liver, masters come into being, how do you come off more lightly than the fellow who is driven to get the strigils by the fear of his owner's strap?*[21]

The *domini*, as described in the remainder of the poem, are greed, luxury, lust, ambition, and superstitition. The question *qui tu inpunitior* comes from Horace, *Sat.* II.7.105:

>   *qui tu inpunitior* illa
> quae paruo sumi nequeunt obsonia captas?

> *How do you come off more lightly when you reach for those delicacies which cannot be obtained at a modest price?*

Again we notice a tighter sequence of thought in Horace. Davus is tempted by a cake; when he gives in to gluttony he is beaten. Horace himself is tempted by expensive dinners; when he gives in to gluttony he eventually ruins his health. Morally there is little to choose between them. Both are guilty, and both are punished. In Persius, however, the analogy between master and slave is not so close. If the slave

---

[21] The idea of corporal punishment comes from the corresponding passage in *Sat.* II.7: *tergo plector* (105). But the actual word used by Persius is *scutica*. It occurs only once in Horace, viz in *Sat.* I.3.119 – shortly before the reference to Crispinus.

is disobedient he is punished. If the 'free' man is dominated by his passions he is made miserable. The gap lies in the fact that the faults are not the same. The slave's fault is apparently disobedience (*cessas, nugator?*) but the free man cannot be censured for disobeying his passions.

This whole section illustrates how, at times, a sequence which was quite straightforward in its Horatian context becomes rather strained when transported to another. By this I do not mean to imply that *all* Persius' transformations of Horace involved a change for the worse. Sometimes he was strikingly successful. There is room, one feels, for a fresh approach to this whole matter, an approach that would try to take account of what each poet was aiming at, and would not, in Marmorale's phrase, regularly make Persius the victim and Horace his unwitting executioner.[22]

The present essay, however, has not been concerned with critical evaluation but with exploring sequences of ideas. The results would suggest that Persius did not as a rule compose with a text of Horace in front of him. Nor, except in a minority of cases, is it likely that the reminiscences were wholly unconscious. It is here that we encounter the basic difference between Persius' mind and the mind of a poet like Keats. When Keats spoke of stout Cortez and all his men 'silent, upon a peak in Darien', he was not thinking of the words used by Robertson to describe that situation,[23] nor did he expect his readers to think of Robertson's or anyone else's history of America. Keats' critic, of course, is entitled to do whatever detective work he likes – and it is always interesting to see the poet's materials in their raw state before they have been transmuted into art – but that has nothing to do with one's immediate response to the poem. In Persius' case, however, the reminiscences are in the main deliberate allusions and are expected to be recognized and appreciated as such. Clearly at some time he committed most of the *Sermones* to memory, and he had them constantly within call when composing his satires. The Horatian phrases, however, are not summoned up in any uniform way. Persius allowed his mind to play over the *Satires* and *Epistles*, moving from one passage to another at the prompting of a name (Crispinus), a phrase (*recto talo*), or a general idea (the rejection of the theatre). And so although the allusion itself may be regarded as deliberate, the process leading to it may often have been only partly conscious. Sometimes too the inter-

---

[22] E. V. Marmorale, *Persio* (Firenze 1963) 6.
[23] Keats, as is often pointed out, confused Cortez with Balboa. See Evans, *Essays and Studies* 16 (1930) 45–6.

mediate stages in that process have been suppressed, so that the reader is suddenly asked to move from (a) to (d) without being shown the stepping-stones (b) and (c). In many cases the stepping-stones cannot be discovered and we simply have to leap and trust to luck. In other cases, as I have tried to show, they can be discovered, and this throws some light on the genesis of the poems.

When we turn our attention from the intermediate stages to the allusions themselves we usually find some rhetorical hyperbole or some conflation of disparate images, some odd extension of grammatical usage or some Stoic habit of thought, which makes it abundantly clear that we are listening to the Neronian, not the Augustan, Flaccus. But this path leads away from the association of ideas towards various forms of stylistic analysis, and that is another matter.

4

TONE
Poets and patrons in Juvenal's seventh satire

We interpret a speaker not only by what he says but by how he says it. Tone is therefore an important element in meaning. Since we cannot hear a writer's voice we must catch his tone from the words themselves. This may not be difficult if the language is our own and the style reasonably simple, but with an ancient author some lexicographical information is often required. Often, too, we need to know the context for which the words were intended and above all the kind of people addressed. Normally the editors supply such information, but sometimes the evidence is not wholly clear and scholars disagree; then we have to try to judge the question as best we can. An example of such a case is the opening of Juvenal's seventh satire.

> Et spes et ratio studiorum in Caesare tantum;
> solus enim tristes hac tempestate Camenas
> respexit...   (1–3)
> nemo tamen studiis indignum ferre laborem
> cogetur posthac, nectit quicumque canoris
> eloquium uocale modis laurumque momordit.
> hoc agite, o iuuenes. circumspicit et stimulat uos
> materiamque sibi ducis indulgentia quaerit.   (17–21)

The hopes and prospects of the arts depend entirely on Caesar. He alone in these times has looked with favour on the dejected Muses...
In future, however, no one who weaves melodious tunes into a web of vocal artistry and has chewed the laurel will be obliged to endure a toil unworthy of his calling. Go to it, my lads; the generosity of our Prince is looking around and urging you on and seeking material for its own exercise.

The identity of Caesar has long been a matter of dispute, but in approaching the problem we need hardly go further back than Nettle-

84

ship, who in 1888 tried to defend the view that the lines were a perfectly straightforward compliment to Domitian (A.D. 81–96).[1] If this were true, *Sat.* 7 would have to be earlier than *Sat.* 4, which mentions the emperor's assassination (v. 153), and also earlier than *Sat.* 2, which speaks of him in the past tense and refers to his incest with his niece as a fairly recent event (29–33). But there are more serious difficulties. In *Sat.* 7.87ff. Juvenal censures the dancer Paris, Domitian's favourite, for his corrupt distribution of patronage. Such an attack is incompatible with Nettleship's view of the opening lines, and indeed could scarcely have been written in Domitian's lifetime. There is also a chronological objection, for since Paris was put to death in A.D. 83 the attack must be dated to about 82. This would mean that *Sat.* 7 was composed at least twenty years before *Sat.* 1. Such a conclusion is exceedingly unlikely. What makes it virtually impossible is the close resemblance between *Sat.* 7.40–9 and Tacitus, *Dialogus* 9, which describes the expense and futility of hiring a hall for a poetic recital. A study of the two passages shows that Juvenal almost certainly borrowed from Tacitus, not vice versa. It is now widely agreed that the *Dialogus* was not written before the first decade of the second century. In that case *Sat.* 7 cannot belong to the period of Domitian.

The identification of Caesar with Domitian might, however, be retained if we interpreted the tone of the passage differently – if, that is, the lines were ironical and really carried a sarcastic attack on the emperor. What, then, would be the poem's relevance in a later period? One answer suggests that Juvenal was using Domitian as an instrument for attacking Hadrian (A.D. 117–38). The two men, it is contended, were alike in their objectionable treatment of poets and intellectuals. Another answer is to admit that the reference to Domitian, like much else in *Sat.* 7, is anachronistic, but to point out that thanks to the publication of works such as Pliny's *Letters*, Suetonius' biographies, and the *Histories* of Tacitus the earlier age had acquired a kind of secondary topicality.

Before considering these conclusions, however, we must ask whether the opening lines can reasonably be taken as sarcastic. In an article published in 1959[2] Helmbold and O'Neil contended that *circumspicit* (20) means 'is on the lookout for' in an unpleasantly self-interested sense, that *stimulat* (20) suggests an element of coercion, that *ducis* (21) is ironical, because a leader in the arts who exerts undesirable pressure isn't really a leader at all, that *indulgentia* (21) implies favouritism,

[1] H. Nettleship, *Lectures and Essays*, second series (Oxford 1895) 132.
[2] W. C. Helmbold and E. O'Neil in *CP* 54 (1959) 100–8.

that the phrase *ducis indulgentia* is an unkind allusion to *Siluae* v. 2.125ff., where Statius gratefully acknowledges Domitian's encouragement, and that *sibi quaerit* (21) also has unfavourable overtones. In the opinion of Helmbold and O'Neil these points 'show clearly [Juvenal's] derogatory intention'. But do they? Whether *circumspicere* is pleasant or not depends on its subject and object. A drug peddler on the lookout for a victim is an unpleasant sight; a benefactor on the lookout for a deserving cause is not. The same applies to *stimulare*: the incentive may be welcome or the reverse. *Dux* is a common word for emperor and, as the authors admit, is often used by Juvenal without sarcasm. Tacitus speaks of Vespasian's *indulgentia* in *Dial.* 9 (a section which, as we have already remarked, was in Juvenal's mind); Pliny frequently pays tribute to the *indulgentia* of Trajan; so it is by no means clear that Juvenal was parodying a particular line of Statius. Again, it is true that in Juvenal 9.92 we hear of a pathic who is anxious to secure the services of a sexual drudge – *bipedem sibi quaerit asellum* – but the moral colouring is supplied by the context; the verb itself is entirely neutral.[3]

One observes that all these points occur in vv. 20-1. But if the compliment to Caesar were ironical Juvenal would have to make this plain in the first three lines. A more recent article maintains that he has in fact done so. The word *spes* in v. 1 is, in G. B. Townend's view,[4] a sarcastic allusion to Calpurnius, *Ecl.* 4.31, which speaks of the hopes aroused by the accession of Nero: *spes magis arridet*. But the expression of hope was conventional on such occasions (Tacitus said the same sort of thing about Trajan in *Agricola* 3), and the verbal link is scarcely strong enough to establish any parodic intention – in fact Townend concedes that it is hardly noticeable. He sees a more striking reminiscence in *respexit* (3), which he relates to Calpurnius, *Ecl.* 4.87-8: *me quoque... Caesar respiciat* ('May Caesar look with favour on me too'). But *respicere* was quite a common verb, and the connection with Calpurnius is far from obvious. No one (to my knowledge) has remarked on it before, and in a footnote Townend candidly admits that he did not notice it himself.

I have been arguing that if the lines are to be taken ironically we must be shown some clear indication in the text, especially as Juvenal's irony usually makes a sharp impact. As far as I can see, no such indication has been discovered. There is also a further point, which concerns the rhetorical emphasis of the passage as a whole. On the straight-

---

[3] Similar arguments are advanced by W. S. Anderson in *CP* 57 (1962) 158, n. 17.

[4] G. B. Townend, *JRS* 63 (1973) 149ff.

forward interpretation Juvenal tactfully excludes the emperor from the criticisms that follow and at the same time obtains a strong white/black contrast: 'Caesar is the only hope; he alone has shown concern at a time when poets were obliged to endure indignities (1–16). True poets need worry no more; Caesar is giving encouragement. But if you expect help from anyone else you may as well give up (17ff.).' The general lack of patronage then becomes the satire's main theme. On the other view the contrast is only between dark grey and black, and the rhetorical point is correspondingly weaker: 'Caesar alone has shown favour to the Muses (in his sinister and undesirable way), at a time when poets were obliged to endure many indignities.'

If, then, the lines do not refer to Domitian, who is Caesar? Of the later emperors there is perhaps nothing that would conclusively rule out Trajan (A.D. 98–117). It has often been remarked that Trajan actually did very little to promote the arts, but in this sort of context one cannot insist on factual accuracy. There is, however, a chronological objection of considerable force. The books of Juvenal's satires as we have them appear to be in sequence. Book I was probably published between A.D. 110 and 115, and Book II (i.e. *Sat.* 6) is normally dated to 116 or soon after. One therefore expects *Sat.* 7 to be later again. This leaves very little time for a reference to Trajan, and one must remember that in his last years he was absent from Rome and had more serious problems to think about than questions of patronage.

There are several considerations, however, which tell strongly in favour of Hadrian (A.D. 117–38). He was a man of genuinely artistic temperament. Eutropius says he was *facundissimus Latino sermone, Graeco eruditissimus*.[5] According to Aurelius Victor he was partial to eloquence and the arts of peace (*eloquio togaeque studiis accommodatior*).[6] Spartianus records his keen interest in poetry, mathematics, art, and music, and states that recitations and various kinds of dramatic performance were given at his dinner parties.[7] One of Hadrian's numerous projects was the re-establishment of the Athenaeum. This institution was described by Aurelius Victor as a school for the liberal arts (*ludus ingenuarum artium*).[8] It contained an auditorium for readings, declamations, and public lectures, and we are told that both Greek and Roman artists were engaged to perform in it. Unfortunately we cannot be sure of the date of its opening. Aurelius Victor says it took place when Hadrian returned to Rome after making peace in the East (*pace*

---

[5] Eutropius VIII.7.2.   [6] Aurelius Victor, *Caes.* 14.1.
[7] Spartianus 14 and 26 (see *Scriptores Historiae Augustae* vol. 1, Loeb).
[8] Aurelius Victor, *Caes.* 14.3.

ad orientem composita). Bardon takes this to refer to the emperor's return after the Jewish revolt, and so he dates the founding of the Athenaeum to about 135.[9] In that case it will have nothing to do with our satire. Highet, however, argues that Aurelius Victor is talking about Hadrian's return from Antioch in 118,[10] and that does seem to be the more natural interpretation of the text. If this is right, then the opening of the seventh satire could have been prompted by the establishment of the Athenaeum a few years later, say in 120. In any case Highet does well to point out that the satire says nothing about the beginning of a new reign or the advent of a new age.[11] It does not read like a coronation poem.

Also, although complimentary, the references to the emperor are brief and restrained. Here, by way of comparison, is a passage from Statius' poem on an equestrian statue of Domitian:

> 'This work fears not the rains of winter or the triple flash of Jove, or the troop from Aeolus' prisonhouse [i.e. the winds] or the slow passage of the years. It will stand while earth and sky remain and Rome's day endures.'

So far so good, though Horace would hardly have been happy to see *exegi monumentum* put to such uses. But this is what follows:

> 'Here, in the silence of the night, when earthly things give pleasure to the gods above, thy family will leave heaven, and gliding down will crowd about thee and exchange kisses. Son, brother, father, and sister will come to embrace thee. One neck will afford room to all the stars of heaven.[12]

That is only a brief example. To Statius the emperor and his possessions are sacred; he is father and ruler of the world. He is beautiful, splendid, and august; his glance is a flame and his countenance radiates light. He is like a constellation. As *dominus* and *deus* he bestows peace and joy on mankind.[13]

Martial also does obeisance. Addressing Domitian at the beginning of Book VIII he says:

> 'All my little volumes, Sir, to which you have granted fame

9 H. Bardon, *Les empereurs et les lettres latines d'Auguste à Hadrien* (Paris 1940) 427.
10 G. Highet, *Juvenal the Satirist* (Oxford 1954), 236–7, hereafter referred to as Highet.
11 Highet 13–14.   12 Statius, *Silu.* I.1.91–4 and 94–8.
13 See K. Scott, *AJP* 54 (1933) 247–59.

(that is, life) make their supplications to you and will be read, I think, for that reason. This book, however, which is numbered eighth in my works, enjoys more frequent opportunities for displaying devotion. Accordingly my talent was not put so hard to work; the subject matter did the writing for me.'

Later, in the final version of his *Panegyricus* (originally delivered in A.D. 100) Pliny descants on the virtues of Trajan:

'What gift of the gods is more excellent or more glorious than an emperor who is pure and holy and most like the gods themselves? If there had been any lingering doubt whether earthly rulers were assigned by the hazards of chance or by some heavenly power, it would assuredly be clear that our emperor had been divinely appointed' (1).

One would like to think that such effusions were beyond Juvenal's powers.

Before leaving the satire's opening verses we should perhaps take up again a question raised earlier. If Caesar in v. 1 is Hadrian, why does the poem contain so many figures from the age of Domitian? No doubt the answer is in part psychological. If we assume that he was born about A.D. 65, then between the ages of sixteen and thirty-one Juvenal lived under Domitian. The events of those years must have made a deep impression on his mind. Again, as Townend rightly points out, the works of Pliny, Suetonius, and Tacitus revived memories for Juvenal and his contemporaries, and also brought the period to life for a new generation which had grown up in the more relaxed atmosphere of Trajan's rule. And yet we should not concentrate exclusively on references to what happened under Domitian. Lucan (79–80), Camerinus (90), and Barea Soranus (91) perished under Nero; Secundus Carrinas (204–5) was banished by Caligula; Theodorus (177) was tutor to Tiberius; with Maecenas (94), Horace (62) and Virgil (69) we are back in the first part of the Augustan age; and Cicero (199) and Ventidius Bassus (199) take us into the republic. Here, as in other satires, Juvenal has illustrated his argument with a wide selection of historical *exempla*; as a result the poem has a range, depth, and force which lift it beyond the merely topical. How far it applied to conditions actually prevailing in the early decades of the second century is a question which we will consider briefly at the end of the essay.

We now return to the opening passage to examine what it has to say about poets. It begins, as we saw, with a ringing assertion which gains weight from being contained exactly within the line:

Et spes et ratio studiorum in Caesare tantum.

There is no other opening like it in Juvenal. Caesar is generous and considerate; he alone has shown concern for the Muses. But what follows?

> cum iam celebres notique poetae
> balneolum Gabiis, Romae conducere furnos
> temptarent, nec foedum alii nec turpe putarent
> praecones fieri, cum desertis Aganippes
> uallibus esuriens migraret in atria Clio.
> nam si Pieria quadrans tibi nullus in umbra
> ostendatur, ames nomen uictumque Machaerae
> et uendas potius commissa quod auctio uendit
> stantibus, oenophorum, tripedes, armaria, cistas,
> Alcitheon Pacci, Thebas et Terea Fausti.   (3–12)

> ...*at a time when popular and famous poets were trying to lease a miserable little bath-house out in Gabii or else bakeries in Rome, and others thought it in no way disgusting or disgraceful to become auctioneers; when Clio herself departed from the vales of Aganippe and took off for the sale-rooms in search of a meal. For if you couldn't find a fivepenny piece in the shade of the Pierian grove you'd be glad to take on Harry the Hammer's name and standard of living, and you'd be better selling what the embattled auction sells to the bystanders – wine-jars, three-legged stools, trunks, book-cases, Paccius' Alcithoe, and the Thebes and Tereus of Faustus.*

Even someone who has read nothing else of Juvenal's will see at once that the satirist's sympathy with the dejected Muses is of a rather peculiar kind. He acknowledges that writers have been forced to earn a living, but he also insists that by taking such jobs they have forfeited a great deal of respect. A reader more familiar with Juvenal will remember that Gabii has been mentioned before as a one-horse town,[14] that men who lease businesses are despicable,[15] and that auctioneers are an odious crew.[16] The characteristic tone is produced by inserting into this grim picture of degradation some stately and romantic phrases like *desertis Aganippes | uallibus* and *Pieria in umbra* which are associated with poetry as a high calling inspired by the Muse. A particularly dense effect is obtained when lofty tragedies with noble old titles are in-

[14] *Sat.* 3.192; 6.56.   [15] *Sat.* 3.31, 38.
[16] *Sat.* 3.157.

cluded in a pile of secondhand junk.[17] It is clear that, however Juvenal
may deplore the decay of patronage, his attitude to the poets is by no
means simple. Nevertheless, he does concede that trade is not the most
squalid way of making money:

> hoc satius quam si dicas sub iudice 'uidi'
> quod non uidisti; faciant equites Asiani,
> altera quos nudo traducit gallica talo.   (13–16)

> *That's better than saying before a judge 'I saw' what you didn't
> see at all. Leave that to our Asian knights who are brought into
> disgrace by one slipper which reveals a bare ankle.*

Anyone in the Roman empire who was an *eques* was really an *eques
Romanus*. Such a man would possess a fortune of at least 400,000
sesterces; he would have considerable prestige in society, and might
even have influence at court. The phrase *equites Asiani* is therefore the
sneer of a native Roman who is dismayed to see foreigners getting rich
while he remains poor.[18] Their money, he concludes, must be a reward
for perjury – and what else can you expect of people who came here as
slaves? But Juvenal doesn't actually say 'came here as slaves'. Instead,
he fastens on a particular physical feature of slavery – the fact that one
ankle still bears the weals of a fetter. Such weals are exposed by the
low shoe which was fashionable at this time.

Thanks to Caesar, then, no poet will be forced to take such uncongenial work. But, again, Juvenal doesn't say 'no poet'. He says

> nectit quicumque canoris
> eloquium uocale modis   (18–19)

– a splendid phrase: 'whoever weaves melodious tunes into a web of
vocal artistry'. But such magnificence is not allowed to stand. Line and
sentence are completed by *laurumque momordit* – 'and has chewed the

---

[17] John Brown, in his *Patronage*, a poem in imitation of Juvenal 7 (London
1820), lists the following items:

> My Lord, a true Canove – a matchless lot!
> A Queen Anne's farthing, and the works of Scott;
> A marble Niobe – what charming grief!
> Madam be quick – a Jove without a leaf.

[18] With Juvenal's *equites Asiani* Serafini compares Claudian, *In Eutrop.*
2.135–6:

> plaudentem cerne senatum
> et Byzantinos proceres Graiosque Quirites.

The text of Juvenal's passage is not certain. I have followed L. A. McKay,
CR 58 (1944) 46. For a defence of *Gallia* instead of *gallica* in v. 16 see
J. G. Griffith, *CR* n.s.l (1951) 138–42.

laurel'. As early as the fifth century it was believed that poetic and prophetic inspiration could be achieved by chewing laurel leaves, the idea being originally, perhaps, that one could get into contact with Apollo by means of his sacred tree.[19] Modern authorities tell us that the practice has no real basis. 'Professor Oesterreich once chewed a large quantity of laurel leaves in the interests of science, and was disappointed to find himself no more inspired than usual.'[20] So reports E. R. Dodds, and we may take it that Juvenal was equally sceptical. What then is the effect of this two-word clause? By speaking of poetry as inspired utterance Juvenal apparently continues the respectful periphrasis that goes before, but at the same time he makes inspiration sound rather silly, implying that it can be induced at will by the simple expedient of chewing leaves. It is perhaps worth noting that some translators, like Charles Dryden (1693) and Gifford (1806), omit the laurel-chewing altogether. Barten Holyday (1673) expands: 'And bit Apollo's verse-infusing bayes'. In modern times too Ramsay (1918) and Green (1967) both translate *laurum* as 'Apollo's laurel' no doubt as a courtesy to the lay reader, but the god's name gives a slight elevation of tone where it isn't wanted. Humphries (1958) avoids this but loses the bathos by reversing the order of lines 18 and 19. Sir Robert Stapylton (1660) is the closest: he speaks of those 'that brouse on laurel', but he supplies no more than a weak paraphrase of the preceding clause.

Caesar is on the look-out for talent, but if you expect help from any other quarter you may as well give up:

> lignorum aliquid posce ocius et quae
> componis dona Veneris, Telesine, marito, (24–5)

Quick, get some sticks, Telesinus, and present your compositions to Venus' husband.

What Juvenal means, of course, is 'put your poems in the fire', but the use of *dona* and the replacement of *igni* by *Veneris marito* suggest a kind of presentation. Like a patron Vulcan will receive the poems, and like a patron he will give no return.

> frange miser calamum uigilataque proelia dele,
> qui facis in parua sublimia carmina cella,
> ut dignus uenias hederis et imagine macra. (27–9)

---

[19] See Sophocles, Frag.897 (Jebb and Pearson) and K. F. Smith on Tibullus II.5.63.

[20] E. R. Dodds, *The Greeks and the Irrational* (Univ. of California 1951) 73.

Break your pen, poor wretch, destroy the battles that have kept you awake – you who are creating lofty poems in your tiny attic in the hope of coming forth to earn a garland of ivy and a famished bust.

It had long been possible for a writer to 'stay awake over' his poem – Ovid has the phrase *carmen uigilatum*, but it was a witty extension of the idea to speak of a poet staying awake over his battles. The battles show, of course, that the man is an epic poet, and Juvenal implies that the loftiest of all genres is appropriately composed in an attic. Yet at the same time the squalor of the attic is brought out by placing *parua* beside *sublimia*. And the poet is reminded that even if his dreams came true, any bust made in his honour would have to be suitably emaciated. As so often the final word carries a sting. If we compare v. 29 with Persius' prologue:

Heliconidasque pallidamque Pirenen
illis remitto, quorum imagines lambunt
hederae sequaces

I leave the daughters of Helicon and pale Pirene to those whose busts are licked by the clinging ivy

we find that Juvenal's *macra* helps to turn ironical humour into sardonic wit.

Perhaps the most interesting phrase, however, is *frange miser calamum*. In Virgil's third eclogue Menalcas is supposed to have broken Daphnis' *calamos*. The context shows, however, that *calamos* means 'arrows': *Daphnidis arcum | fregisti et calamos* (12–13) – 'You broke Daphnis' bow and arrows.' In Calpurnius the breaking of *calami* is brought into connection with patronage, for in 4.23 Corydon is said to have given this gloomy advice: *frange puer calamos et inanes desere Musas*, 'Break your *calami* my lad, and abandon the empty-handed Muses.' Here *calami* are pipes, as is shown shortly after: *quid enim tibi fistula reddet | quo tutare famem?* 'For what recompense will your pipe bring you whereby you may ward off hunger?' The next stage is represented by Martial ix.73.9. A cobbler has come into a rich man's inheritance, and so Martial curses his own occupation: *frange leves calamos et scinde, Thalia, libellos* – 'Break your worthless *calami* and tear up your books, Thalia.' Here *calami* means 'pens', a sense which was only implied in Calpurnius. I do not know whether the plural form and the mention of Thalia (who was the Muse of Virgil's eclogues as well as of Martial's epigrams) retain a dim recollection of pastoral. But in any case with Juvenal's *frange miser calamum* the separation is complete.

So in these passages instead of saying the same thing, as so often, in different words, the poets have contrived to say different things with the same words.[21]

The section ends on a more subdued note. The ageing and impoverished poet thinks of the years that could have been spent in more active and rewarding work: *aetas | et pelagi patiens et cassidis atque ligonis* – 'an age which could put up with the sea, the helmet, or the spade'.

> 'Then a weariness enters the heart, then old age, still with its power over words but without a rag to its back, curses itself and its Muse.' (34–5)

Within the context of the poem these are the wistful reflections of a man who is weary and disenchanted with the life he has led in the capital: 'I'd have done better to join the army and get away from it all.' But, someone may say, does Juvenal really mean this? Are there not other passages where he takes a less rosy view of the soldier's life? This, of course, is a very large question; here one can only make a few observations on how it might be handled. First, let us consider a few other lines – all from later satires:

> 'From here (viz from the common people) comes the hard-working young professional soldier who marches to the Euphrates or to the eagles that keep guard over the conquered Dutch.' (8.51–2)

> 'It is fine to present your country and people with a citizen if you see to it that he serves his country, making a contribution on the land or in the conduct of peace and war.' (14.70–2)

> 'The spoils of war – a breastplate nailed to a tree of victory, a broken helmet with its cheek-piece dangling down, a yoke

---

[21] The whole passage came into Ben Jonson's mind when he was writing the Apologeticall Dialogue appended to *The Poetaster*:

O, this would make a learn'd and liberal soul
To rive his stained quill up to the back
And damn his long-watched labours to the fire.
. . .
I that spend half my nights and half my days
Here in a cell to get a dark pale face
To come forth worth the ivy or the bays,
And in this age can hope no other grace –
Leave me! There's something come into my thought
That must and shall be sung high and aloof,
Safe from the world's black jaw and the dull ass's hoof.

with its pole snapped off, the flagstaff from a surrendered galley, a dejected prisoner on a triumphal arch – these are regarded as superhuman blessings.' (10.133–7)

'In those days the rough soldier didn't know how to appreciate Greek art. When a city was captured and he found some cups by a great metal-worker in his share of the loot, he would break them up to provide gay brasses for his horse.' (11.100–7)

'Let's consider the advantages shared by all military men. Not least is the fact that no one in civilian clothes would dare beat you up. If *he's* beaten up he won't let on; he wouldn't dare show a magistrate the gaps where his teeth have been knocked out, or the dark lumpy bruises on his face, or the one surviving eye which the doctor doesn't guarantee to save.' (16.7–12)

Now it might be possible, I suppose, though not very profitable, to make a synthesis of these and other passages and to present the result as 'Juvenal's view of army life'. It might also be possible, at least with some topics, to find a significant difference between earlier and later comments and so to infer a development in the satirist's ideas. But the first thing is to ask what abuse is under attack in each particular case. In the examples before us Juvenal speaks wistfully (though impersonally) about the army in Satire 7, because he is sick and weary of the client-poet's life. He writes admiringly of the proletarian soldier in 8 because he is attacking a peculiarly stupid instance of snobbery. In 14 he is criticizing parents who fail to bring up their children properly, and so he says 'It's fine to have a family if they are trained to be useful, but all too often...' In 10 we are asked to recognize that military glory, like all grandiose aspirations, is nothing but vanity. In 11 the soldier is represented as an uncouth philistine, but he is *praised* for such behaviour because Juvenal is castigating the luxury of later times. It is only in 16 that the army is Juvenal's main target. Accordingly it receives the full brunt of the satirist's indignation. All this simply illustrates the fact that the tone of a given passage is largely governed by the writer's immediate purpose. Having said this, I would not want to make the further assertion that one cannot draw *any* conclusions from the satires about Juvenal's outlook and personality – that is surely taking scepticism too far. But because Juvenal is such a master of rhetoric, general statements about him must be based on a particularly careful examination of tone and context.

In the next twelve lines (36–47) the spotlight moves from poets to patrons, and so we shall leave that passage aside for the moment. Juvenal then continues: rich men are mean, but in spite of that:

> nos tamen hoc agimus tenuique in puluere sulcos
> ducimus et litus sterili uersamus aratro.
> nam si discedas, laqueo tenet ambitiosum
> scribendi cacoethes et aegro in corde senescit. (48ff.)

> *Yet we still keep at it, driving furrows through the thin dust and turning over the sea shore with our barren ploughs. If you try to get away from it, the craving for literary prestige holds you in a noose and becomes a chronic disease within your mind.* [The text of 50–1 is uncertain]

I have quoted this passage not only for its physiological imagery, but because it shows once again how complex Juvenal's attitude is. The futility of ploughing the sand is a common idea. Why then do poets continue to write? Not for any rational purpose but rather because of a pathological obsession. Clearly this cannot be taken as an appeal for sympathy. Moreover, for the first time Juvenal now acknowledges that he himself belongs to this afflicted company.

He then goes on to say that the true poet cannot function in such conditions:

> 'The exceptional poet (*uatem egregium*) who has no ordinary vein of talent (*publica uena*), who doesn't produce anything that's widely available (*expositum*) or strike familiar songs from a common mint (*communi moneta*) – the sort of man I cannot point to but only feel – he is the product of a mind free from anxiety and untroubled by bitterness, a mind that loves the woods and is fit to drink from the Muses' spring.' (53–9)

After these noble lines Juvenal introduces a jarring note – deliberately, because he is moving back down to the practical point of his argument:

> 'Gloomy poverty cannot sing in a Pierian grotto (*sub antro Pierio*) or grasp the thyrsis (*thyrsum contingere*) when she lacks the money which the body requires day and night.'

With the phrase *sub antro Pierio* the thought of Horace has entered Juvenal's mind, for in *Odes* III.4.40 Horace had spoken of the Muses in their *Pierium antrum*. As we shall see, Juvenal's *thyrsum contingere* may also owe something to Horace's *parce graui metuende thyrso* (*Odes*

II.19.8). After the mention of the body and its food it is not so steep a drop to the concluding epigram, in which Horace appears in person:

> Satur est cum dicit Horatius 'Euhoe!'

> *Horace's stomach is full when he cries 'Hail, Bacchus!'*

This is a direct reference to *Odes* II.19.5 and 7 (*Euhoe*, and *Euhoe, parce Liber*); and the second of these lines continues *parce gravi metuende thyrso*. Juvenal cleverly chooses two of the most 'mantic' passages of Horace, who normally operates on a much more conversational level. The contrast with *satur* is thus made amusingly effective – we can hardly help visualizing the short, rather tubby, figure intoning *Bacchum in remotis* after a good dinner. Boileau rendered the idea as follows:

> Un auteur qui, pressé d'un besoin importun,
> Le soir entend crier ses entrailles à jeun,
> Goûte peu d'Hélicon les douces promenades;
> Horace a bu son soûl quand il voit les Ménades.
>
> (*AP* 4.179–82)

Although satirical, there is no resentment in Juvenal's picture, and the same is true of the reference to Virgil which follows:

> 'Where can genius find room, except when your heart is disturbed (*uexant*) by poetry alone and is carried away by the lords of Cirrha and Nysa, refusing to admit more than a single concern (*curas*)? It takes a lofty soul which is not in a state of shock (*attonitae*) at the prospect of buying a blanket, to envisage chariots and horses and the faces of gods, and to describe how the Fury looked when she dumbfounded the Rutulian.' (63–8)

Here the words in brackets have a dual function. They refer both to mental worry and to poetic inspiration. Again the characteristic tension is achieved by tossing a cheap blanket into the scene of divine enthusiasm. It is probably a mistake to look for a specific passage of the *Aeneid* describing chariots and horses, but with *facies deorum* Juvenal is already thinking of the tremendous scene in *Aen.* 7.447–8 in which Turnus is overwhelmed at the sight of the Fury Allecto:

> tot Erinys sibilat hydris
> tantaque se *facies* aperit.

> *so many are the Fury's hissing snakes; so monstrous the face that reveals itself.*

97

Juvenal continues:

> 'If Virgil had been without a slave-boy (*puer*) and decent
> lodgings, all the snakes (*hydri*) would have dropped from the
> Fury's hair; her trumpet (*bucina*), bereft of sound, would
> have blared forth no deep note.' (69–71)

The snakes come from the Virgilian lines already quoted, and the
trumpet from vv. 519–20, which speak of the call given forth by
Allecto's *dira bucina*. So much is clear, but it is perhaps possible to go a
step further. Why did Juvenal fasten on this particular passage of
Virgil? There are others as fine, and after the reference to Apollo in
v. 64 we might perhaps have expected an allusion to the scene of divine
possession in *Aen*. 6. One suspects that after thinking of the Bacchic
passage in Horace his mind moved on to a Bacchic passage in Virgil.
This was to be found in *Aen*. 7, where Amata is stirred to a frenzy by
Allecto. Rushing to the hills, she cries *Euhoe Bacche!* (389) and claims
that her daughter takes up the thyrsis for the god – *mollis tibi sumere
thyrsos* (390). The passage ends *reginam Allecto stimulis agit undique
Bacchi* (405) 'Allecto drives the queen far and wide with her Bacchic
goad.' These lines may well have supplied a bridge to the following
scene, in which Allecto assails Turnus. This, after all, is the only
occurrence of *Euhoe* in the whole of Virgil.

Whether this speculation seems credible or not, the lines about
Virgil certainly produce the type of tension already noted; for next to
the terrible Fury with her snakes and trumpet stands a slave-boy – and
the very prosaic requirement of decent accommodation.[22] The *tolerabile
hospitium* may be a deliberate understatement in view of what ancient
sources tell us about Virgil's circumstances. He had, it seems, a house
on the Esquiline near Maecenas' mansion, and also a villa in Campania.[23] The unspecified *puer* raises a more interesting point. Gifford
translates:

> Those snakes, had Virgil no Maecenas found,
> Had dropped in listless length, upon the ground.

That, of course, won't do. But Charles Dryden has:

> If Virgil's suit Maecenas had not sped,

[22] *Hospitium* in the sense of 'accommodation' is a humble word. See *TLL*
3040–1.

[23] Suetonius, *Virgil* 13. Maecenas' generosity to Virgil and Horace is
praised in the *Laus Pisonis* 230–45. See *Minor Latin Poets* (Loeb)
289–315.

And sent Alexis to the poet's bed,
The crested snakes had dropped upon the ground,
And the loud trumpet languished in the sound.

This rendering is based on the story found in Suetonius (*Virgil*, 9) that Alexis in the second eclogue was really Alexander, a boy presented to Virgil by Asinius Pollio. Did Juvenal have this romantic anecdote in mind when he wrote v. 69? One's first impulse is to dismiss the idea as nonsense, but then one recalls that Alexis is mentioned several times in Martial, usually in connection with patronage. The most important passages are:

> sed non et ueteres contenti laude fuerunt,
>   cum minimum uati munus Alexis erat; (v.16.11–12)

> *But our ancestors were not content with words of praise. Then the least gift that a poet might expect was an Alexis.*

> (Paraphrase) if Martial were given a Corinna or an Alexis he would write poetry comparable to Ovid's and Virgil's. (VIII.73.10)

> (Paraphrase) You wonder why today there are no geniuses like Virgil. Well, if there were Maecenases there would be Virgils too. Virgil lamented the loss of his farm and stock. Maecenas smiled and removed his poverty:

> Accipe diuitias et uatum maximus esto;
>   tu licet et nostrum, dixit, Alexin ames.

> *'Here is plenty of money – be the greatest of poets; you may also love my Alexis', he said.*

> At the sight of Alexis Virgil forgot about the *Eclogues* and *Georgics* and was inspired to write the *Aeneid.* (VIII.56)

In view of these passages it is hard to deny that Juvenal thought of Alexis – especially since he wrote *puer*, not *servus*. He nevertheless realized that the figure of Alexis and the associations that went with him were quite inappropriate to this context. The argument, after all, is that Virgil could not have written the *Aeneid* if he hadn't had a roof over his head and someone to do the housework. The point is ruined if we think of a long-haired fancy-boy decanting Falernian. Juvenal therefore suppressed the name, and the *puer* became an ordinary slave.[24]

[24] In *Sat.* 9.64 Naevolus too has a single slave-boy to keep house.

If then, says Juvenal, Horace and Virgil lived in decent comfort, how can we expect Rubrenus Lappa to reach the same heights as the old tragedians when Atreus compels him to pawn his coat, along with his cup and saucer?

> poscimus ut sit
> non minor antiquo Rubrenus Lappa coturno,
> cuius et alueolos et laenam pignerat Atreus?
>
> (71–3)

The stately metaphor of the tragic buskin is immediately undermined by the picture of destitution in the next line. But again the destitution is treated comically, for the use of Atreus as subject of *pignerat* allows us to imagine the king himself pawning the poet's crockery.

In his chapter on the seventh satire Highet makes the important point that Juvenal does not complain that the intellectuals are neglected. 'He does not say that their poems are ignored or misunderstood by the stupid bourgeois. On the contrary. He says their poetry is loved dearly and applauded with enthusiasm.'[25] The last point is perhaps slightly overstated (only *some* poets are popular), but it is certainly true that Juvenal's main complaint is financial. Poetry may bring you fame but it won't buy your groceries.

> Contentus fama iaceat Lucanus in hortis
> marmoreis, at Serrano tenuique Saleiio
> gloria quantalibet quid erit, si gloria tantum est?　(79–81)

> *Lucan may be content with fame as he lies at ease in his marble gardens, but what use is glory, however great, to Serranus and thin Saleius if it is only glory?*

One cannot tell what Juvenal thought of Lucan's *Civil War*, but the picture of the poet lounging in luxury is not devoid of malice. Statues, fountains, colonnades – there is so much marble that you forget about the grass. Of the translations I have seen only Holyday keeps the metaphor: 'Lucan may in his marble gardens lie │ content with fame.' But some of its force was remembered by Hall at the opening of his sixth satire:

> When Lucan stretched on his marble bed
> To think of Caesar and great Pompey's deed.
>
> (*Virgidemiarum* 6.1)

Of the other two poets, Serranus and Saleius, we know very little.

[25] Highet 107–8.

Quintilian tells us that they both died rather young (x.1.89–90). Saleius Bassus, he says, had a powerful poetic talent (presumably he wrote epic). Tacitus adds that he was an admirable man and an accomplished poet (*Dial. 5*). More important is the information that he was given an exceptional gift of 500,000 sesterces by Vespasian (*Dial. 9*). To judge from the context in Tacitus and from Juvenal's argument, Bassus was previously destitute. The next instance is provided by Statius:

> curritur ad uocem iucundam et carmen amicae
> Thebaidos, laetam cum fecit Statius urbem
> promisitque diem: tanta dulcedine captos
> adficit ille animos tantaque libidine uolgi
> auditur. sed cum fregit subsellia uersu,
> esurit, intactam Paridi nisi uendit Agauen.   (82–7)

> *People rush to hear the attractive voice and music of the beloved* Thebais, *when Statius has delighted the public by fixing a day.*[26] *He holds their hearts enthralled by his sweetness; and the crowd listen to him in rapture. But after he has brought the house crashing down with his poetry,*[27] *he goes hungry, unless he sells his virgin Agave to Paris.*

The main line of argument is clear enough: Statius gets no adequate reward for his epic, and that is deplorable. So in a sense we are invited to sympathize with Statius. Yet once again Juvenal does not convey a simple emotion. The whole passage is given an ironical tone by the use of an extended metaphor.[28] As there is a slight pause after *amicae*, the

---

[26] Statius would have been reciting the *Thebais* shortly after A.D. 80, and the sale of his *Agave* must have taken place before the death of Paris in 83 (Dio LXVII.3.1). Assuming Juvenal was born about A.D. 65, he would have been in his teens when these events took place, and probably still living at Aquinum.

[27] It comes as a surprise to find the phrase *fregit subsellia* translated in *The Dunciad*. Talking of Henley (3.201–4) Pope says:

> How fluent nonsense trickles from his tongue!
> How sweet the periods neither said nor sung!
> Still *break the benches*, Henley, with thy strain,
> While Sherlock, Hare, and Gibson preach in vain.

On Henley see Isaac D'Israeli, *Calamities and Quarrels of Authors* (London 1881) 59.

[28] The erotic imagery was noticed by Pichon, *De Sermone Amatorio* (Paris 1902) 6. It was already implicit in Stapylton's translation:

> To their dear Thebais the people throng,
> And to the sound of his inchanting tongue,

first line suggests that a song recital is being given by an attractive *meretrix*, who then turns out to be a poem, viz Statius' epic on Thebes. The role of charmer is then taken over by Statius himself, who delights the city by promising a day, just as a *meretrix* would promise a night. He holds the audience in a quasi-erotic spell (*dulcedine, libidine*). Then, after receiving a wild ovation – he starves. There must be a pause after *uersu*, so *esurit* comes with added force. It is, moreover, a dactylic word filling the first foot, and it is followed by another pause before the sentence is finished. As far as I can discover, that effect is unique in Juvenal. The erotic imagery is completed in the last line: to earn his bread Statius must sell his new play *Agave* to Paris, the emperor's favourite ballet-dancer. On the whole it seems likely that Paris, rather than Statius, is pictured as the brothel-owner. But they are both involved in the same squalid deal.

Such evidence as there is would suggest that Juvenal had reservations about his fellow-poet. The latter's work must surely be included in the contemptuous dismissal of epic in Satire 1, Juvenal can hardly have condoned his gross flattery of Domitian, and there are good grounds for believing that the fourth satire contains a parody of one of Statius' court poems.[29] Admittedly, within his chosen field (whether one admired it or not) Statius had acquired a position of some distinction, and so his case could be used, with a certain amount of exaggeration, to illustrate the plight of a literary artist in a society reluctant to support him. Nevertheless, as we have seen, even when Juvenal asks us to deplore Statius' poverty, he does so in a way which puts the poet in a rather dubious light. Roman satire had long been suspicious of writers who set out to attract large audiences.[30]

What has been said about the ambiguous tone of the seventh satire may all seem rather obvious. And indeed it *is* obvious. My only defence for saying it is that no one else appears to have done so.[31] In general surveys of silver age poetry the satire is summed up in terms such as

> When Statius with the promise of a day
> O're joyes the town; for in so sweet a way
> He reads his poem, that to here it spoke
> A lust affects the soul; yet when he broke
> The benches with strong lines, he must for bread
> To Paris sell Agave's maiden-head.

29 See Valla's note on *Sat*. 4.94; also Highet 79 and 259 n. 12.
30 Cf. Horace, *Sat*. 1.10.73 and Persius *Sat*. 1.2–3.
31 H. A. Mason did not happen to discuss this satire in his article on Juvenal in *Critical Essays on Roman Literature*, 'Satire', ed. J. P. Sullivan (London 1963). But I imagine that he, like many others, would take the poem more or less as I do.

these: 'The accession of Hadrian has swept all the storm-clouds from the author's sky. But in the unhappy days but lately passed away the poet's lot was most miserable. His work brings him no livelihood; his patron's liberality [what liberality?] goes but a little way.'[32] 'Satire seven laments the inadequacy of the remuneration received by members of the learned professions.'[33] 'Number seven deals with the woes of students and teachers of art and letters.'[34] 'The poem is a growl of discontent over the present condition of literature, which does not pay. Patrons are mean and poverty chills authorship.'[35]

More detailed studies have remarks like the following:

> 'But here is another change of outlook. When he wrote Book 1, he was decisively unsympathetic towards serious poetry; now he thinks of it as a noble occupation which deserves encouragement. He said then that it was a useless occupation and added that the results bored him to death. Now he admires the poet who pawns his overcoat and dishes to keep him alive while finishing his tragedy...'[36]

> 'In 1.1–21 and 3.5–9 he was an indignant satirist fulminating against reciting poets. In 7.39–47, however, he plays the role of a "compassionate satirist" deploring the ill-treatment which a reciter receives from a niggardly patron.'[37]

One scholar speaks about the *infinita tristezza* of vv. 32–5,[38] and another, after quoting the same lines, says:

> 's'arrachant à la tristesse dont on dirait que l'accablement l'a fait un instant fléchir, Juvénal développe sa pensée sur la pénurie matérielle où languissent tant de ses confrères en poésie'.[39]

---

[32] H. E. Butler, *Post Augustan Poetry* (Oxford 1909) 295.

[33] W. C. Summers, *The Silver Age of Latin Literature* (London 1936) 78.

[34] H. J. Rose, *A Handbook of Latin Literature*, third ed. (London 1966) 408.

[35] J. Wight Duff, *A Literary History of Rome in the Silver Age*, second ed. (London 1960) 489. The quotation from Duff's paraphrase is brief but representative. The same sort of remarks are to be found in Friedländer's introduction, trans. J. R. C. Martyn (Amsterdam 1969) 19, and in U. Knoche, *Die Römische Satire* (Göttingen 1957) 92.

[36] Highet 107. Although the present essay tries to add a further element to the interpretation of *Sat.* 7 as given in *Juvenal the Satirist*, I gladly acknowledge a debt to Highet's book, which after a quarter of a century has no competitor.

[37] R. E. Colton, *Class. Bull.* 42 (1966) 84.

[38] A. Serafini, *Studio sulla satira di Giovenale* (Firenze 1957) 190.

[39] P. de Labriolle, *Les satires de Juvénal* (Paris 1933) 220.

Needless to say, there is some truth in these observations. But in view of the text, as examined above, are they not rather misleading? For if we leave out the element of sardonic wit, which is directed at poets *as well as* patrons, we are in effect altering what Juvenal has said. The point is not confined to Satire 7. In his chapter on Satire 3, entitled 'L'avvocato dei poveri e degli oppressi', Serafini says Juvenal is 'il poèta della povera gente: egli sente e condivide le sofferenze di tutti i derelitti della società'.[40] He is echoed by an American scholar who contends that Juvenal's greatest contribution to *satura* was his 'sense of pathos': 'the urban poor are considered seriously, their problematical existence is examined, probed, and painted . . .

> nil habet infelix paupertas durius in se
> quam quod ridiculos homines facit.
>
> [*unfortunate poverty involves nothing so harsh as the fact that it makes men ridiculous*]

Thus the poet's aphorism. Yet it is the rich who are ridiculous in the poet's eyes, not the poor. The latter enjoy dignity, for it is they whom the poet takes seriously.'[41] Now the two lines just quoted are preceded by the following:

> quid quod materiam praebet causasque iocorum
> omnibus hic idem, si foeda et scissa lacerna,
> si toga sordidula est et rupta calceus alter
> pelle patet, uel si consuto uolnere crassum
> atque recens linum ostendit non una cicatrix?   (147–51)
>
> *What about the fact that the same poor man provides everyone with the material and the occasion for jokes, if his cloak is ripped and filthy, if his toga's grubby, and if one of his shoes gapes open where the leather is split, or if, where the wound has been sewn together, multiple scars draw attention to the coarse thread that's only a few days old.*

Like all good passages, that suffers in translation. But surely, whatever social complaint it may entail, it must also be seen as a splendid piece of comic writing. After saying that the poor man's clothes look as if they'd been in a battle, Juvenal then protests that poverty makes a man look ridiculous!

40 A. Serafini, *Studio sulla satira di Giovenale* 318.
41 C. Witke, *Latin Satire* (Leiden 1970) 132.

Earlier in Satire 3 Juvenal condemns Greek immigrants at length for their abominable flattery. We assume that the poor native Roman is too proud and too honest to compete, until we read:

> haec eadem licet et nobis laudare, sed illis
> creditur. (92–3)

We too may praise the same things, but they *are* believed!

In vv. 126ff. Juvenal complains bitterly about having to hurry out before dawn – it's all so futile because a Praetor will get there first and greet the childless old ladies before you. So the poor man is not less contemptible, but merely less favourably placed. Again, what an outrage that a rich man's slave can afford to buy the favours of a Roman lady – while the son of a free citizen has to think twice before paying for a common whore (132–6)! It may well be true that in a general sense Juvenal is on the side of the poor. But having Juvenal on your side was not always a comforting or reassuring experience.

A last illustration may be given from Satire 5, where the point is made much more brutally. There the weight of Juvenal's attack falls on the obnoxious Virro, who humiliates his poor clients by serving them with inferior food and drink. The patron's meanness, gluttony, and malevolence are pilloried in an attack lasting 150 lines. But Juvenal has carefully forbidden us to read the poem simply as a denunciation of Virro and his like; for in the opening verses he says 'Are you not *ashamed* to be dependent on a rich patron for your dinner? There's more dignity in the life of a beggar'. And at the end we read:

> Ille sapit, qui te sic utitur. omnia ferre
> si potes, et debes.

> *The man who treats you like that knows what he's doing. If you can tolerate it, you deserve the lot.*

It is relevant here to recall one of the few pieces of hard evidence about Juvenal's life. In the eighteenth epigram of Book XII Martial pictures him wandering restlessly in the Subura or trudging hot and weary up to the doors of his wealthy patrons. So although the fifth satire may represent a ferocious caricature, it seems to be based, however indirectly, on the poet's own experience.

As the present chapter is concerned only with poets and patrons, there is no need to examine in detail what Juvenal says about historians, lawyers, and teachers. It is enough to point out that the tone remains the same. Historians are wasting their time because no one will pay them; but if these lines are anything to go by, Juvenal thought little of historiography. Lawyers are said to be grossly underpaid; they are also described as a profession of fools and liars. It is a scandal that teachers of rhetoric should be so impoverished; but Juvenal's description makes teaching itself seem ridiculously dull and trivial. The elementary teacher's life is even worse. He is cooped up in a smelly little room before daybreak; he has to take legal action to recover his miserable fees; and he is expected to have an encyclopedic knowledge of nugatory facts (who was Anchises' nurse?). Higher expectations are also entertained:

> exigite ut mores teneros ceu pollice ducat,
> ut si quis cera uoltum facit; (237–8)

> *Demand that he shape their young characters as it were with his*
> *thumb, like a man who makes a face out of wax.*

These verses, based on a line of Persius (5.40), are straightforward and dignified. What follows remains at the same level:

> exigite ut sit
> et pater ipsius coetus (238–9)

> *Demand that he be a father to the entire group.*

Excellent, but what does this high parental role involve? Simply preventing the little brats from masturbating. Once again, if we leave out the wit and the double vision, and talk only in terms of protest and compassion, we are bound to give a sentimental reading of the poem.

In the first hundred lines it is noticeable that Juvenal has achieved variety by switching our attention from poets to patrons. Thus Caesar is introduced in 1–2 and again in 20–1; a rich miser is mentioned in 30–2, an allegedly typical patron in 36–47, Numitor in 74–8, and finally Paris in 88–97. In 36f. we find:

> accipe nunc artes, ne quid tibi conferat iste,
> quem colis et Musarum et Apollinis aede relicta.

The choice of *colis* along with the phrase *aede relicta* seems to imply that the poet has changed his devotions from one patron deity to another. If so, the lines might be rendered in some such way as this:

> *Now I want to tell you of the devices he employs to avoid giving*
> *you any support – I mean the man for whose service you have left*
> *the temple of the Muses and Apollo.*

The *auarus* dislikes spending money on poets, because he is a poet himself. Here Juvenal contrives a crescendo of absurdity:

Ipse facit versus (*he writes poetry himself*) atque uni cedit
Homero (*indeed he yields second place only to Homer*) | propter
mille annos (*in deference to Homer's thousand years*).

As often the climax is postponed to the beginning of the following line.
Juvenal then continues:

> 'If the sweet prospect of fame impels you to give a recitation,
> he allows you the use of a building with damp-spots on the
> walls – a house which is pressed into service though it has
> been locked up for years and the door makes a noise like a
> herd of frightened pigs.[42] He's willing to provide freedmen
> to sit at the end of each row, and he'll place the loud voices of
> his attendants strategically around the hall. But none of your
> lordships will provide the cost of the benches, or the seats
> which are balanced on their hired supports, or the front-row
> chairs which have to be carried back after the show.' (39–47)

As we mentioned earlier, this may be compared with a passage in
Tacitus, *Dialogus* 9, in which one of the speakers remarks that a poet
who wants to recite has to round up an audience: he is out of pocket
because he must borrow a house (*domum mutuatur*), get the room
ready, hire seats (*subsellia conducit*), and distribute programmes. Now
as Tacitus' speaker is talking about the futility of poetry as a means of
making money, and as the poet chosen as an illustration is Saleius
Bassus, whom Juvenal mentions in v. 80, it seems almost certain that
Juvenal has this section of Tacitus in mind. But it is more important for
our purpose to notice how Juvenal gives the material a comic elaboration. The house is not just a house – it is a dilapidated dump with a
creaking door; seats are fastened precariously on to a raised framework; and the chairs have to be returned. (Does *reportandis* suggest
that the star has to wait behind and help carry the furniture out to the
owner's wagon?)

In vv. 74–8 we hear of the patron Numitor:

non habet infelix Numitor quod mittat amico,

Poor Numitor has nothing to send to his friend.

Some Roman readers probably knew who Numitor was, and so could
interpret the words at once. We have to wait until the next line:

[42] In v. 42 I have translated Jessen's conjecture *porcas* for *portas*. It is
certainly Juvenalian in spirit, and it provides more point than the
traditional reading. See Highet 271.

Quintillae quod donet habet

He does have something to give Quintilla.

So *infelix* is ironical and Numitor is not so poor as he seems. The contrast in behaviour is denoted not by a *sed* but by a formal chiasmus – *non habet* (a), *quod mittat* (b), *amico* (c), *Quintillae* (c), *quod donet* (b), *habet* (a). The juxtaposition of Quintilla with *amico* shows that she is Numitor's *amica*, i.e. his mistress. There is also just possibly a distinction between *mittat* (a cool way to treat a friend) and *donet* (a personal presentation).

But Juvenal has not yet finished with Numitor:

> 'Nor was he short of enough money to buy a lion (already tamed) which demanded enormous quantities of meat. No doubt a beast doesn't cost as much, and a poet's guts are more capacious.'

A splendid conclusion, which impressed Gibbon: 'if wit consist in the discovery of relations natural without being obvious, that of the poet and the lion is one of the wittiest possible'. The neglect of the poet in favour of the lion is given extra prominence by the fact that the beast (*belua*) is allowed to function as the subject of its own verb. The poet is not. His guts (*intestina*) are used instead.

In v. 88 Juvenal again returns to patronage. He has been talking about Statius' selling the libretto of his *Agave* to Paris, the emperor's favourite. What, we may ask, would a dancer want with a libretto? At performances, it seems that the lyrics were sung by a chorus with musical accompaniment, while the story itself was interpreted by a ballet-dancer. So on this occasion we are to imagine Paris purchasing (perhaps indeed commissioning) a libretto on the theme of Agave, the Theban queen who murdered her son Pentheus in a fit of Dionysiac frenzy. Still speaking of Paris, Juvenal continues:

> ille et militiae multis largitus honorem
> semenstri uatum digitos circumligat auro.
> quod non dant proceres, dabit histrio, tu Camerinos
> et Baream, tu nobilium magna atria curas?
> praefectos Pelopea facit, Philomela tribunos.   (88–92)

He also confers positions of military rank, and puts on poets' fingers the gold ring earned by six months' service. What the aristocracy refuses a dancer will bestow. Are you sedulously paying your respects to Barea and the Camerini and the great houses of the nobility?[43] *It is Pelopea that appoints our Prefects, Philomela our Tribunes.*[44]

A number of separate points must be kept in mind here. First, Paris has been compared metaphorically to a brothel-keeper who buys a young girl as a slave. Secondly, Juvenal is referring to the farce whereby military commissions (which involved promotion to the rank of *eques*) were conferred on people with no military qualifications, who were never going to fight. Thirdly, he is pointing to the further scandal that such commissions were to be obtained simply by currying favour with a ballet-dancer. As Highet remarks, 'The particular point of the attack, then, was that the dancer Paris had far more power at court than members of the old aristocratic families, and that the best way to obtain a post or promotion in the army was to toady to him.'[45]

That, however, is not the whole story. We must remember that unlike the aristocracy Paris does give patronage – not only to Statius, but to other poets as well. Macleane goes as far as to say that Juvenal's remark is 'kindly said and kindly meant'.[46] Other references to Paris in Dio, Suetonius, and Juvenal testify to the man's immense popularity.[47] And Martial's epitaph on him is in no way unfavourable.[48] This is the aspect Juvenal has in mind when he continues:

[43] Barea Soranus, an aristocrat with republican sentiments, was condemned to death in A.D. *66* under Nero. The Camerini were an old patrician family of the *gens Sulpicia*. One member was put to death under Nero for manifesting family pride (Dio LXII.18). It may be that Juvenal was led to those names by the fact that there was also another Paris, living in the time of Nero. (See Smith's *Dictionary of Greek and Latin Biography*). The death of this Paris is described by Dio in the very section noted above.

[44] Pelopea was a name borne by several princesses of Greek mythology. (See Smith's dictionary under Pelopeia.) Any of them could have been made the subject of a ballet. The story of Philomela and Procne is told by Ovid in *Met.* 6.424ff.

[45] Highet 24–5.

[46] A. J. Macleane in his commentary (London 1857) 172.

[47] Dio LXVII.3; Suetonius, *Domitian* 3.1; Juvenal 6.82–7 and the scholiast's note.

[48] Martial XI.13. The relevant lines are:

> urbis deliciae, salesque Nili,
> ars et gratia, ludus et uoluptas,
> Romani decus et dolor theatri,
> atque omnes Veneres Cupidinesque
> hoc sunt condita, quo Paris, sepulchro.

> *The city's darling and the Nile's wit, art and grace, delight and fun, the glory and grief of the Roman stage, every Venus and every Cupid, are buried here in Paris's grave.*

haut tamen inuideas uati quem pulpita pascunt.
quis tibi Maecenas, quis nunc erit aut Proculeius
aut Fabius, quis Cotta iterum, quis Lentulus alter? (93–5)

*But you shouldn't resent a poet's getting his bread and butter from
the stage. Who nowadays will be a Maecenas or a Fabius to you?
Who another Cotta or a second Lentulus?*

So the passage is typically complex: the decay of traditional patronage
may be measured by the fact that poets have to rely on a ballet-dancer
to save them from starvation; it is Paris who confers rank and prestige; but nowadays an artist must accept help from any quarter, for
respectable patrons no longer exist. A poet like Statius is therefore,
according to Juvenal, in the mortifying position of owing a heavy debt
of gratitude to a man whom he thoroughly despises.

Finally, after that indignant series of rhetorical questions, Juvenal
descends to a calmer tone, first with a neutral statement ('then a man's
genius was matched by his rewards') and then with a smiling conclusion:

                    tunc utile multis
pallere et uinum toto nescire Decembri   (96–7)

*Then many found it profitable to acquire a pallor and to forget
about alcohol for the whole of December.*

That is how Horace used to talk, and he may have influenced Juvenal's
phrasing. Actually the reminiscences may begin a little earlier, in v. 91:
tu nobilium magna atria curas? ('Do you attend the great halls of the
aristocracy?'), which seems to recall *Epist.* 1.19.39–40. Horace there
says:

non ego, *nobilium* scriptorum auditor et ultor,
grammaticas ambire tribus et *pulpita* dignor

*I listen to distinguished writers and pay them back; I do not deign
to canvass the academics on their platforms.*

Juvenal corrects this attitude: nowadays one shouldn't look askance at
anyone who makes a living from *pulpita* (93); after all, there are no
Maecenases around.[49] From Maecenas Juvenal switches back to
Horace, who in *Sat.* II.3 is supposed to have left Rome in December
during the revelry of the Saturnalia to do some serious writing. On the
Sabine farm he is interrupted by Damasippus, who says:

[49] Proculeius also comes from Horace. See *Odes* II. 2.5.

sobrius ergo
dic aliquid dignum promissis   (*Sat.* II.3.4–5)

Well, then, in this sober condition write something as good as your
promises.

By means of these Horatian echoes Juvenal has effected a diminuendo
which brings the passage to a close.

In the discussion so far little has been said of the poet's imagery. Yet
in various subtle ways imagery can play a part in the creation of tonal
effect. This is, naturally, a large subject.[50] Here I shall note only one
general type, that which might be broadly termed 'personification'.
The examples all come from the seventh satire.

1. A man is figuratively associated with another man.

(*a*)   Rufum quem totiens Ciceronem Allobroga dixit   (214)

Rufus, whom (the class) so often called the Allobrogian Cicero.

Here Rufus is merely *called* Cicero.

(*b*)   Quis tibi Maecenas, quis nunc erit aut Proculeius
aut Fabius?   (94–5)

Who will now be a Maecenas, who nowadays will be a Proculeius
or a Fabius to you?

Here one man is in a figurative sense *identified* with another.

(*c*)   Surgis tu pallidus Aiax   (115)

You rise to your feet, a pale-faced Ajax.

Here the relation is one of apposition; there is not even an *ut* to
separate the two terms.

We come now to cases where some kind of entity is described as be-
having in a human manner.

2. Perhaps the simplest type is where a traditional personification is
exploited in a novel and amusing way, e.g.

(*a*)   cum desertis Aganippes
uallibus esuriens migraret in atria Clio   (6–7)

When Clio left the vales of Aganippe and took off for the sale-
room in search of a meal

i.e. poets took jobs with auctioneers.

[50] A useful discussion is provided by W. S. Anderson in *AJP* 81 (1960)
243–60.

(b)   quae

componis dona Veneris, Telesine, marito   (24–5)

Present your compositions, Telesinus, to Venus' husband.

3. Sometimes a country is personified by the use of its name, e.g.

nutricula causidicorum

Africa   (148–9)

Africa, that lawyers' nursemaid.

4. Sometimes a literary work is personified by the use of its title, e.g.

praefectos Pelopea facit, Philomela tribunos   (92)

Pelopea *creates Prefects*, Philomela *Tribunes.*

5. Sometimes a declamation is personified by its theme, e.g.

cuius mihi sexta

quaque die miserum dirus caput Hannibal inplet   (160–1)

*His 'Hannibal the terrible' fills my unfortunate head at five-day
intervals.*

6. In one interesting case poetry-books are personified by the authors'
   names:

cum totus decolor esset

Flaccus et haereret nigro fuligo Maroni   (226–7)

*When Flaccus was all discoloured and Maro blackened with a
layer of soot,*

i.e. copies of Horace and Virgil were read at school before dawn by
the light of the schoolboys' lamps.

These cases have all involved names. We now come to phrases in
which various things are described in human terms:

7. Where an object behaves like a person:

(a)   domus seruire iubetur   (41)

a house is ordered to be at your service,

(b)   haut tamen inuideas uati quem pulpita pascunt   (93)

*Yet you shouldn't resent a bard's receiving his bread and butter from
the stage.*

8. Where an event or function behaves like a person:

et uendas potius commissa quod auctio uendit
stantibus   (10–11)

And you'd be better selling what the embattled auction sells to the by-standers.

9. Where a part of the body functions on behalf of a person:

(*a*) nimirum et capiunt plus intestina poetae   (78)

    and no doubt a poet's guts hold more,

(*b*) tunc immensa caui spirant mendacia folles   (111)

    Then their capacious bellows (i.e. their lungs) puff out endless lies.

10. Where an unhealthy condition behaves like a person:

laqueo tenet ambitiosum
scribendi cacoethes   (51–2)

The craving for literary prestige holds you in a noose.

11. Where men's voices are treated by metonymy as persons:

[scit] magnas comitum disponere uoces   (44)

He can distribute the loud voices of his attendants.

12. Where an accomplishment is treated as a person:

rara in tenui facundia panno

Eloquence doesn't often wear threadbare rags.   (145)

13. Where a time of life behaves like a person:

defluit aetas
et pelagi patiens et cassidis atque ligonis   (32–3)

That age flows past which could put up with the sea, the helmet, and the spade.

14. Where the statue of a man behaves like a man:

ipse feroci
bellatore sedens curuatum hastile minatur
eminus et statua meditatur proelia lusca   (126–8)

He himself sits on his fierce charger aiming his drooping spear from long range and practising for battle from his one-eyed statue.[51]

---

[51] Describing a statue as if it were a man is a favourite device; cf. the opening of *Sat*. 8 and the famous passage about Sejanus in *Sat*. 10.61–4. *cont.*

These passages all show various entities being treated as men. The technique is one of direct association. That is, our attention is not called to the fact that a comparison is about to be made. We are not actually told that *x* is *like y*, but are suddenly confronted with the fact that *y* has been substituted for it. This is just one of the many factors which contribute to the liveliness and novelty of Juvenal's style.

To conclude this discussion of the satire's tone let us compare half a dozen English passages in which the writer is complaining about patronage.

1. Spenser, *The Shepheardes Calendar*, October:

> Cuddie: Piers, I have pyped erst so long with payne
> That all mine Oten reeds bene rent and wore:
> And my poore Muse hath spent her spared store,
> Yet little good hath got, and much less gayne.
>
> .   .   .
>
> But ah Mecoenas is yclad in claye,
> And great Augustus long ygoe is dead:
> And all the worthies liggen wrapt in leade,
> That matter made for Poets on to play.

Sad, gentle, nostalgic and hopeless, Cuddie reminds us of Moeris in Virgil's ninth eclogue: *nunc uicti, tristes, quoniam fors omnia uersat* (5). The complaint is muted and melancholy – a tone which is right for pastoral but the very antithesis of satire.

2. Hall, *Virgidemiarum* 1.1.11–14:

> Nor can I crouch, and writhe my fawning tayle
> To some great Patron, for my best availe.
> Such hunger-starven Trencher-Poetry,
> Or let it never live, or timely dye.

Hall is angry with poets who accept a humiliating position, but unlike Juvenal he dissociates himself from them. Juvenal, moreover, does not complain about the custom of flattering the rich. It is perhaps worth adding that Hall is well aware of the Roman satiric tradition – his 'fawning tayle' comes from Persius 4.15.

In the translation of the lines from *Sat.* 7 given here we are to imagine the spear as made of wood which bends in the course of time; one of the eyes has fallen out, leaving an empty socket. It is not clear, however, why the statue of a living man should be in such a bad state of repair. J. G. Griffith has suggested in *CQ* 19 (1969) 382–3 that Aemilius is aiming a bow with one eye shut. But, as he himself points out, it is hard to find examples of statues of mounted archers from this period.

3. Thomas Nash, *Pierce Pennylesse* (pronounced 'purse penniless') 8:
   'This is the lamentable condition of our times, that men of arte
   must seek almes of cormorants, and those that deserve best be
   kept under by dunces, who count it a policie to keep them
   bare, because they should follow their books the better.'

Nash has much of Juvenal's energy, but his contempt is directed
solely against the wealthy patrons; the men of arte are blameless.

4. Sir John Harington, *Letters*:[52]

   'How my poetry may be relished in time to come, I will not
   hazard to say. Thus much have I lived to see, and (in good
   sooth) feel too, that honest prose will never better a man's
   purse at court; and had not my fortune been in *terra firma*, I
   might, even for my verses, have danced barefoot with Clio and
   her schoolfellows until I did sweat, and then have gotten
   nothing to slake my thirst but a pitcher from Helicon's well.'

Unlike Juvenal, Harington is autobiographical. The first two sentences are direct and without irony, but the rest is more Juvenalian
in tone; and indeed the references to Clio as a Muse of Poetry and
to Helicon's well suggest that Harington may have recalled vv. 6–7
of the seventh satire.

5. Burton, *Anatomy of Melancholy*:[53]

   'Why do we take such pains? Why the insane desire to turn
   pallid over mere paper? If there be no more hope of reward,
   no better encouragement, I say again, Break your trifling
   pens, Thalia, and destroy your books; let's turn soldiers, sell
   our books, and buy swords, guns and pikes, or stop bottles
   with them...and rather betake ourselves to any other course
   of life, than to continue longer in this misery.'

This is quite close to Juvenal – partly because so much of it is derived from him. We notice, however, that for the 'break your pens'
motif Burton has gone directly to Martial.

6. Johnson, *Letter to the Earl of Chesterfield*:

   'Is not a patron, my lord, one who looks with unconcern on a

---

[52] Sir John Harington, *Letters and Epigrams*, ed. N. E. McClure (Phila-
delphia 1930) 100. Cf. his *Nugae antiquae* 1.168: 'I have spent my time,
my fortune, and almost my honesty, to buy false hope, false friends, and
shallow praise.'

[53] R. Burton, *Anatomy of Melancholy*, ed. Dell and Jordan-Smith (New York
1927) 269.

man struggling for life in the water, and when he has reached ground, cumbers him with help? The notice which you have been pleased to take of my labours, had it been early, had been kind; but it has been delayed until I am indifferent, and cannot enjoy it, till I am solitary and cannot impart it, till I am known and do not want it. I hope it is no very cynical asperity not to confess obligations where no benefit has been received, or to be unwilling that the Publick should consider me as owing that to a Patron which Providence has enabled me to do for myself.'

This well-known passage differs from Juvenal in several obvious ways – e.g. it is addressed to a specific patron and written by a man who has succeeded in surviving by his own efforts. But the main contrast lies in the measured dignity of Johnson's utterance – that same dignity which converted Juvenal's tenth satire into *The Vanity of Human Wishes*.

Having made some effort to ascertain the tone of *Sat.* 7, we may wonder how far Juvenal's allegations were justified. Is it true that by the year 120 (or thereabouts) patronage had completely collapsed? Or are we dealing with the hyperbole of a disgruntled declaimer? No proper answer can be given, since we have so little in the way of contemporary evidence. Some writers like Florus, Favorinus, and Suetonius were certainly employed by Hadrian, and that, as far as it goes, bears out what Juvenal says. The same would be true of jurists like Salvius Julianus and Sextus Pomponius. But what we really want to know is whether any writers were supported by patrons *other* than the emperor. Men like Silius Italicus, Pliny, and Tacitus do not affect the question, since they belonged to the senatorial order and had no need of patronage. The same is true of writers mentioned by Pliny, such as Octavius Rufus and Sentius Augurinus. Others referred to in the *Letters*, like Pompeius Saturninus and Passennus Paulus, were Roman knights.

Some help can be obtained, however, by going back twenty-five years or so to the time of Martial and Statius. In that period we meet the same complaints. A friend of Martial's, who hopes to make a living in Rome, says he will attend the houses of the great. 'That', replies Martial, 'has supported hardly two or three people. The rest of the crowd are pale with hunger' (III.38). Again, Martial says 'There [in the Forum] coins chink, but around our platforms and barren chairs there is only the smack of kisses' (I.76). He himself is read throughout the empire, including Britain, but *quid prodest? nescit sacculus ista meus* 'what use is it? My purse knows nothing of that' (xi.3). Yet Martial survived, and so did Statius. As they had no private means, and as there was no book-trade as we understand it, they had to rely on patronage.

The people who supplied this patronage have been studied very closely in a recent dissertation by Dr Peter White,[54] and he has kindly allowed me to abstract the following points from it. Of the people whom Martial addressed, just over twenty can be identified as senators, and three as important equestrian officials. Of these, however, several are mentioned only once or twice, presumably because they failed to provide more than temporary assistance. Since the rest are not complimented on their public achievements, and since their careers were largely undistinguished, it is clear that their patronage was of a social rather than political kind, a fact which is readily understandable in a state where the emperor did not welcome any rivals to his own prestige. Apart from these figures, Martial mentions at least seventy-five other potential patrons – i.e. people who are treated with deference, described as wealthy, and canvassed for favours. In the case of Statius, if we omit the emperor and the poet's own family, eighteen people are honoured, of whom seven are senators. The latter, however, are mostly young men at the beginning of their careers. With the one exception of Rutilius Gallicus, Statius does not address the emperor's governors or advisers. Often he emphasizes the peacefulness of his patrons' lives; in fact, according to White, approximately half the men addressed in the *Siluae* are explicitly associated with quietism. Another point which emerges is that the circles in which Martial and Statius moved hardly overlapped. Only six possible patrons in Martial reappear in Statius. If one considers Pliny's correspondents the same holds good. Of fifty 'literary' friends mentioned by Pliny only five are found in Martial, while the circles of Pliny and Statius do not touch at all.

So we must imagine quite considerable numbers of heterogeneous patrons, some of them only temporary, making small contributions to the poets of the day. How effective such patronage was depended of course on the number seeking it. Though Martial and Statius survived, we may believe them when they say others didn't. Good patrons were always rare. Writing in the late 80s or early 90s Statius thanks Manilius Vopiscus for his hospitality, compliments him on his handsome estate (*Silu.* 1.3) and calls him 'a very cultured man, one who is rescuing literature, now almost disappearing, from neglect' (*Silu.* i.Pref.). Pliny, too, speaks of Titinius Capito as 'one who is retrieving

<hr/>

[54] Peter White, *Aspects of Non-Imperial Patronage in the Works of Martial and Statius*, Diss. Harvard 1972.

and re-establishing literature, which is now in decay' (VIII.12.1).
When due allowance is made for genre, these statements are not so far
removed from Juvenal's. One must also bear in mind the various passages in which Martial, Juvenal and Pliny comment on the frequency of
recitations.[55] Assuming, as one surely must, that such comments have a
solid basis of truth, one infers yet again that a certain amount of assistance was available but not enough to satisfy the demand. No wonder,
then, that writers looked back with nostalgia to the age of Horace,
when a successful poet might be given a country house with eight servants and an income for life. Yet even then there weren't many patrons
like Maecenas, and *he* was known to be selective. We may be sure that
the pest on the Sacred Way was not the only artist to be disappointed.[56]

It is not hard to speculate on some of the general factors which produced the situation outlined above. The old republican aristocracy was
gone; even the families who had come to prominence under Julius
Caesar and Augustus no longer had any influence. And so there were
no rich men with a tradition of patronage behind them. Even if there
had been, the emperors would not have tolerated anything that might
seem to challenge their primacy. Again, because of Hadrian's foreign
policy, fewer careers were available in the army. At home, security and
prosperity had produced too many educated men. Even if they had been
willing to take up other, less intellectual, work, there was no guarantee
that commerce would absorb them. And so they spent their time in an
undignified and often futile quest for patronage.[57] These, as I say, are
merely general observations. I am not qualified to offer a deeper
analysis, nor is that part of our present purpose. But I hope enough has
been said to show that the picture of the poet–patron relationship in
satire seven is neither an accurate portrait nor a piece of grotesque
fantasy. Like many other Juvenalian sketches it is best described as a
faithful caricature.

[55] See Mayor's note on Juvenal, *Sat.* 3.9.
[56] Horace, *Sat.* I.9.
[57] The situation in Juvenal's day offers some parallels to that which existed
in the seventeenth century. In 1611 Bacon warned James I against encouraging education – it would produce too many over-qualified people
(a disconcertingly modern opinion). The end of the war with Spain
caused some writers to dwell on the dangers of peace. Then too commerce
and industry were not sufficiently developed to meet the problem. Many
writers were destitute, and some were imprisoned for debt. See L. C.
Knights, *Drama and Society in the Age of Jonson* (repr. London 1962)
Appendix B.

5

ARCHITECTURE
Theories about Virgil's *Eclogues*

The purpose of this chapter is to present various types of architectural theory and to suggest ways of assessing them. It will be convenient to use for illustration a work of which the over-all design has been a matter of debate. Since, in the last twenty-five years, a great deal of debate has centred on Virgil's *Eclogues*, and since they also happen to be the first extant collection of that kind,[1] they appear to be the most suitable choice. We shall not be concerned, except incidentally, with the structure of individual pieces or passages. Here and there such matters are still open to question, but no one denies that certain stuctural features exist, and in most cases their nature is obvious enough – e.g., in the first five lines of *Ecl.* 1 we have a chiastic arrangement of *Tityre – tu – nos – nos – tu – Tityre*, the two songs of *Ecl.* 5 each contain twenty-five verses, and *Ecl.* 10 begins and ends with a set of eight verses (3 + 5 and 5 + 3). But when we consider the collection as a whole the situation is not so clear.

Before we discuss the main problem, two preliminary questions must be stated. First, did Virgil collect the poems himself? The grammarian Probus says he did: *Bucolica scripsit, sed non eodem ordine edidit quo scripsit.*[2] Earlier testimony is provided by Ovid. In *Amores* 1.15.25–6, written not long after Virgil's death, he says that Tityrus and the crops and the arms of Aeneas will continue to be read as long as Rome remains head of the world she has conquered:

> Tityrus et segetes Aeneiaque arma legentur
> Roma triumphati dum caput orbis erit.

Here Ovid is referring to the *Eclogues* and the *Aeneid* by quoting a key

---

1 I am referring to collections of poems in the same metre made by the poet himself. This formulation avoids the question whether Catullus arranged his own poems.
2 Probus, Thilo–Hagen 3.328.10.

word from the opening line of each. If Naugerius' *segetes* is right, the same applies to the *Georgics*. If the MSS reading *fruges* is correct, that could represent a lapse of memory; otherwise the reference to the *Georgics* must be seen as an allusion rather than a quotation. At any rate it looks as if our *Ecl.* 1 stood first in the edition used by Ovid. This is confirmed by *Georg.* 4.566, where Virgil himself refers to the first line of *Ecl.* 1 in order to denote the work as a whole:

> Tityre, te patulae cecini sub tegmine fagi.

Finally, we know from the opening of *Ecl.* 10 that it was intended to be the last poem in the book:

> Extremum hunc, Arethusa, mihi concede laborem.

We may therefore assume that the *Eclogues* were published by Virgil in their present order. And so if any clear principle of arrangement emerges it may be fairly attributed to the poet's own intention. A further conclusion might also follow. If the arrangement turned out to be one of prominence and importance, we might well have to consider the book itself as a kind of poem with an extra meaning over and above the meaning of its separate parts.

Secondly, why should there be ten eclogues? The usual answer is that there were ten poems in Virgil's copy of Theocritus. This is based on a remark of Servius in the introduction to his commentary: *sane sciendum vii eclogas esse meras rusticas, quas Theocritus x habet.*[3] Servius is not quite so helpful as he appears. He does not say that Virgil wrote ten eclogues because he possessed ten idylls of Theocritus, but that he wrote seven pure pastorals whereas Theocritus wrote ten. Yet if we grant that all the eclogues are in some sense pastoral (which all the idylls certainly are not), we may still suppose that Virgil chose to write ten pieces because he found ten pastoral idylls in the works of Theocritus, namely 1–11 omitting no. 2.[4] This does not mean that Virgil knew only those idylls; in fact he alludes to nearly all of them. But it was part of his technique for extending the genre to incorporate non-pastoral elements from Theocritus into his own eclogues.

In view of our ignorance about the work of Cornelius Gallus we cannot be sure that Virgil was the first Roman poet to make a collection of ten pieces, but it is true that several later collections consist of multiples of ten – e.g. Horace, *Satires* I (10), *Epistles* I (20), *Odes* II (20), III (30); Tibullus I (10); Ovid *Amores* II (20). This may well have been

---

[3] Thilo–Hagen 3.3.20–1.
[4] There are good reasons for believing that *Idylls* 8 and 9 were not written by Theocritus; but Virgil treats them as if they were.

due to Virgil's influence. On the other hand there can hardly have been anything mandatory about the number ten; otherwise we should not have seventeen epodes and eight satires (Book II) from Horace, and four georgics and twelve books of the *Aeneid* from Virgil himself.

Assuming, then, that Virgil published the *Eclogues* in their present order, can we detect the principle on which he arranged them? Certain possibilities, which are reasonable enough in theory, can be quickly ruled out. The poems might have been arranged according to the names of the shepherds who appear in them. But when the names are tabulated this is seen to be untrue.[5] Or again, the poems could have been set out according to their predominant moods. But if we characterize each piece as sad, happy, or mixed, we do not obtain anything that could be called a pattern.[6] It is true that K. Büchner sees in each half of the work a movement from the lighter, more peaceful, to the heavier, more emphatic, and more agitated.[7] But is 1 really lighter and more peaceful than 3? Or 7 heavier and more agitated than 6?

It has sometimes been held that the order is based on the poems' geographical setting. Thus R. S. Conway writes as follows: 'His *Eclogues*, we found, are arranged so that those with odd numbers have all Italian subjects, and those with even numbers have subjects beyond Italy.'[8] A note on this refers us back to an earlier passage, where we read: 'Virgil...has chosen...five poems with a local [i.e. Mantuan] setting [viz 1, 3, 5, 7, 9], and five with a foreign setting [viz 2, 4, 6, 8, 10], and arranged them alternately.'[9] These two passages say quite different things. We will consider only the earlier and more detailed contention. According to this there are two categories of eclogue: Mantuan and foreign. But on inspection there proves to be no specifically Mantuan reference in 1, 3, or 5; also 'foreign' is an imprecise term, including as it does Sicilian, Arcadian, and Greek.

Let us recall the main items of evidence. *Ecl.* 2 has a Sicilian background, to judge from v. 21 where Corydon boasts:

[5] 1. Meliboeus, Tityrus; 2. Corydon; 3. Menalcas, Damoetas; 4. None; 5. Menalcas, Mopsus; 6. Silenus; 7. Meliboeus, Corydon, Thyrsis; 8. Damon, Alphesiboeus; 9. Lycidas, Moeris; 10. Gallus.

[6] 1. Mixed; 2. sad; 3. happy; 4. happy; 5. mixed; 6. happy; 7. happy; 8. mixed; 9. mixed; 10. sad.

[7] K. Büchner, Pauly–Wissowa VIII A 1, 1257: 'aber deutlich ist wohl auch, dass die beiden Hälften von Leichterem, Ruhigerem zu Schwererem (daher Stellung von 9), zu dem Emphatischsten, Bewegtesten hinführen'. Although unable to follow him on this point I owe a great deal to Büchner's article.

[8] R. S. Conway, *Harvard Lectures on the Vergilian Age* (Harvard 1928) 139.

[9] R. S. Conway, *ibid.* 16 n.2.

mille meae Siculis errant in montibus agnae

a thousand lambs of mine roam on Sicily's mountains.

Sometimes, however, as in 3 and 5, no facts are given about the poem's location. Conway thought that because Menalcas was mentioned in a Mantuan setting in 9 he must therefore be pictured in a similar setting in 3 and 5. But this line of argument is fallacious, because Menalcas is not a consistent character throughout the book, and even the setting of 9 is by no means firm. In other eclogues the background is so large and general as to be quite irrelevant. The prophecy in 4 embraces the Roman world as a whole, and the capture of Silenus in 6 takes place in the realm of Greek folk-tale. Most often the references are mixed in such a way as to frustrate geographical enquiries. Thus in 7 Arcadian shepherds (4 and 26) sing by the river Mincius in N. Italy (12–13). In 8.6–13 Virgil, presumably in Naples, addresses a Roman general who is on his way home from Illyricum;[10] Damon's song has an Arcadian background, to judge from the reference to Mount Maenalus in vv. 22–4 and from the refrain:

incipe Maenalios mecum, mea tibia, uersus

begin with me, my pipe, a song of Maenalus.

The song of Alphesiboeus is set vaguely in the countryside, as may be seen from the fact that the girl tries to prevail on her lover to return from the town.

In 9.27–8 we are in the district around Mantua (*Mantua uae miserae nimium uicina Cremonae*), but towards the end Lycidas calls attention to the calmness of the sea:

et nunc omne tibi stratum silet aequor, et omnes,
aspice, uentosi ceciderunt murmuris aurae   (57–8)

and now before you the whole sea lies level and silent and look, the gusts of the noisy wind have all fallen still.

[10] The general is usually identified with Pollio, who campaigned against the Parthini in 39 B.C. But since the Parthini lived near Dyrrachium (Appian 5.75) it is hard to see why Pollio should have returned to Italy via Trieste instead of crossing to Brundisium. This has led G. Bowersock to identify the general with Octavian, who in 35 B.C. campaigned in the district of Trieste (*HSCP* 75 (1971) 73–80). On the other hand Virgil's general had already achieved a reputation as a tragedian (9–10). This fits Pollio well (Horace, *Sat.* 1.10.42–3; *Odes* II.1.9–12) but hardly Octavian, in spite of Suetonius, *Aug.* 85.2. No doubt the matter will be debated during the next few years. Commitment is not necessary for our purpose. See now W. Clausen, *HSCP* 76 (1972) 201–5.

This points to Sicily, rather than Mantua, which is nowhere near the sea;[11] and the presence of a tomb in v. 60 is a literary reminiscence of Theocritus 7.11.[12]

In 1 we are told that Tityrus has visited Rome (19ff.), but we are not told where he lives. Usually scholars infer a Mantuan setting from 9 because both poems mention evictions. This can be supported by some of the references to landscape, e.g. 46–8:

> fortunate senex, ergo tua rura manebunt.
> et tibi magna satis, quamuis lapis omnia nudus
> limosoque palus obducat pascua iunco.

> *You lucky old man! So the land will still be yours. And it's big enough for you, even though all your pastures are covered by bare rock and by the marsh with its muddy reeds.*

Yet other features, like the bees of Hybla (54), the high rock (56), the cave (75) and the lofty mountains (83) recall Sicily, and the names of the shepherds and their girls are, of course, Greek. A hundred years ago, when such a viewpoint was uncommon, John Conington wrote as follows:

> 'When Castelvetro, in the sixteenth century, asserted that the favourite trees of the *Eclogues*, the beech, the ilex, the chestnut, and the pine, do not grow about Mantua, subsequent critics were ready to reply that the features of the country may have changed, and that surely Virgil must know best. But such reasoning will hardly avail against the absence of the green caves in which the shepherd lies, or the briary crags from which his goats hang, or the lofty mountains whose

---

11 These lines look like an elaboration of Theocritus 2.38: ἠνίδε σιγῇ μὲν πόντος, σιγῶντι δ'ἀῆται 'look, the sea is silent and silent are the winds'. R. Hanslik, *WS* 68 (1955) 14 sees them as a reminiscence of Theocritus 7.57–9. I prefer the older view, but both passages of Theocritus support the interpretation of *aequor* as 'sea'. Moreover, *silet* and *stratum* are appropriate to the sea (cf. *Aen.* 5.763 and 821; 1.164; and 5.127 cited by G. Williams, *Tradition and Originality in Roman Poetry* (Oxford 1968) 320), whereas they are inappropriate to a plain. They are also unsuitable to large expanses of flood water. The question was discussed by G. Jachmann in his important article 'Die dichterische Technik in Vergils Bukolika' in *Neue Jahrbücher* 49 (1922) 101–20, especially 113–14.

12 The dead man is called Brasilas in Theocritus, Bianor in Virgil. We don't know why Virgil chose that name. One guess, by S. Tugwell in *CR* 13 (1963) 132–3, is that he was thinking of *Greek Anthology* 7.261, in which a mother speaks of Bianor her dead son.

lengthening shadows remind him of evening. These are the unmistakable features of Sicily, and no illusion of historical criticism will persuade us that they have changed their places, strange as it is to meet them in conjunction with real Mantuan scenery, with the flinty soil of Andes, and the broad, lazy current of the Mincio.'[13]

In 10 the poet Gallus is described as pining away on a lonely hillside, apparently in Arcadia (14–15); the Italian Silvanus and the Arcadian Pan come to reason with him (24–6); in his reply Gallus wishes he could have been an Arcadian shepherd with his girl beside him; then to our surprise he laments that now he is on military service:

> nunc insanus amor duri me Martis in armis
> tela inter media atque aduersos detinet hostis.   (44–5)

Now the mad love of stern war keeps me in arms with weapons all around and the enemy out in front.

A little later (52ff.) he declares his intention of living in the woods or roaming over Mt Maenalus with the nymphs; or perhaps he will hunt wild animals. Finally (60ff.) he admits that none of these activities will cure his love; no part of the world, however remote, is free from Love's dominion.

There are many difficulties in this eclogue, but the right starting point is surely the fact that Gallus was himself a poet. In addition we must remember the hint given by Servius in his note on v. 46: *hi autem omnes uersus Galli sunt, de ipsius translati carminibus* – 'these are all verses of Gallus, taken from his poems'. It is true that Servius cannot be interpreted quite literally, because Gallus wrote in elegiac couplets. But we are entitled to believe that Virgil took over certain phrases and motifs from Gallus' work and embodied them in an eclogue written specially for him. This means that the Gallus presented by Virgil is based on Gallus as he appeared in his own poems. He can be described as dying of love because he had written of himself in those terms. He had also presumably spoken sadly about the demands of a soldier's life (a theme found in later elegy) and even reproached himself with his calling; he can therefore be imagined as doing so in Virgil's eclogue (44–5). His intention of living in the woods and roaming with the nymphs is also to be understood in a literary sense; for in the immediately preceding lines he has said:

[13] J. Conington, p. 10 of the Introduction to his commentary on the *Eclogues*, fifth edition (London 1898).

ibo et Chalcidico quae sunt mihi condita uersu
carmina pastoris Siculi modulabor auena.

*I shall go and play on the Sicilian shepherd's pipe the songs I
composed in Chalcidic verse.*

In other words he will write poetry in Theocritus' style instead of
Euphorion's; the woods he will dwell in are the woods of pastoral. So
too, when he finally concedes that living with the nymphs in Arcadia is
no cure for love (60–1) he adds:

iam neque Hamadryades rursus neque carmina nobis
ipsa placent; ipsae rursus concedite siluae.

*Now once again the forest nymphs and even poems have no
pleasure for me; away with you once again, even ye woodlands.*

That is, he will not write of himself as a shepherd/lover in a pastoral
setting. The explanation for the shifting background of *Ecl.* 10 is
therefore to be sought in literature, not in geography.

To sum up. If the actual setting of the *Eclogues* is something which
Virgil has so often blurred and confused, then that cannot have been the
basis for his arrangement of the poems.

Another theory, which would save a lot of speculation if true, was
proposed rather tentatively by R. Helm, namely that except for 1 the
order of the eclogues is chronological.[14] There are, however, one or
two fairly strong objections. The known chronological facts are few.
In 5.85–7 the shepherd Menalcas says to Mopsus:

hac te nos fragili donabimus ante cicuta;
haec nos 'formosum Corydon ardebat Alexin',
haec aedem docuit 'cuium pecus? an Meliboei?'

*I will give you first this slender reed. This taught me 'Corydon
was burning for the lovely Alexis' and also 'Who owns the flock?
Is it Meliboeus'?'*

This shows that 2 and 3 preceded 5. Apart from this we know that 4
belongs to 40 B.C., 8 to 39 (if not later) and that 10 was written last.

Now for Helm to be right 4 would have to come before 5, but in the
passage quoted above Virgil seems to be referring rather proudly to *all*
his previous eclogues. Although 4 is rather dignified pastoral (*paulo*

---

[14] R. Helm, *Bursians Jahresbericht* (1902) 21–2. According to W. Port,
Philologus 81 (1926) 283–4, the same view was held by Mancini,
Stampini and P. Jahn.

maiora canamus) it is still a pastoral. The Sicilian Muses invoked at the beginning are the Muses of Theocritus, the woods in v. 3 are the woods of pastoral, and much of the prophecy is conceived and pre- sented in pastoral terms – e.g. vv. 18–30, 40–5, and 55–9. Therefore if 4 already existed one would have expected it to be included along with the references to 2 and 3. Furthermore, to state the matter in as un- controversial a way as possible, it is hard to believe that the deification of Daphnis in 5 and the mention of his worship (65ff.) had absolutely nothing to do with the deification of Julius Caesar in 42 B.C.[15] If there is any connection, then 5 antedates 4. Since 4 and 1 are now both out of order, the chronological theory loses its appeal.

In the foregoing argument I have said nothing about the sequence of 6, 7 and 8, or about the relation of 1 to 9. This is because there is no evidence to justify any firm conclusion. It would be a waste of time to tabulate all the suggested schemes. Here are six, simply for the sake of illustration (I have omitted 2, 3, 5, and 10, because their position is known):

Krause:	7, 6, 9, 1, 4, 8
Cartault:	7, 4, 6, 8, 1, 9
Goelzer:	4, 6, 7, 8, 1, 9
Witte:	9, 1, 4, 8, 6, (with 7 at the very beginning)
Bayet:	7, 1, 9, 4, 6, 8
Büchner:	9, 1, 6, 4, 8, 7

Since we know so little about the exact order of the *Eclogues* we cannot hope to chart the spiritual development of the poet or his characters. And so when we find it stated in a well known essay that 'Virgil's shepherds, on the other hand, – and it is charming to follow the steady progress from eclogue to eclogue – become increasingly more delicate and sensitive'[16] we must remember that in spite of the indicative mood we are not reading a statement of fact.

We come now to a view which has long been held and which might have some truth in it, namely that the *Eclogues* are arranged on a formal principle according to which one kind of poem alternates with another. The details have been formulated in different terms. Wagner saw the pattern as an alternation of *carmina amoebaea* with *carmina non amoebaea*.[17] This is hardly satisfactory, for a *carmen amoebaeum* is

---

[15] See P. Grimal, *Mélanges Picard* (Paris 1949) 406–19.

[16] B. Snell, 'Arcadia: the Discovery of a Spiritual Landscape', printed in *The Discovery of the Mind*, trans. T. G. Rosenmeyer (Oxford 1953) 287.

[17] Heyne–Wagner, Vol. 1, part 1 (1830) 59–60 in a note on Spohn's Prolegomena.

properly speaking a poem made up of responses in which one speaker tries to outdo the other. Of the *Eclogues* number 3 is fully responsive (the presence of a third party as a judge would not count as an objection); 7 is fully responsive, but the exchanges are reported by a narrator; 5 is partly responsive in that the song of Mopsus (20–44) is answered by that of Menalcas (56–80); 9 is responsive in a few places, but only indirectly, through quotations – e.g. at 23–5 and 27–9; 1 is not responsive at all. Furthermore if we consider the even numbers, 8 must be classed as a *carmen amoebaeum*, since Alphesiboeus answers Damon (*responderit* in v. 62) in an equal number of lines.

The way to another formulation was prepared by Schulze.[18] Although he used the term *carmen amoebaeum* ('1, 3, 5, 7, 9 sind *carmina amoebaea*, Wechselgesänge zwischen zwei Hirten...'), he had already said in the previous sentence 'es ist ferner zu beachten, wie regelmässig Eclogen in dialogischer Form mit andern abwechseln'. This idea occurs again in Cartault ('nous voyons que les Égl. 1, 3, 5, 7, 9 sont des dialogues; au contraire les Égl. 2, 4, 6, 10 sont des monologues'[19]), and it has often been repeated since. Cartault concedes that according to this theory 8 ought to be a monologue, but isn't. For him this proves only that Virgil was doing his best to arrange material which was already complete; he did not write the pieces to fit the scheme and therefore one could not expect the result to be entirely symmetrical. This last point will come up again later, but in the meantime it should be noted that the classification of 2, 4, 6, and 10 also raises difficulties. Of these only 4 is a pure monologue; 2 is a reported monologue; 6 might be called a monologue containing a summary of another monologue; 10 could not be called a monologue at all.

Finally, Klotz saw the distinction in terms of dramatic as opposed to narrative pieces: 'dramatische und erzählende Idyllen wechseln in regelmässige Folge'.[20] But 1, a conversation between two shepherds in which one relates his good fortune and the other his bad, is dramatic in a very different sense from 3, in which two herdsmen exchange banter and then compete for prizes in a singing context. The two songs which make up the greater part of 5 could hardly be termed dramatic, for one has no effect on the other; and, as Klotz admits, in 7 (which might be called dramatic in the same sense as 3) the contest is presented within a narrative framework. Again, to take the even numbers, although

[18] K. P. Schulze, *Jahrbücher f. klassische Philologie* 131 (1885) 866.
[19] A. Cartault, *Étude sur les Bucoliques de Virgile* (Paris 1897) 53. Cf. J. Bayet, *Mélanges de la littérature latine* (Rome 1967) 136.
[20] A. Klotz, *Rh.Mus.* 64 (1909) 326.

Corydon's song in 2 is reported by Virgil the poem as a whole is not a piece of narrative; the same objection applies just as strongly to 8 and 10.

In view of this discussion it may be helpful to list very briefly the main formal features of the *Eclogues*. (The verb 'report' is used to mean 'present verbatim'.)

1. Dialogue between two shepherds: non-responsive: longest speech 15 vv.
2. Introductory narrative by Virgil (5 vv.), who then reports a love-lorn shepherd's song.
3. Dialogue between two shepherds: responsive: longest speech 12 vv. This is followed by a responsive song-contest in couplets, introduced and concluded by a third shepherd.
4. Virgil speaks throughout, foretelling the coming of a new golden age: no reported speech, except for v. 46.
5. Dialogue between two shepherds: longest speech 4 vv. This is followed by two responsive songs (25 vv. each) separated by a few lines of dialogue. Concluding dialogue of 10 vv.
6. Introductory statement by Virgil concerning pastoral poetry and Varus (12 vv.); further narrative by Virgil relating the capture of Silenus (18 vv.). Virgil then summarizes the songs of Silenus. The summary includes two short passages of reported speech.
7. A shepherd narrates how he was present at a song-contest (20 vv.) He then reports the contest, which is in responsive quatrains, and adds two concluding lines.
8. Virgil announces his intention to report a song-contest (5 vv.): he then addresses a Roman general (8 vv.) before going on to set the scene (3 vv.). He reports two responsive songs (46 vv. each), separating them by two verses of comment.
9. Dialogue between two shepherds: occasionally but indirectly responsive: longest speech 10 vv. Lines of song are quoted from a third shepherd.
10. Introductory and concluding passages (8 vv. each) addressed by Virgil to Arethusa and the Muses. These frame a song for the love-lorn Gallus, which is partly narrative, partly reported dialogue, but mainly a report of Gallus' own words.

With this list before us it may be instructive to recall a classification made by Servius which has not, as far as I know, figured in modern discussions. In his introduction to *Ecl.* 3 Servius distinguished three types of poem: one (A) in which only the poet's characters spoke, another (B) in which only the poet spoke, and a third (C) in which both the poet and his characters spoke. In the *Eclogues*, he says, all three types are found; *Ecl.* 1 represents the first, *Ecl.* 4 the second, and *Ecl.* 10 the third.[21] Now Servius did not use this classification to understand the *Eclogues'* arrangement, but if he had he would have seen that numbers 1, 3, 5, 7, and 9 (and only they) belonged to type A. The sequence is regular enough to suggest that it might have been deliberate, though it could hardly be said to constitute a very significant system of classification; also some further principle would be needed to explain the position of the individual pieces.

Yet another approach to the architecture of the *Eclogues* lies through an examination of their subject-matter. One particular form of this approach involves a comparison between each eclogue and the various idylls of Theocritus on which it is based. In 1885 K. P. Schulze took as his starting-point the remark of Servius already quoted, namely that seven of the eclogues were purely pastoral. In three, Servius goes on to say, Virgil departed from the pastoral genre: *in tribus a bucolico carmine sed cum excusatione discessit*. On the strength of this observation Schulze distinguishes two classes (1) 'purely pastoral, viz. 2, 3, 5, 7, 8, and 9 with which 1 is connected', and (2) 'poems in which the pastoral element recedes more into the background and in which the poet sings of loftier themes, viz. 4 and 6, with which 10 is connected'.[22] He then maintains that 2, 3, 5, 7, 8, and 9 are studies in the manner of Theocritus, and that 4 and 6 are inserted into this series on the principle of *uariatio*. 'And so we obtain the following symmetrical and doubtless intentional arrangement:

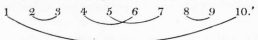

In spite of appearances, this is not a symmetrical arrangement. If 4 is separated from the half-way line by one eclogue, the same ought to be true of 6. Therefore in the interests of symmetry 6 and 7 ought to change places. Moreover, if we grant that 2, 3, 5, and 7 are 'purely pastoral', the same can hardly be said of 8 and 9. The second part of 8 is indeed sung by a shepherd, but it is not really his song. It is the song of a girl who is trying to win back her lover by magic spells. Although the lover is called Daphnis he has no other pastoral features, and although the girl lives in the country and makes some references to it

[21] Thilo–Hagen 1.29.18–30.3. Cf. Probus, Thilo–Hagen 3.329.10–15.
[22] Schulze, *Jahrbücher f. klassische Philologie* 131 (1885). 866.

(e.g. the heifer in 86ff., the woods and corn in 97ff.) her song has very little in the way of pastoral colouring. The reason is, of course, that it is based on a *non*-pastoral poem of Theocritus (*Id.* 2). Likewise the evictions mentioned in 9 prevent it from being 'purely pastoral'. The main difficulty, however, concerns the first and last pieces. Does Schulze mean to connect 10 with 6 or with 1? In fact it goes with neither. And what is the status of 1? If it is really related to 9 the pattern is further impaired.

A rather different scheme was proposed by Kroll.[23] He took 2, 3, 5, 7, and 8 as Theocritean imitations and distinguished them from 1, 4, 6, 9, and 10, in which Theocritean influence was, he said, either secondary or negligible. This theory would yield the pattern

A   B   B   A   B   A   B   B   A   A

which shows a fair degree of symmetry. But what is meant by 'Theocritean'? Evidence which would help us to use this term with some degree of precision has recently been published by S. Posch.[24] In his third table Posch shows the number of passages in each eclogue derived from the first eleven idylls of Theocritus. The figures are:

3 (79), 2, (48), 7 (44), 8 (42), 5 (41), 10 (34), 1 (20), 9 (17), 4 (6), 6 (3).

One must, however, take account of the length of each poem. When this is done the figures are:

3 (0.712), 2 (0.658), 7 (0.629), 5 (0.456), 10 (0.442), 8 (0.385), 9 (0.254), 1 (0.241), 4 (0.095), 6 (0.035).

This shows that the main divisions come between 7 and 5, between 8 and 9, and between 1 and 4. The resulting groups are 3, 2, 7; 5, 10, 8; 9, 1; 4, 6. On the basis of Theocritean allusions, therefore, it seems impossible to uphold Kroll's distinction. No. 10 is misplaced. And the figures show that there is a far bigger difference between 8 and 7 (which Kroll classes together) than between 8 and 9 (which he separates). There are also clearly difficulties in classifying 4 and 6 with 1 and 9.[25]

[23] W. Kroll, *Studien zum Verständnis der Römischen Literatur* (repr. Darmstadt 1964) 228–9. Originally published in *Neue Jahrbücher* 19 (1916) 93–106.

[24] S. Posch, *Beobachtungen zur Theokritnachwirkung bei Vergil* (Innsbruck–Munich 1969) 15–27.

[25] This is perhaps the place to notice the theory of K. Witte, propounded in *Der Bukoliker Vergil* (Stuttgart 1922) 40–1. After fixing the positions

But perhaps the eclogues could be arranged on the basis, not of their allusions, but of their situations. This idea seems to underlie one of the theories advanced by Brooks Otis:

> 'The eclogues clearly fall into three main categories: the fully Theocritean poems (2, 3, 7, 8); the Theocritean poems with a specifically Roman, contemporary bearing (5, 10); and the non-Theocritean poems (1, 4, 6, 9). All, it is true, show Theocritean influence in that all are, to a greater or lesser degree, indebted to Theocritus' style or manner...But these considerations do not in the least alter the facts [sic] that 2, 3, 7, 8 are directly based on Theocritean models; that 5 and 10 use a Theocritean original (the first Idyll) in a very special, Roman way; and that 1, 4, 6, 9 are not based on actual Theocritean models (with perhaps some slight qualification for 9) but derive instead from obviously non-Theocritean sources or ideas.'[26]

When Otis speaks of 2, 3, 7 and 8 being 'directly based on Theocritean models', he seems to have in mind the situations described in the poems. Thus the picture of the doleful Corydon complaining about the indifference of his beloved (*Ecl.* 2) may be said to be based on similar pictures of Polyphemus in idylls 6 and 11; the encounter of Menalcas and Damoetas in 3, and that of Corydon and Thyrsis in 7, recall corresponding encounters in idylls 4, 5, and 8. But the case of *Ecl.* 8 is not so easy. The address to the Roman general in vv. 6–13 has to be left aside, and it must be admitted that the matrimonial element in Damon's song – i.e. the situation of the jilted fiancé – has no prototype in Theocritus.

Turning to Otis' second category, we find that the first idyll provides only a very loose connection between 5 and 10. In 5 the opening conversation between Menalcas and Mopsus (1–19) and their exchange of presents at the end (81–90) owe almost nothing to Theocritus' poem; the lament (20–44) begins at the point where the first idyll ends – i.e. at the death of Daphnis; and Menalcas' song about the shepherd's apotheosis (56–80) is Virgil's own contribution. The description in

of 1, 3, 8, 9, and 10 on other grounds, Witte says that Virgil then tried to make the 'Greek' and the 'Roman' poems alternate as much as possible. He therefore put 4 and 6 in their present positions and filled the gaps with the 'Greek' poems 2, 5, and 7. But it seems very odd to classify 6 as 'Roman' merely on the strength of the address to Varus.

[26] B. Otis, *Virgil: A Study in Civilized Poetry* (Oxford 1964) 128–9.

10.9–30 of the surroundings in which Gallus is pining away and of the various characters who come to reason with him is indeed based on *Id.* 1.66ff. But after v. 30 the eclogue goes its own way for another forty-seven lines. Again, Otis maintains that eclogues 5 and 10 use the first idyll 'in a very special, Roman way'. This might suggest a certain similarity of treatment, yet the differences are surely more striking. In 5 the Roman element consists of a few veiled allusions to Julius Caesar, whereas in 10 the presence of Gallus is ubiquitous and acknowledged. Also the purport of the allusions in 5 is national and political, whereas the presentation of Gallus in 10 has a personal and literary function. Further differences will be noted later.

Finally, if we are looking for an eclogue which is based predominantly on a single idyll, and which at the same time uses that idyll in a very special, Roman way, we can hardly overlook no. 9. According to Posch, this poem contains ten allusions to the seventh idyll, and also offers the same kind of setting, viz a country walk. The Roman treatment is seen in the mention of Varus (26–7), Caesar (47), and two contemporary poets (35), and more particularly in the references to the tragic events taking place around Mantua and Cremona.

In view of these points Otis' categories are not wholly convincing.

We now come to the most ingenious and elaborate theory of the plan underlying the *Eclogues*. Since it was first advanced by P. Maury in 1944[27] it has been accepted with various degrees of qualification by such distinguished scholars as Perret, Duckworth, Otis, R. D. Williams, and Skutsch. Basically the contention is that the eclogues are built on two mutually supporting principles, viz topical and arithmetical correspondence. Before rehearsing the details, it is worth looking very briefly at some observations made by E. Krause in 1884,[28] because they provide, as it were, the germ of Maury's theory.

According to Krause eclogues 1 and 9 belong together because they both represent the troubles which afflicted Italy at the time of the proscriptions, and also they are written in a purely dramatic form without any intervention on the part of the poet. Eclogues 3 and 7 are both responsive singing-matches. Numbers 4 and 6 stand some distance away from strict pastoral, and they deal with contemporary people in an elevated style. In 2 and 8 the woes of love are presented. Number 5 stands by itself, unrelated to any of the others. The plan as a whole is represented thus:

---

27 P. Maury, *Lettres d'Humanité* 3 (1944) 71–147.
28 E. Krause, *Quibus temporibus quoque ordine Vergilius eclogas suas scripserit* (Berlin 1884) 6.

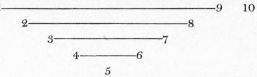

One notices here that three different principles are invoked – form, style, and subject. This would not satisfy anyone who wished to find a single unifying idea. Secondly, no attempt is made to relate the various sets of pairs to one another. Krause is content to say that Virgil's main concern was to prevent similar eclogues from standing next to each other. Thirdly, there are certain difficulties of detail, e.g. 4 and 6 are not the only pieces that refer to contemporary people, nor are 2 and 8 the only ones to deal with love. Number 5 is left on its own, and apparently 10 has no place in the scheme at all – Krause simply says it was composed last, as if that were enough to explain why it could not be included. Maury has therefore some reason for finding Krause's theory inadequate: 'il n'a pas compris lui-même l'importance de sa découverte, qui est restée stérile' (90 n. 1).

Maury's own theory, which apparently came to him with all the excitement of an independent discovery, may be summarized as follows: eclogues 1 and 9 correspond, because they are both concerned with the ordeals of the land (*les épreuves de la terre*). Numbers 2 and 8 present ordeals of a different kind – *les épreuves de l'amour*. 'C'est le drame passionel après la tragédie politique' (78). The lovers are tormented by a passion which cannot be cured by reason or morality; nor can it be consoled by poetry itself. The next stage is that of *la musique libératrice*. After describing the singing contests of 3 and 7, which take place in a world of sunshine and security, Maury concludes: 'ces libations de musique essentielle...délivrent l'homme des servitudes des siècles de fer, le purifient des passions et des souillures de la terre, elles lui permettent de se réaliser et de s'accomplir, et, l'arrachant au cercle odieux des nécessités, l'orientent déjà vers les hautes demeures dont il garde la nostalgie' (84). Higher still are eclogues 4 and 6, which provide supernatural revelations. The first comes from the Sibyl (the voice of Apollo) presenting the glorious future, and the second from Silenus (the mask of Dionysus) interpreting the terrible past. Finally, on the pinnacle of this structure we have number 5, which concerns the dead and risen Daphnis/Caesar. At the last stage of the journey, between his Sibyl and his Silenus, Virgil has placed this ideal picture to serve as a subject of meditation and a model of perfection (89). When represented schematically, the whole structure forms what M. Maury calls *une chapelle bucolique*:

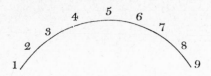

There can be no doubt that this is a highly ingenious theory, and many scholars would say that it was confirmed by certain numerical correspondences to which Maury drew attention. The more important of these correspondences will be considered presently, but first we must look more closely at Maury's treatment of the eclogues' subject matter. And even before that we have to face the obvious question: what has happened to number 10? Unlike Krause, Maury does have an answer, yet one cannot help feeling that he finds the poem something of an embarrassment. He says more than once that it did not figure in Virgil's original plan.[29] When it is left aside, number 5 can be regarded as the centre of the remaining nine. Thus on p. 89 Maury refers to 5 as 'une seule églogue, isolée, sans contrepartie'. And on p. 99 he says 'les Bucoliques ne sont qu'un seule poème en neuf strophes'. One has the impression that it would have suited Maury very much better if number 10 had never been written; indeed one wonders why it *was* written, since the scheme was apparently complete without it.

Nevertheless, Maury does succeed in finding a function for 10. According to him, Gallus is to be seen as the anti-type of Daphnis in 5. As such he has no part in the spiritual ascent. Having allowed himself to be seized by an *indignus amor* he is excluded from the bucolic chapel and stands disconsolately at the door. 'Gallus s'oppose à Daphnis comme l'amour profane à l'amour sacré, l'homme de chair imparfaitement initié, à l'idéal de l'homme rénové dont il garde toujours la nostalgie dans les brumes et les frimas de son exil' (107).

Let us now look quickly at the corresponding pairs. Is it fair to sum up the first eclogue as 'the ordeals of the land'? Such a heading seems to overstress the grim side of the poem, which has, after all, as much to do with restitution as with eviction. However, one may admit that the first eclogue is largely concerned with the re-assignment of land. The same is not true of the ninth. Out of sixty-seven verses no more than twenty (viz 1–16 and 26–9) refer to the troubles around Cremona. For the rest we are in a world of pastoral song. So any correspondence between the poems is of a much looser kind than Maury supposes.

---

29 See, in particular, p. 74: 'la *Xe Bucolique* (Gallus) est un postscriptum, ajouté par Virgile au moment de la publication de son receuil. . . un poème que j'avais droit de supposer étranger au programme arrêté par Virgile.' Cf. 100–1.

In *Ecl.* 2 a shepherd-poet sings a lament about unrequited love. This
has, it is true, a fair amount in common with Damon's song in 8. But
Damon's song takes up less than half the poem. The other song – that
of Alphesiboeus – is quite different in tone. It is not a lament; the girl
is determined to get Daphnis back, and she believes in the end that she
has succeeded (*ab urbe uenit*). There is a further point. If Corydon's
song has something in common with that of Damon, it has also something in common with the song of Gallus in 10. *Sollicitos Galli dicamus
amores*, says Virgil in his introduction to that poem. That ought surely
to suggest *les épreuves de l'amour*. Moreover, although Gallus is represented as a vastly more sophisticated lover than Corydon, the two
resemble each other in their response to suffering. Tender, sensitive,
defeated, and prone to self pity, they both give the impression of being
elegiac lovers in a pastoral setting.[30]

No one will deny the resemblance between 3 and 7, and there is much
to agree with in Maury's observations about these delightful poems.
But the elevated general meaning which he assigns to them is hardly
supported by anything in the text itself. When the reader encounters
the cheerful accusations of theft, sodomy, and vandalism at the beginning of 3, he is not aware of being lifted above all earthly concerns.
Nor, for that matter, is there any indication within 2 or 8 that Virgil is
pointing the way to higher things. However, it might be argued in
reply that the additional, spiritual, meaning is conferred by the placing
of the poems within the pattern. We are therefore thrown back on the
question: how convincing are the details of Maury's symmetrical
design?

In the case of 4 and 6 we are told that both poems are supernatural
revelations. But this is a very weak connection, and in fact they have
almost nothing in common. 4 is a prophecy, 6 is not; 4 claims to be
more elevated than pastoral usually is (*paulo maiora canamus*), 6 claims
to respect the normal boundaries of the genre (*deductum carmen, tenui
harundine*); 4 is concerned with the future of Rome in history, 6 with
the world's mythological past as described in Alexandrian poetry; in 4
Virgil speaks *in propria persona*, in 6 he uses a narrator; 4 has one large
theme, 6 has half a dozen small ones. Now if Maury were arguing

---

[30] See C. Fantazzi, *AJP* 87 (1966) 171–91. In the grouping proposed by
G. Stégen *Commentaire sur Cinq Bucoliques de Virgile* (Namur 1957)
chap. 6, 1 goes with 9, 2 with 10, 3 with 7, 4 with 6, 5 with 8. There
is certainly a formal similarity between 5 and 8. Both are composed
of large contrasting panels. I have discussed the other pairs in the text.
Some have, indeed, genuine points of comparison. But even if we accepted
all the groupings proposed by Stégen we would still not have anything
that could be called a regular pattern.

simply that in arranging the eclogues Virgil grouped 4 and 6 together because neither resembled any of the other pieces, that might just be acceptable. But in fact he is maintaining that the common features of 4 and 6 are so central and substantial that the poems can be seen as supporting a superstructure of mystical religious affirmation. One is reminded of the old schoolboy riddle: 'Why is a mad dog like a tin of condensed milk?' Answer: 'Because neither can ride a bicycle.'

We move on to numbers 5 and 10. Is Gallus the anti-type of Daphnis? If he is, and if, as Maury imagines, he stands at the entrance of the *chapelle bucolique*, then surely he is on the wrong level. As a casualty of love he ought by rights to be hanging outside a first-floor window. A less frivolous objection is the fact that it is not easy to relate the two figures in any significant way. In *Ecl.* 5, as Maury himself points out, Daphnis is not portrayed as a lover, nor do we hear anything about either the cause or the circumstances of his death.[31] Virgil is interested only in its effects – the grief of man and nature. This grief is balanced by joy at the shepherd's apotheosis. How then are we to compare or contrast this vague superhuman figure with Gallus, a living poet? The fact that they are both derived in very different ways from Theocritus' first idyll is not enough to establish the direct and substantial relationship required by Maury. Finally, Maury's theory entails the belief that Virgil is in some way censuring the behaviour of Gallus as represented in the tenth eclogue. 'La plus belle des églogues amoureuses de Virgile... contient implicitement la condamnation d'une vie et d'une poésie asservies à l'amour et ruinées par l'amour même' (103). But surely this is most unlikely. To judge from v. 3 (*neget quis carmina Gallo?*) Gallus had requested a poem from his friend. Can we really believe that Virgil replied with a rebuke, however gently phrased? On the contrary, the poem was meant as a mark of the highest respect, and it has usually been understood as such.

In view of these objections, the solemn religious superstructure which Maury built on the eclogues does not seem convincing. Certainly if the book had such an exalted character it eluded the poet's friend, who praised the work for possessing *molle atque facetum*, 'the qualities of tenderness and elegance' (Horace, *Sat.* 1.10.44).

Although he discards Maury's religious interpretation, Brooks Otis retains his corresponding pairs. At the same time he proposes, as we saw, a three-fold division into Theocritean, Theocritean-Roman, and

---

31 In Theocritus Aphrodite is the cause of Daphnis' death. Venus is not given the same role by Virgil, perhaps because he wanted to hint at a relationship between Daphnis and Caesar.

non-Theocritean. And he holds both these theories in conjunction with a third:

> 'It is clear (whatever else may not be clear) that *Eclogues* 1–5 are relatively forward-looking, peaceful, conciliatory and patriotic in a Julio-Augustan sense. *Eclogues* 6–10, on the contrary, are neoteric, ambiguous or polemic, concerned with the past and emotively dominated by *amor indignus*, love which is essentially destructive and irrational and is implicitly inconsistent with (if not hostile to) a strong Roman-patriotic orientation.'[32]

But are these contentions really so clear? In presenting his case Otis has summarized the eclogues in contrasting pairs. Let us look briefly at a few of his précis. *Ecl.* 1 is summed up as follows: 'exile revoked: praise of the new god; bitterness assuaged by hospitality; complete fusion of bucolic and Roman-Augustan themes'. But if we must have summaries surely this would be more accurate: 'exile revoked for one shepherd but not for another; praise for the new god by the luckier of the two, a bitter complaint about the evictions on the part of the less fortunate (64–78); hospitality granted for a single night before an untold period of homeless wandering; incomplete fusion of bucolic and Roman-Augustan themes which has caused considerable difficulties at various points, e.g. 27ff. and 45'. *Ecl.* 2 is described thus: 'the cure of unworthy love by the recovery of reason'. But it is not clear that Corydon achieves more than a temporary cure, for at the beginning we are told that he constantly wandered into the woods to sing his song (*assidue ueniebat*). If he ever did find another, less scornful, Alexis (73), that would I suppose have been peaceful and conciliatory, though hardly forward-looking and patriotic in a Julio-Augustan sense.

Ecl. 3 ('Amoebaean contest starting in crude abuse and *ending* in a peaceful non-decision by an umpire') is contrasted with 7 ('Amoebaean contest *ending* in defeat of the harsh Thyrsis, victory of the mild Corydon'). Even if one agrees that Thyrsis is harsh (or 'bitter and harshly emphatic'[33]) it is hard to see why a decision in favour of his mild opponent should make the piece in some way less positive than number 3, which ends in a draw.

[32] B. Otis, *Virgil*, 130–1.
[33] B. Otis, *Virgil*, 143. For a detailed discussion of the seventh eclogue see V. Pöschl, *Die Hirtendichtung Virgils* (Heidelberg 1964) chap. 3.
Various scholars have found fault with the lines spoken by Thyrsis. On a few points I think the criticisms are valid, if over-solemn. But one has to be careful. Did Virgil mean us to infer that half the eclogue was made up of inferior poetry spoken by an objectionable character?

As we have already dealt with 5 and 10, that leaves only the supposed contrast between 4 ('the new age: return of the *Saturnia regna*') and 6 ('the former age: passing of the ancient *Saturnia regna* into a series of unnatural *amores* and *metamorphoses*'). In connection with 6 one need only recall a few points which were made by O. Skutsch in 1969.[34] Answering the suggestion that there is a picture of continuous degeneration following the tale of Pasiphaë, he says: 'There is nothing particularly sinister about Atalanta picking up the golden apples and losing the race, or sinful about the Heliads weeping over the death of their brother and being turned into alder trees' (164). Otis sees a chronological sequence of events moving away from the golden age. To this Skutsch answers: 'If anyone sets out to make a chronological sequence, he should not put the *Saturnia regna* after the flood, and he should certainly not put the *Saturnia regna* after Pyrrha and before her uncle and father-in-law Prometheus' (164). Again, 'the supposed movement away from the *Saturnia regna* arrests itself far back in the mythological age of Greece, and the only mention of modern times, which ought to be even more corrupt, shows Gallus in happy communion with the entourage of Apollo' (165). These are serious objections to Otis' views of 6, and to them must be added another, general, consideration, also noted by Skutsch: 'If I were a poet and wanted to represent five positive aspects of one thing or another and five negative aspects, would I really put all the negative aspects in the second half of my book and let the reader sink into gloom and despair? The answer is obviously No' (161).

Skutsch's own view is based on Maury's sets of pairs, but it denies, as we have just seen, any of the extra dimensions envisaged by Maury and Otis. For Skutsch, the main factor which relates 1 to 9, 2 to 8 etc. is numerical – an idea also advanced by Maury. If we think only of the totals yielded by each pair we get the following scheme:

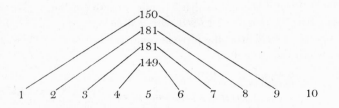

34 O. Skutsch, *HSCP* 73 (1969) 153–69.

Some readers may well feel that this diagram puts the whole matter beyond doubt. As it happens, I am not myself wholly convinced, but I admit that Skutsch has argued the case with great skill and also that one cannot simply turn one's back on the figures, saying 'I don't like that sort of thing.' To introduce a reasonable element of doubt we should have to establish at least one of the following points: (a) that the totals were due to chance, (b) that the numerical scheme was in some way unsatisfactory, or (c) that the same figures could be used to support another theory.

(a) The first approach was taken by Marouzeau.[35] On examining the Fables of La Fontaine he found that the first ten came very close in length to the last, and that with 'a little adjustment' the totals were exactly equal. In between came two fables, each of twenty-eight verses. Moving on to Gautier, *Émaux et camées*, Marouzeau found that numbers 9 and 13 dealt with similar themes (*thèmes de galanterie*) and contained 18 quatrains each; numbers 10 and 12 (*inspiration marine*) had each 8 quatrains; and the centre piece, number 11, consisted of 10 quatrains. The five poems therefore presented a completely symmetrical pattern, but Marouzeau and the colleagues whom he consulted were convinced that these effects were entirely fortuitous.

In the nature of things the type of argument used by Marouzeau cannot be conclusive. It can, however, engender doubt. Skutsch would reply that in the *Eclogues* chance can be ruled out, because the numerical pattern 'accompanies and confirms the pattern observed in the content' (159). This would be entirely convincing if the content-pattern were itself complete. But, as we have seen, it isn't. Whatever way we look at the problem, chance does seem to have played *some* part in the overall design. If one accepts the Maury–Skutsch numerical scheme as basic and intentional, then a feature like the alternation of *non propria persona/propria persona* must surely be fortuitous.

(b) First, a textual point in *Ecl.* 8. In the interests of exact symmetry within the poem Skutsch cuts out v. 76. He may, of course, be right, though he admits elsewhere that one can't be sure of exact symmetry. The more usual procedure, however, has been to insert another line of the refrain after v. 28, as in the latest Oxford text. If this is done, *Ecl.* 8 has 110 lines, and at once the correspondence 181 : 181 disappears. Secondly, if we keep Skutsch's totals, 149 and 181 might seem rather unlikely numbers for Virgil to choose: 150 and 180 would, one imagines, have been more obvious. Skutsch's answer here is that the

[35] J. Marouzeau, *REL* 23 (1945) 74–6.

total 149 could not have been changed without wrecking the internal symmetry of 4 and 6. This is a very strong argument in the case of 4, which is constructed on the basis of the number seven $(3 + 7 + 7 + 28 + 7 + 7 + 4)$; it is not quite so strong in the case of 6, in which the structure is less intricate and regular. The natural divisions would seem to be 12, 18, 10, 20, 13 $(3 + 8 + 2)$, 13 $(8 + 5)$, giving an over-all scheme of 30, 30, 26. In any case the conclusion would be that Virgil attached less importance to the symmetry of the book than to the symmetry of individual pieces. As for the total of 181, Skutsch believes that this was produced in the first place by grouping 3 with 7, and that later Virgil added eleven lines to 2 in order to obtain a similar total for 2 and 8.[36] Without those eleven lines 2 would have remained perfectly symmetrical $(5 + 13 + 9 + 8 + 9 + 13 + 5)$. So in this case Virgil *was* prepared to sacrifice the regularity of a single poem to the general design of the book. However, the question why Virgil should have accepted the totals of 149 and 181 cannot finally be answered. Skutsch is justified in maintaining simply that Virgil did accept them. But we are also justified in thinking them a little odd. Thirdly, there is the problem of *Ecl.* 10. The structure is not regular, the most likely divisions being 8, 22, 19, 20, 8. As it was apparently the last to be composed one would surely have expected the poet, if he was so concerned with general symmetry, to write a piece which, when added to *Ecl.* 5, would produce a total of 149 or 181, or an intermediate figure of 165. Now this last figure was well within his grasp. He could have reached it (and at the same time achieved internal symmetry) by making *Ecl.* 10 two verses shorter. But he never did.

More generally, although in the Maury–Skutsch plan there may be one exact correspondence and one near miss in the five totals, the length of the individual eclogues is very irregular. This fact is obscured by Skutsch's neat diagram, but it becomes plainer if we fill in the following numbers under each poem: 83, 73, 111, 63, 90, 86, 70, 108, 69, 77. It is plainer still if we draw the ten eclogues as a row of vertical lines on squared paper; no. 1 reaches just above the eighth square, no. 2 just above the seventh, and so on. When we look at that row of lines and read the totals underneath, it is hard to concede that the Maury–Skutsch plan for the book is really analogous to the clear, simple plans discernible within separate poems. All one can say, I think, is that if Maury and Skutsch are right, the plan is so obscure that it can hardly be thought to have had any aesthetic function for the reader.

(*c*) Consider now another possibility, which I have not seen developed

36 O. Skutsch, *HSCP* 74 (1970) 95–9.

though no doubt it has occurred to many readers: Virgil decided to arrange his book in two halves, without aiming at mathematical symmetry. He saw that two eclogues contained over a hundred lines; so they would naturally occupy the central position in each half. On either side he would put the two small pairs (i.e. the sixty-line and seventy-line pairs) and on the outside the two intermediate pairs. That was the *basic* plan, but which member of a pair should go in which half? Of the two eighty-line pieces the one referring to Octavian would naturally come first, whether or not it was written earlier. In the case of the next two pairs there was no problem, because chronology and subject-matter gave the same answer: 2 should come before 7 and 3 before 8. (By referring to subject-matter I mean that in the book as a whole 3 would not be allowed to follow 7, because of the similarity in subject-matter; and 8 would not have been placed next to 2.) The same consideration (i.e. *uariatio* based on subject-matter) decided the position of the two sixty-line pieces: the eclogue with the section on land-confiscation would go in the second half. With the final pair there was again no problem: the piece beginning *extremum hunc, Arethusa* would obviously come last. The resulting scheme looked like this:

(1)	83	86	(6)
(2)	73	70	(7)
(3)	111	108	(8)
(4)	63	67	(9)
(5)	90	77	(10)

If that, or something like it, was what Virgil planned, certain other effects must be due to chance, e.g. that Corydon sings in 2 and 7, that Pollio (if it *is* Pollio) is honoured in 3 and 8, that the sum of $1 + 2$ (156) = the sum of $6 + 7$ (156) and $1 + 3$ (194) = $6 + 8$ (194), and that various other totals are extremely close. If the reader does not wish to believe that the connection of 5 and 10 with Theocritus' first idyll is due to chance, it is easy to imagine that 10 was written with that connection in mind. Finally, if the general plan was already formed when 10 was being composed, why didn't Virgil make the poem twelve lines longer and so produce two halves of 420 verses? Because, as we assumed at the outset, he was not interested in exact mathematical correspondences.

The object of this paper has been to present and assess the main theories regarding the architecture of the *Eclogues*. If pressed for my own opinion I would say that, while some of the cruder proposals mentioned at the beginning were clearly wrong, a few of the others were in some degree plausible. I have in mind:

(a) The theory that eclogues from which Virgil is absent alternate with those in which the poet speaks *in propria persona*. More detailed positions could be explained by using *uariatio* as a subsidiary principle.

(b) The theory that we have a series of pairs bracketing *Ecl.* 5, which in its turn is balanced by *Ecl.* 10, and that this pattern is supported by arithmetical correspondences. (Maury's theory, reduced and refined by Skutsch.)

(c) The theory that the Eclogues fall into two halves containing corresponding pairs based on length. Here again, *uariatio* is used as a subsidiary principle.

As far as I can see, each system has at least one defect, and none is so superior to the others as to be obviously Virgil's own. If this conclusion is correct, it would follow that the final pattern of the book was not, after all, a matter of primary importance to the poet; otherwise he would surely have taken more trouble to make it clear.

The theories discussed above were put forward to answer the question 'Why did Virgil place the eclogues in their present order?' All the proposals, whether based on subject-matter, form, or length, treated the poems as separate wholes. Naturally this in no way precludes a different approach, whereby one examines various themes, concepts, or images, which recur throughout the book – e.g. the *locus amoenus*, the pathetic fallacy, the presentation of gifts, and (most general of all) pastoral song.[37] The latter type of enquiry, however, is not really 'architectural' since it is not designed to account for the shape of the book. If used for that purpose it tends to cause confusion.

To provide a further illustration of the distinction I have in mind, let us take the first book of Horace's *Satires*, which was being written at much the same time as the *Eclogues*, and, like them, consists of ten poems. Now everyone agrees that the first three pieces go together; they are all homilies or 'diatribes' on moral themes. Equally clearly, 4 is connected with 10; they, and only they, are about satire as a literary genre. We therefore have these groupings:

1   2   3   4   5   6   7   8   9   10

The reason why this scheme is generally acceptable is that the common factors connecting the pieces are large, bold, and simple. The same is

37 See C. Becker, *Hermes* 83 (1955) 314–49.

true of the scheme which Boll discerned in the arrangement of the second book of *Satires*,[38] viz:

1	consultations	5
2	rural simplicity	6
3	Stoic sermons	7
4	follies of gastronomy	8.

Boll's scheme, however, is complete, unlike our scheme for Book 1, to which we must now return. What other connections can be established? There is a certain amount to be said for bracketing 5 (the journey to Brundisium) with 9 (the encounter with the pest). Both are light-hearted, non-didactic pieces, set in the same milieu, i.e. the circle of Varius, Viscus, Virgil, and Maecenas. And in each case the poet is both narrator and actor. It is also not unreasonable to link 7 with 8. Both are fairly short and amusing anecdotes building up to a single climax, and in the treatment there is a similar tension between style and content. The poet plays no part in either story.

In joining 7 to 8 and 5 to 9 I am not denying that there are points of comparison with other pieces. I would only say that these are the main connections, and even these are less prominent than those which link 1 with 2 and 3, and 4 with 10. The scheme would now look like this:

```
1     2    3      4    5    6    7    8    9    10
└──┴──┘        └────┴─────────────────┘
```

But what about 6? This poem is best described as an autobiographical homily, which means that, taken as a whole, it does not quite belong either to the homilies or to the autobiographical pieces. Of the homilies it stands closest to number 1. As the first poem is on the penalties of acquisitiveness and the sixth is on the penalties of ambition, both have a good deal to say about contentment. And both poems begin with an address to Maecenas. Of the autobiographical satires, the nearest relative to 6 is 4. In 4 Horace bases his views of satire on his own personal experience; in 6 he bases his views of ambition on his own personal experience. Each poem contains an important passage on the training he received from his father. In view of all this, some readers may wish to draw in dotted lines connecting 6 with both 1 and 4. Yet that still does not produce what we have agreed to call an architectural pattern. The problem would be somewhat easier if 6 came after 3, and much easier if 6 stood between 7 and 8. But, as it is, there is no complete pattern and we must assume that Horace did not intend to supply one.

The other type of enquiry has been conducted in recent years by

[38] F. Boll, *Hermes* 48 (1913) 143–5.

several well-known scholars. Van Rooy, while expressing agreement with all the traditional schemes, has elaborated certain connections between 1 and 2, 3 and 4, 5 and 6, 7 and 8.[39] He assures us (and who will doubt him?) that other connections exist between 2 and 3, 4 and 5, etc. In addition, he points out similarities between 4, 7, and 10, and he refers with approval to an article by Buchheit which associates 7 with 9.[40] Anderson adds his contribution by joining 8 to 7 and 9.[41] And Ludwig extends the method so as to establish links between Books 1 and 2.[42] Now, as one would expect, there is a good deal in all these articles that is sound and convincing. But what they are doing, I would submit, is examining the *texture*, not the architecture, of the book. For if every piece is in some way related to every other, we are still left with the problem why they have been placed in one particular order.

It is natural that the more often one reads the *Satires* the more aware one becomes of recurrent words, topics, and opinions. But some care and discrimination are needed in deciding what to make of any given case. First, is the connection really there, or has it been excogitated by one's own or someone else's ingenuity? If it is there, how significant is it, and what in fact does it signify? Last of all, and most important for our purpose, do such reminiscences indicate that the book was conceived and written as a complex whole, with every echo planned, or do they simply reflect the preoccupations of a single mind at a certain period of its activity? In my view the second explanation is by far the more probable.

To sum up. An architectural theory should, ideally, be concerned with poems as wholes. It should present a plan which will explain why the poems are in this and not another order. Such a plan will, one assumes, be part of the poet's intention. And the features of the plan will be large, bold, and simple, so that if they are not immediately noticed by the reader they are nevertheless immediately discernible when pointed out. As a general rule, the more subtle an architectural theory is, and the more it tries to explain, the less persuasive it becomes.

[39] C. A. Van Rooy, *Acta Classica* 11 (1968) 38–72. Cf. *Acta Classica* 13 (1970) 7–25, 45–59; 14 (1971) 67–90.
[40] V. Buchheit, *Gymnasium* 75 (1968) 519–55.
[41] W. S. Anderson, *AJP* 93 (1972) 4–13.
[42] W. Ludwig, *Poetica* 2 (1968) 304–25.

6
THEORY
Sincerity and mask

A few years ago the distinguished American critic Lionel Trilling published a series of lectures entitled *Sincerity and Authenticity*.[1] At the beginning he called attention to two responses which we are aware of when reading an ancient work of literature: 'How like us those people were! How little human nature has changed!' and at the same time 'How different in their way of life, their thoughts, and their moral assumptions!' So far so good. But after that Trilling went on to concentrate exclusively on the second response, proposing the idea that 'at a certain point in its history the moral life of Europe added to itself a new element, the state or quality of self which we call sincerity' (2). It then emerges that the crucial point in history was the late sixteenth and early seventeenth century and that the country where this momentous change took place was England.

Now when confronted with such a large and surprising statement we naturally assume that the writer is using his key terms in a deliberately strange or provocative way, and so we read on with our critical antennae on the alert. Trilling tells us that 'sincerity' as he understands it is restricted to certain phases of culture.

> 'For example, we cannot say of the patriarch Abraham that he was a sincere man. That statement must seem only comical. The sincerity of Achilles or Beowulf cannot be discussed: they neither have nor lack sincerity. But if we ask whether young Werther is really as sincere as he intends to be, or which of the two Dashwood sisters, Elinor or Marianne, is thought by Jane Austen to be the more truly sincere, we can confidently expect a serious response...'

I am still not quite sure what Trilling means. In the twenty-second

[1] L. Trilling, *Sincerity and Authenticity* (Oxford 1972).

chapter of Genesis we are told that God tested Abraham by commanding him to sacrifice his son. When Abraham made as if to obey, the angel of the Lord restrained him, saying: 'Now I know thou fearest God.' Why is it comical to suppose that Jehovah was testing Abraham's sincerity? Again, if it is true that the sincerity of Achilles cannot be discussed, does the same apply to Odysseus? And surely, whatever opinions may be held about fictional heroes, it makes perfectly good sense to ask whether Alcibiades or Cicero or Seneca was a sincere man.

If we confine ourselves to the basic meaning of 'sincere' – i.e. 'not dissembling one's real view, feeling, or attitude' – then it need hardly be said that sincerity and its opposite were thoroughly familiar to the ancients. According to Cicero the first requirement of friendship is that there should be no feigning or insincerity – *ne quid fictum sit neue simulatum*[2] – and the same thought lies at the bottom of Plutarch's essay on how to distinguish a flatterer from a friend. In Terence's *Eunuchus* (175) Phaedria says to Thais *utinam istuc uerbum ex animo ac uere diceres* ('I only wish you spoke that phrase sincerely and from the heart') – an idea echoed later by Catullus in no. 109:

> di magni, facite ut uere promittere possit,
> atque id sincere dicat et ex animo

> *Ye gods, grant that she may be able to make that promise truly, and to say it sincerely and from the heart.*

So there we have three Latin equivalents for sincerely.

Sometimes connected with sincerity was the rather vague idea that a man's speech reflects his character. I say 'rather vague', because formulations of the idea which look similar turn out to mean different things. We may start with a passage of Seneca in which the ideas of sincerity and appropriateness come together. He is telling his friend Lucilius that a personal letter should be easy and informal like conversation, not self-consciously 'stylish'. Sincerity, he says, is the main thing: *quod sentimus loquamur, quod loquimur sentiamus; concordet sermo cum uita* (*Epist.* 75.1–4) – 'Let us say what we think and think what we say. Our words should be in harmony with our lives.' A different idea is found in a fragment of Menander (66, Körte), which says ἀνδρὸς χαρακτὴρ ἐκ λόγου γνωρίζεται 'a man's character is revealed by his speech'. This assertion has little to do with sincerity, for it appears to mean that a good man reveals his goodness and a bad man his badness.

---

2 Cicero, *De Amicitia* 65. Cf. Ennius, *Trag.* W.7–9 (based on *Iliad* 9.313); Horace, *Sat* 1.3.62; Seneca, *Epist.* 24.19 (*turpe est aliud loqui aliud sentire*).

A line of Terence's is less sweeping: *quale ingenium haberes fuit indicio oratio* (*Heaut.* 384) – 'What you said was an indication of your character.' As far as one can judge (because the words are not reported in the play) it is the content of the girl's remarks that is being referred to rather than her manner. In his *Brutus* (117) Cicero mentions a rugged character called Q. Aelius Tubero, whose life was austere and in harmony with his philosophy; *sed ut uita sic oratione durus incultus horridus* – 'but in his speech, as in his life, he was harsh, untrained and rough'. That is a matter of style rather than content. Tubero's sincerity is not mentioned, though it seems to be implied. In Juvenal 4.82 we hear of Vibius Crispus, a member of Domitian's court – a nice old man whose eloquence was gentle, like his character (*cuius erant mores qualis facundia*). But could such a man be called sincere? Juvenal clearly thought not, though he didn't blame him: 'He never struck out against the current; he wasn't one of those citizens who could speak frankly what was in his mind and risk his life for truth.' A different notion again is found in Seneca's fortieth epistle, where he says that a philosopher should talk as he lives – calmly: *pronuntiatio quoque, sicut uita, debet esse composita*. That is a matter of delivery (2). Later the area of reference is widened: 'What are we to think of the mind of a man whose speech is whipped up and allowed to run away and can't be reined in?' A disorderly way of speaking shows a disorderly mind (6–7). Quintilian says the same about orators, exploring the moral implications a little further: when you see certain men ranting and wrangling in court you infer from their mental attitude (*mentis habitu*) that they are as reckless in taking on cases as they are in pleading them. *Profert enim mores plerumque oratio et animi secreta detegit. nec sine causa Graeci prodiderunt, ut uiuat, quemque etiam dicere* (xi.1.29–30) – 'A man's way of speaking generally reveals his character and his inner mentality. There are good grounds for the Greek proverb that speech and life go together.' This clearly anticipates Buffon's dictum: *le style est l'homme même*.[3]

A long, but not very penetrating, discussion of the idea is found in Seneca, *Epist.* 114, which asks why certain periods have seen the emergence of a degenerate style. The answer proposed is that such a style is a symptom of moral corruption: *talis hominibus fuit oratio qualis uita* (1). Maecenas is chosen as an illustration: his walk, his effeminacy, his exhibitionism, and his decadent poetic style all come from the same defect of character. As if this weren't enough, Seneca goes on to say that his poetic diction was as sure a sign of depravity as his loose

---

[3] Buffon, *Oeuvres philosophiques*. ed. J. Piveteau (Paris 1954) 503. It is perhaps worth observing that this is the correct form of the dictum.

clothes, his entourage, his house, and his domineering wife! Leaving aside the unfairness and crudity of Seneca's attack, one can't help noticing that if the principle were so universally valid the problem of sincerity would be conveniently removed. For deception would be impossible. We shall refer to the matter again later on. For the moment it may be useful to point to an antidote (though not perhaps of the most salubrious kind). In his second satire Juvenal complains about men who outwardly follow the Stoic way of life – collecting busts of Chrysippus, cutting their hair short, wearing a stern expression, and condemning vice – while all the time lending themselves to sexual perversion.[4]

So far we have been talking about sincerity in the fundamental sense of frankness or candour. But the word is also used by Trilling and other modern critics in a number of extended meanings. One of the commonest of these stands opposed to artifice and is therefore akin to plainness and simplicity. The relationship can be seen by putting Matthew Arnold's view of Homer as 'eminently plain and direct' beside the judgement of Leigh Hunt, who admired 'the passionate sincerity...of the greatest early poets such as Homer and Chaucer'. In a similar vein John Churton Collins compared Catullus to Burns, claiming that 'both were distinguished by sincerity and simplicity'.[5] It is easy to see how stylistic adornment, whether grandiose or sentimental or merely vain, may convey an impression of falseness; and if the critic is primarily interested in states of mind he may account for this falseness by alleging that the writer was in some way insincere.

Now a distrust of artifice was a recurrent feature of ancient literary criticism.[6] All the major philosophies held that an elaborate manner was unsuitable for imparting information. The rhetorical theorists emphasized that for argument and demonstration one ought to cultivate the plain style. And satirists were suspicious of epic and tragedy because an elevated diction seemed out of touch with reality. Even critics who admired the grand style, like Cicero, Longinus, and Quintilian, were well aware of its pitfalls. The speaker might assume a pompous manner, contriving long periods with involved antitheses and striking

---

4 Cf. Democritus 53a; Persius, *Sat.* 1.9–11; Quintilian I pref. 15.
5 Leigh Hunt, *Imagination and Fancy*, fourth ed. (London 1871) 5. The whole passage connects sincerity with simplicity. J. C. Collins, *Ephemera Critica* (London 1901) 347. It is interesting to note that in Arnold's view Chaucer failed to achieve 'high and excellent seriousness' (*Essays in Criticism*, second series (London 1898) 33); Burns also failed (*ibid.* 45, 48–9).
6 See J. F. D'Alton, *Roman Literary Theory and Criticism* (repr. New York 1962) 130–3, 391–4, 536–7.

figures, when the occasion called for something simple. And even on great occasions a man of mediocre talent could not be sure of success; he might aim at grandeur and merely become swollen: *professus grandia turget* (Horace, *AP* 27). But when the ancients detected falseness they usually interpreted it as a failure of taste or a breach of decorum, not as a sign of insincerity. And perhaps they were wise. For it may be very difficult to relate defects of style to defects in the speaker's attitude – especially in tragedy, where the writer is not speaking *in propria persona*. The plain style may also pose problems, for the apparent simplicity may be the result of intense effort and careful revision. A successful poet, says Horace (*Epist.* II.2.124), will give the impression of playing and will suffer agony in the process: *ludentis speciem dabit et torquebitur*. An inferior poet may, of course, give the impression of being in pain, and that is why some people have advocated composing quickly so as to preserve the directness and spontaneity of the original impulse. The danger here is that unless the writer has thought hard beforehand a rapid method of composition may only obscure what he wants to say. Sincerity, like truth, may require a degree of artifice.

The term 'sincerity' has also been used as the opposite of imitation. In his *Principles of Success in Literature* G. H. Lewes states that 'whatever is sincerely felt or believed...will always maintain an infinite superiority over imitative splendour'. Later he adds 'If the purpose of literature be the sincere expression of the individual's own ideas and feelings, it is obvious that the cant about "the best models" tends to pervert and obstruct that expression.'[7] The more normal and logical contrast is between *originality* and imitation, but one can see how a novel treatment or tone or style may come to be regarded as the writer's own, in contrast to what he has taken over from somebody else. The point is clearer in the case of artifacts. This vase or painting is original and authentic, that is an imitation – perhaps even a fake.

In the nineteenth century, when this way of thinking was common, most Latin poetry was condemned as derivative and second rate. Even satire, the one native genre, did not escape. In fact Juvenal was particularly unfortunate. Since he was found to have drawn many of his observations from the commonplaces of the rhetorical schools, his poetry was clearly not original. But if it wasn't original, it must have been a work of imitation, which meant that it could not be wholly genuine and sincere. And if Juvenal was not sincere in his condemnation of vice he must therefore have been morally disreputable. Today

---

[7] G. H. Lewes, *Principles of Success in Literature*, ed. by T. S. Knowlson (London n.d.) 103 and 114.

this sounds merely amusing, but the line of reasoning (if that is the right word) has been documented by David Wiesen,[8] and there is still a trace of it in Marmorale's book, which first appeared in 1938.[9]

Since we can still draw on the legacy of Pound and Eliot, there is no need to illustrate or defend the creative employment of a literary tradition, but a few observations may be in order on the hazards of using 'sincere' as the opposite of 'imitative'. First, church-going people should be wary of the antithesis, for if it is imitation to make use of a common fund of ideas then no Christian preacher can ever be sincere. Nor is the materialist in any position to be complacent, for on this criterion Lucretius turns out to be the most insincere of Latin poets, since his whole philosophy is taken from Epicurus. Again, Greek authors also went in for imitation. As Longinus says: 'Was Herodotus the only "most Homeric" writer? Surely Stesichorus and Archilochus earned the name before him. So, more than any, did Plato, who diverted to himself countless rills from the Homeric spring.'[10] Therefore the Greeks too must have been guilty of insincerity.

There are many degrees of imitation. Talking of his *Epodes*, Horace conceded that he had taken over the metre and vehemence of Archilochus, but not his words or his subjects (*Epist.* 1.19.24–5). If he *had* taken over his words and subjects, he would, I suppose, have produced a translation. That is the closest type of imitation and therefore presumably the least sincere. But is Catullus' version of Sappho (*ille mi par esse deo uidetur*) a palpably insincere poem? And if we class that as an exception are we to rule out the possibility that a translator may feel genuinely at one with his author?

> United by this sympathetic bond,
> You grow familiar, intimate and fond;
> Your thoughts, your words, your styles, your souls agree,
> No longer his interpreter, but he.

So Roscommon.[11] Leaving translations aside, one thinks of Terence's adaptations of New Comedy, Virgil's allusions to Homer and Ennius, Ovid's use of Nicander, and Petronius' parody of the Greek romances – the list could easily be extended. Each procedure is different. To lump them all together and label them 'insincere' would be a total absurdity. Finally, although they acknowledged that various types of imitation

---

8 D. Wiesen, *Latomus* 22 (1963) 440–71.
9 E. V. Marmorale, *Giovenale* (1938, second ed. 1950).
10 Longinus 14.3–4, trans. D. A. Russell (Oxford 1965).
11 Roscommon, *Essay on Translated Verse* (1684), ed. J. Spingarn, *Critical Essays of the Seventeenth Century* (1908) vol. 2. 300.

were legitimate and necessary, Roman poets from Ennius on often laid claim to originality. Lucretius could talk of making his way to fresh springs of poetry – *integros accedere fontis* (*DRN* 1.927) – because no one had yet presented Epicurus' philosophy in verse, Virgil sang the song of Ascra (i.e. the didactic poetry of Hesiod) through Roman towns (*Georg.* 2.176), and Horace boasted of being the first to adapt Aeolian verse to the tunes of Italy – *princeps Aeolium carmen ad Italos | deduxisse modos* (*Odes* iii.30.13–14). Within his chosen genre the poet had to make a fresh contribution. Thus Virgil did not merely write Theocritean idylls in Latin; he developed pastoral in a number of highly significant ways. The same principle of *aemulatio* lay behind Ovid's changes in love elegy, and led, in a more restricted way, to Persius' transformations of Horace. Feeble copying was recognized for what it was, and there were several protests against the use of trite and boring mythological themes, of which the most famous comes at the beginning of Juvenal's first satire:

> 'No one knows his own house better than I know the grove of Mars and the cave of Vulcan near Aeolus' crags. What the winds are up to, what shades are being tortured by Aeacus, from what land someone else is conveying the golden prize of a stolen bit of sheepskin, what monstrous ash-trees are being hurled by Monychus – this information is shouted by Fronto's plane-trees, his shuddering marble statues, and his pillars cracked by countless readers.'

But although many unkind things were said about second-rate imitators (*seruum pecus*), such men were not called insincere. And so a good deal of confusion was avoided.

Sincerity has also been combined in modern times with seriousness and earnestness to form a contrast to what is frivolous and shallow. The best known example is probably Matthew Arnold's phrase 'the high seriousness which comes from absolute sincerity'.[12] Speaking of the *Vates*, whether priest or prophet, Carlyle called him 'a man...in earnest with the Universe, though all others were but toying with it'. Such a man, says Carlyle, 'is a *Vates*, first of all, in virtue of being sincere'.[13] Another example is Quiller-Couch's remark on the third canto of Byron's *Childe Harold*: 'Who can fail to perceive the sudden deepening

[12] M. Arnold, *Essays on Criticism*, second series (London 1898) 48.
[13] T. Carlyle, *On Heroes and Hero-worship*, lecture 3 'The hero as poet' p. 100. Cf. his remark on Rousseau:"with all his drawbacks...he has the first and chief characteristic of a Hero: he is heartily in earnest' (227).

of the voice to sincerity...? Who can fail to feel that out of mere Vanity Fair we have passed at one stride into a region of moral earnestness, into acquaintance with a grand manner, into a presence?'[14]

I doubt if anyone has ever found Roman literature deficient in seriousness. Readers are more likely to have groaned beneath its *grauitas*. But here we ought perhaps to distinguish between two propositions: 'seriousness is a *sign* of sincerity' and 'seriousness *constitutes* sincerity'. In the first case, if by seriousness we mean a serious manner, the Romans would have admitted that the proposition was often, but not always, true. Various poets assert that they are speaking in earnest, that what they say comes from sincere feeling. Thus Ennius proclaims that his cup of burning verses is 'drawn from the marrow of his bones' (*medullitus*),[15] Lucilius writes 'from the bottom of his heart' (*ex praecordiis*),[16] and Persius affirms his devotion to his teacher Cornutus in terms of quite embarrassing earnestness.[17] Yet, as far as I can see, the Romans did not *equate* seriousness with sincerity. One reason for saying this is that sincerity was not used as the opposite of frivolity. And this was very prudent; for the essence of insincerity is the wish to mislead (whether oneself or others), and therefore frivolous poetry which does *not* aim to mislead ought not to be called insincere. In the seventh poem of his *Amores*, Book II Ovid complains to his mistress in an injured tone that she has accused him of seducing her maid, Cypassis. What a monstrous idea! How could any gentleman sleep with a slave? And anyhow, common prudence would rule out an intrigue with his own girl's hairdresser. The very next poem is addressed to Cypassis herself, and it opens with the question 'Who gave us away?' It is sad to see distinguished scholars taking this witty charade as evidence of Ovid's duplicity. To give another illustration: the term *dissimulatio* was regularly applied to criminal fraud (e.g. Cicero, *De Off.* 3.61 and 64), but the same word was used without disapproval to denote irony: 'It is witty *dissimulatio*', says Cicero, 'when in your whole style of speaking you keep up a solemn joke, your words at odds with your meaning' (*De Orat.* 2.269). In the latter case there was no intent to deceive, and so the speaker, however flippant, could not be called insincere.

In his *Lectures on Poetry*, which were delivered in Latin between 1832 and 1841 and later published in English, John Keble maintained that the prerequisite of what he called 'primary poetry' was to be true to

---

[14] Quiller-Couch, *Studies in Literature* (Cambridge 1922) 14. Thackeray thought otherwise: 'That man *never* wrote from his heart', *Notes of a journey from Cornhill to Grand Cairo*, chap. 5.

[15] Ennius, *Saturae* W.6–7.   [16] Lucilius, W.670–1.

[17] Persius, *Sat.* 5.21–9.

oneself. This basic honesty, he said, underlay all genuine and keenly felt emotion and also 'transparently sincere poetry'.[18] Trilling, too, takes the famous injunction 'to thine own self be true' as the starting point of his investigation, observing that the self became important in an epoch which saw a sudden efflorescence of the theatre, and that the problems of authenticity were explored most memorably by dramatic characters like Hamlet and Iago. Historically, the late sixteenth and early seventeenth centuries dissolved feudalism and reduced ecclesiastical authority, while increasing urbanization and encouraging social mobility. Calvinists advocated plain speaking and called on men to scrutinize their inner life – a habit which found expression in numerous diaries and spiritual journals. Better housing brought more privacy; Venetian glass mirrors (manufactured in England from the early seventeenth century) reflected a clearer image, and men began to paint self-portraits and write autobiographies.

All this, I take it, is acceptable to historians of the period. What I should like to question, however, is the proposal that such developments amounted to 'something like a mutation in human nature' (19) and that in the sixteenth or seventeenth century 'men became individuals' (24). In our enquiry we shall try to keep in mind the main features I mentioned a moment ago. Not all of them have Roman parallels – e.g. the decay of the church's authority – but several do: in particular, urbanization, social mobility, privacy, and introspection. The discussion will make little reference to Greece, partly for reasons of space, but mainly because these essays are about Latin literature. Even within this field I have made no systematic study. The illustrations are drawn from well known passages which one is likely to come across in general reading.

First, a preliminary point. 'The development of the individual' when used in a historical context, is a phrase that calls to mind a section of Burckhardt's famous work *The Civilization of the Renaissance in Italy* – a section which is referred to by Trilling. But apart from the fact that Burckhardt dated the development to fourteenth- and fifteenth-century Italy, it is not at all clear that he wished to deny the existence of individuals in classical antiquity. Granted, he says that before the renaissance 'man was conscious of himself only as a member of a race, people, party, family, or corporation – only through some general category'. But in that whole passage he is talking of the middle ages.

---

[18] J. Keble, *Lectures on Poetry*, Eng. trans. (Oxford 1912) vol. 1.69. Cf. Carlyle's remarks on Burns: 'The chief quality of Burns is the *sincerity* of him. So in his Poetry, so in his Life', *On Heroes and Hero-worship*, lecture 5 'The hero as man of letters' p. 236.

'*In the middle ages* [my italics] both sides of human consciousness...
lay as though dreaming or half awake beneath a common veil...man
was conscious of himself only as a member of a race etc. It was in Italy
that this veil dissolved first...Man became a spiritual individual, and
recognized himself as such.'[19]

Taking up some of Trilling's smaller points, one may start from the
fact that Latin literature, in much the same sense as English literature
of the eighteenth century, was the product of an urban society. By the
time of Augustus Rome had a population of about a million, as London
had just before 1800. The writers who have survived were members of
either the senatorial or the equestrian class, or else were connected
with those classes through the ties of patronage. Such men were used to
working in a considerable degree of privacy and comfort. They also
knew what they looked like. Lucretius has a long passage on reflections, in which he describes how by multiple mirrors unseen parts of a
house can be brought, as it were, into the room. He also notes how a
horizontally concave mirror returns the correct image to the observer –
i.e. if you are holding a book in your left hand, the reflected figure will
also have a book in *his* left hand.[20] Seneca speaks of full-length mirrors
(*specula totis paria corporibus*).[21] And Suetonius' biography of Horace
reports that the poet's bedroom was fitted with mirrors to provide reflections of the various goings on.[22] That passage may not tell us anything about Horace, for Suetonius indicates that the story was just a
rumour. But it does tell us something about mirrors. This and other
evidence makes it doubtful whether the glass products of seventeenth-
century England had quite such a revolutionary effect on the human
mind as Trilling supposes.

We come now to the idea that a man only existed as part of a group.
When the educated layman hears the phrase 'ancient Rome', he sees a
picture of stern-faced men leading armies or addressing assemblies,
constructing bridges and harbours, or making money from trade and
commerce. It is easy to forget that one of the major philosophies regarded all such activity as misguided.[23] The quietism of Epicurus, as

---

19 J. Burckhardt, *The Civilization of the Renaissance in Italy*, trans.
   Middlemore (Mentor Paperback 1970) 121. Burckhardt's thesis is not
   fully accepted by medievalists. See C. Morris, *The Discovery of the
   Individual 1050–1200* (London 1972), chapters 1 and 4.
20 Lucretius *DRN* 4.269–323; see Bailey's notes.
21 Seneca, *Nat. Quaest.* I.17.8. Magnifying mirrors are mentioned in
   1.16.2.
22 Suetonius vol. 2 (Loeb) 488.
23 Epicurus, *Principal Doctrines* 14, Frag. A 58 and 81, *Life* 119 (Bailey).
   The diffusion of Epicurean teaching in Rome is shown by Cicero, *De Fin.*

opposed to the imperial ideal, was summed up by Lucretius in *DRN*
5.1129–30 (Bailey):

> ut satius multo iam sit parere quietum
> quam regere imperio res uelle et regna tenere.
>
> *And so it is much better to stay quiet and obey than to desire to rule
> men's affairs with authority and to hold power over kingdoms.*

Many citizens shaped their lives by this doctrine, many others held it
as a kind of option which they could take up in times of weariness and
disillusion. A more extreme form of withdrawal was represented by
the Cynics, who renounced not only public life but the social organization as a whole. For good reasons or bad, such men were willing to
endure hardship and beggary rather than submit to the constraints of
civilized life. Coming back within society again, we can easily find other
men, who turned away from public life, not for philosophical or economic reasons, but simply because they found it uncongenial. When Ovid
was about twenty he abandoned the legal career which would have led
to posts in government service, and much to his father's disgust devoted himself to poetry and pleasure. A generation earlier Horace took
a similar decision when offered a job as Augustus' secretary. Before
him Cicero had done much of his writing and thinking in enforced re-
tirement. One cannot believe that the individuality of such men was
absorbed by family, class, state, or anything else. If someone had asked
Cicero 'Are you significantly different from everyone in the land?' he
would probably have answered 'Yes, and considerably superior to
most.'[24]

These are some of the more obvious practical examples. If we want
theoretical evidence for the idea of the individual we may start from
Cicero's *De Officiis* 1.107ff. Nature, he says, has endowed us with two
characters. One we share with other human beings; the other is assigned separately to each individual – *proprie singulis est tributa.* He
goes on to mention differences in physique, appearance, and temperament, and he is clearly not thinking simply of types, because he uses
the names of well-known personalities as illustrations. He concludes by
saying that there are countless other differences of nature and disposition – *innumerabiles aliae dissimilitudines naturae morumque* (109): it is
up to everyone to choose the life and career that suits his own *natura*

2.44, *Tusc.* 4.7, and *De Off.* 1.29. That it was not an anti-aristocratic
school is established by A. Momigliano, *JRS* 31 (1941) 149–57.

[24] Apart from Cicero's *Letters*, there are extensive autobiographical
passages in *Brutus* 301–30; *Pro Sestio* 36–54, and *De Domo* 3–31. All
this illustrates the great man's interest in himself.

(110ff.). From this passage of the *De Officiis* we can move back to Panaetius and on to Seneca, Epictetus, and Marcus Aurelius.[25] Nor was the idea confined to the Stoics. In the fifth century Democritus had recommended the man in quest of cheerfulness (εὐθυμία) not to choose activities beyond his powers and natural capacity.[26] Epicurus apparently said the same sort of thing,[27] and Plutarch develops the idea in his περὶ εὐθυμίας (473A).

Another important channel for the same notion was the tradition of Hippocratic medicine.[28] The treatise *On Ancient Medicine* says the doctor must know how each person will react to various types of food and drink.[29] The names recorded in the *Epidemics* are those of real people, and the writer bases his treatment on 'the common nature of all and the particular nature of each individual' (I.xxiii) – exactly the same division as we found in Cicero. Success in the arts also depended on the correct assessment of one's own abilities. Cicero remarks that 'actors select not the best plays but the ones most suited to themselves... Rupilius, whom I remember, always played in *Antiopa*, Aesopus rarely in *Ajax*'.[30] Early in the *Ars Poetica* Horace urges the budding writer to make sure his shoulders are equal to the weight of his subject (*AP* 38–40). And Ovid, appealing to the old Delphic maxim 'Know yourself', advises the lover to make the most of his strong points: 'If you have a nice skin, recline with your shoulder visible; if you sing artistically, sing; and if you drink artistically, drink' (*AA* 2.504ff.). The same interest in individual peculiarities can be found in educational theory, in the work of the physiognomists, and above all in the development of portraiture, whether in coins, statues, or painting.[31]

25 Seneca, *De Tranquill.* 6.2, 7.2; Epictetus, *Discourses* I.2; M. Aurelius IV.32.
26 Democritus 3. See K. Freeman, *Ancilla to the Pre-Socratic Philosophers* (Oxford 1956) 92.
27 Plutarch, *On Tranquillity of Mind* (περὶ εὐθυμίας) 465 F.
28 See W. A. Heidel, *Hippocratic Medicine, its Spirit and Method* (New York 1941) 63 and 76 and reff. Compare also O. Temkin's translation of Soranus' *Gynecology* (Baltimore 1956) 18–19.
29 *On Ancient Medicine*, trans. by W. H. S. Jones (Loeb) xx, 22–3, cf. 35ff.
30 Cicero, *De Off.* 1.114. Looking back on Catiline's conspiracy Cicero says that the role he played in suppressing it was necessary but distasteful: *illam uero grauitatis seueritatisque personam non appetiui, sed ab re publica mihi impositam sustinui* (*Pro Murena* 3.6); cf. *Pro Sulla* 3.8.
31 For educational theory see Quintilian II.8 and Musonius Rufus chap. 1 (*YCS* 10 (1947)) 1ff.); for the physiognomists see E. C. Evans, *HSCP* 46 (1935) 43–84 and *TAPA* 72 (1941) 96–108; for portraiture see E. Strong, *Roman Sculpture* vol. 2 (London 1911) chap. 15, and the illustrations in G. Hanfmann, *Roman Art* (New York Graphic Society, Connecticut, n.d.); also V. H. Poulsen, *Roman Portraits* (Copenhagen 1962).

Coming now to the matter of social change, one could point out that although Rome is rightly regarded as a stratified society, enormous changes took place between, say, 75 B.C. and A.D. 75. A ceaseless if irregular movement continued from slavery to freedom;[32] the industrious or the lucky made money in trade or property or military service, and moved into the equestrian order. By acquiring useful friends or marrying into the right families or winning the emperor's approval others climbed the *cursus honorum*, and many new men reached the consulship. With all this change going on people had to learn new modes of behaviour. Social success depended at least to some extent on adaptability, and this favoured a flexible rather than a rigid personality. In his seventeenth epistle (23) Horace says of Aristippus that he was suited to every style of life and every level of prestige and prosperity:

Omnis Aristippum decuit color et status et res.

In the following poem Horace gives advice on how a client should behave toward his patron. When all allowance has been made for irony, the basic message of the epistle is clear enough: you won't get far unless you're tactful and obliging. Those who failed to adapt and assimilate were the target of snobbish disapproval, whether on account of their manners, their speech (as with Catullus' Arrius), their clothes, or their personal appearance. Nasidienus in Horace, *Sat.* II.8 is a goodnatured man who has made enough money to risk inviting guests like Maecenas to dinner, but who is so lacking in *savoir faire* and a sense of humour that his party becomes a memorable fiasco. Trimalchio in Petronius' *Satyricon* is a more fully delineated example of the same type. Social advancement was a searching test of character. Cicero, who knew what he was talking about, speaks of those 'who once behaved decently but have been changed by rank, power, or success, and now refuse to have anything to do with their old friends, cultivating new ones instead' (*De Amicitia* 54). That is seen as a change of *mores*, which I suppose we would translate as 'disposition' or 'personality'.

It was recognized that the *mores* of young people were especially apt to change. Talking about characterization in drama Horace says:

aetatis cuiusque notandi sunt tibi mores,
mobilibusque decor naturis dandus et annis   (*AP* 156–7)

The behaviour patterns of each age-group should be indicated; and you should represent appropriately the changes wrought in men's nature by the passage of the years.

[32] For the social relations of freedmen see S. Treggiari, *Roman Freedmen during the Late Republic* (Oxford 1969), chapters 6 and 7.

'The beardless young man', Horace continues, 'can be shaped like wax for the worse. He is given to high thoughts and strong urges, and is quick to abandon his crazes.' Education was important because bad habits might be acquired early. Sometimes parents were at fault; their children would see undesirable things going on at home – things which would become a habit and eventually part of their nature. *Fit ex his consuetudo inde natura*, as Quintilian says.[33] At other times the teacher might corrupt his charge – hence the importance of choosing men of decent character as tutors.[34] Young men in their late teens were particularly impressionable; after putting on the *toga uirilis* they might easily get into bad company and start a life of dissipation.[35] Yet, as Cicero emphasizes in the *Pro Caelio*, most would come through this phase and grow into responsible citizens.[36]

Later, too, moral improvement might be achieved in various ways – in particular by study, contemplation, and friendship. In his sixth epistle to Lucilius Seneca says: 'I am conscious that I am being not only improved but transformed (*transfigurari*).' He then offers to send the books he has been reading, with the edifying passages marked, and he concludes by inviting Lucilius to come and benefit from his company. (He doesn't quite put it like that, but it's clearly what he means.) The opposite process can be inferred from Seneca's comments on the degrading effects of gladiatorial shows (*Epist.* 7): 'When I go', he says, 'I never bring back the same *mores* as I had before.' He then proceeds to give a vivid account of the shows, dwelling on their brutalizing influence. In this passage, incidentally, *animus*, *ingenium*, and *mores* are used without any important distinctions. There were other factors, too, which might bring about a change of character. Misfortune and the burden of age are mentioned by Laelius in Cicero's *De Amicitia* (33); we have already spoken of the effects of power and success.

These are gradual processes, whether for good or ill. But occasionally the change might be sudden and dramatic. One thinks of young Polemo, who on his way home from a bibulous party happened to hear a lecture on temperance by Xenocrates and at once became devoted to sobriety and virtue (D.L. 4.16). Metrocles was on the point of suicide when he was saved by Crates and became a new man (D.L. 6.94). A comic treatment of the same phenomenon is given in a satire of Horace

---

33 Quintilian i.2.8; cf. *frequens imitatio transit in mores* (i.11.3) – 'constant imitation becomes second nature'; and Democritus 33 and 242.
34 See Quintilian ii.2.15; Cicero, *Pro Cael.* 6–11; Pliny, *Epist.* 3.3.
35 See Persius, *Sat.* 5.30–5; Apuleius, *Golden Ass*, book 11.15.
36 See Cicero, *Pro Cael.* 47; cf. Lucilius W.450–2.

(II.3), which describes how Damasippus was transformed from a casualty of commerce into a Stoic sage. According to A. D. Nock conversions to philosophy were more common than conversions to religion. But in antiquity the border between the two was not clearly marked. The message of Epicurus, for instance, was surely as much a religion as a philosophy. But even if we keep the distinction, there are several interesting cases which Nock himself mentions.[37] The most unexpected is perhaps that of C. Valerius Flaccus who, according to Livy (XXVII.8.5–6), became Flamen Dialis and who when his *animus* was seized with a concern for rites and worship at once put off his *antiquos mores*. Plutarch (*De sera numinis uindicta*, 563) has the story of Aridaios of Soli, who appeared to die, saw a vision of the next world, was brought back to life, and became a new man, taking the name of Thespesios. The most famous story of that kind in Latin literature is, of course, the tale of Lucius, who in Apuleius' novel goes through a series of degrading and farcical adventures in the form of an ass before regaining his human shape and becoming a devotee of Isis. It may perhaps be inadmissible to go further afield and include a man like St Paul. But for all his Jewish origins it is worth remembering that as a native of Tarsus Paul was well within the ambit of Greek culture. He also had connections with Rome in that he had a Roman name and was a Roman citizen. Not all scholars, however, share Ramsay's confidence that he spoke Latin.

In spite of all this, it is a well known fact that changes of character, even of a gradual kind, were not often acknowledged by ancient historians and biographers. Tacitus (*Ann.* 6.51) divides the *mores* of Tiberius into five phases: (1) excellence under Augustus, (2) hypocrisy while Germanicus and Drusus survived, (3) a mixture of good and evil until his mother died, (4) the revelation of his cruelty but not yet of his lust in the period of Sejanus' influence, (5) the indulgence of every kind of wickedness when he followed simply his own *ingenium*. In other words, essentially Tiberius had always been as he was at the end. The same sort of allegation is made a number of times by Suetonius, though in a more haphazard way. Plutarch, too, usually works with the notion of a fixed personality. Speaking of Philip V of Macedon, he says:

'Philip *seems* to have been an instance of the greatest and strangest alteration of character; after being a mild king and

---

[37] A. D. Nock, 'Conversion and adolescence', printed in *Essays in Religion and the Ancient World*, ed. Z. Stewart (Oxford 1972) vol. 1.

a modest youth he became a lascivious man and a most cruel tyrant. But in *reality* this was not a change of nature, but a bold revelation, when it was safe to do so, of the wickedness which his fear had for a long time obliged him to conceal.' (*Aratus* 51.4)

A few qualifications, however, are necessary. First, the historians do, occasionally, give us glimpses of another view by imputing it to someone else. Tacitus, for instance, puts into the mouth of Lucius Arruntius the opinion that Tiberius had been shattered and changed by absolute power – *ui dominationis conuulsus et mutatus* (*Ann.* 6.48). Suetonius quotes from a speech in which Tiberius promises to be consistent and never to change his character as long as he remains of sound mind (*Tib.* 67.3). In Plutarch's life of Pericles (38.2) we hear that Theophrastus discussed the question whether men's characters change with circumstances and whether their behaviour diverges from virtue as a result of ill health. Secondly, the historians sometimes hint that they themselves are not wholly satisfied with the static theory. Plutarch is particularly revealing. Commenting on Sulla's later cruelty as compared with his former moderation, he wonders whether a man's nature can be changed by fortune, or whether power simply reveals a wickedness already present (30.5). So too a piece of untypical harshness on the part of Sertorius prompts the suggestion that good intentions (προαιρέσεις) and natures (φύσεις) can sometimes be perverted as the result of great and undeserved misfortunes (*Sertorius* 10.4). Thirdly, however inadequate their psychological theories may have been, Tacitus, Suetonius, and Plutarch did as a rule present the *facts* of change in such a way as to enable later scholars to construct more plausible interpretations. In the case of Tacitus I am thinking not just of the large portrait of Tiberius, but also of smaller sketches like those of Otho, Petronius, and Lucius Vitellius, who all behaved with unexpected energy and integrity when posted abroad. And one mustn't forget Vespasian – the one emperor who changed for the better.[38]

From change we move to complexity, and here we encounter another idea, a refinement on the one attributed to Burckhardt; it is conveniently formulated in the work of Paul Delany, to whom Trilling is much indebted. Delany sees the chief novelty of renaissance humanism in 'the emergence of men who are able to imagine themselves in more than one role, who stand as it were outside or above their own per-

---

[38] Otho (*Ann.* XIII.46.3), Petronius (*Ann.* XVI.18.2), Lucius Vitellius (*Ann.* VI.32.4), Vespasian (*Hist.* I.50.4). This section owes much to A. Wardman, *Plutarch's Lives* (London 1974) chap. 4.

sonalities, who are protean'.[39] How far the protean personality was known in the millennium before the renaissance is a question for medievalists to decide. My only concern is to recall that the type was well known in classical times. As Tacitus is fresh in our minds we may think of Licinius Mucianus (*Hist.* 1.10) who 'displayed a mixture of luxury and industry, of affability and insolence, of good and wicked accomplishments'.[40] Now this kind of thing was not, of course, in the best tradition. The ideal Roman type – so often associated with the early republic – was tough and austere, straightforward and reliable, consistent, predictable, and homogeneous. No doubt this idea, assisted by Stoic thought, was for a long time a living force, and influenced the upbringing and behaviour of many generations. Yet for all its conservatism Rome could not escape the effects of progress. Cicero in one passage goes so far as to say that the old type was almost superhuman: 'Such men, I think, were the famous Camilli, Fabricii, Curii, and all those who made Rome so great from its small beginnings. But virtues of that kind are no longer to be found in our social behaviour, scarcely even in our writings.'[41] Although exaggerated, the words contain a measure of truth.

In Greece, of course, the manysided and devious personality had long been recognized. There is a direct line of descent from Odysseus, the Homeric archetype, down through Alcibiades, branching out into the flatterers, parasites, and malcontents of Hellenistic literature. In Rome from the middle of the second century on, as society became more mixed and complex and the scope of people's activities widened, the protean personality became more common. Such men were not always rendered ineffective by their varied interests. Sulla, one recalls, spent his leisure in the company of actors and comedians without any apparent loss of dynamism.[42] Maecenas was a shrewd politician. (Whatever Seneca may say in *Epist.* 114, we may be sure that when Octavian went east to Actium and Egypt he did not leave Rome in the charge of a mere fop.) The most manysided man of all was, of course, Julius Caesar – general, orator, diarist, scholar, critic, womanizer, and wit.

Yet such versatility usually excited distrust. In his *De Amicitia* (65) Cicero, himself not the most simple of men, remarked that a complex and devious character could not be relied on – *neque enim fidum potest esse multiplex ingenium et tortuosum.* The philosophical schools regularly

[39] P. Delany, *British Autobiography in the Seventeenth Century* (London 1969) 11.
[40] Cf. Sallust on Sulla, *Jug.* 95.
[41] Cicero, *Pro Cael.* 39–40; cf. *De Amic.* 62.
[42] See C. Garton, *Phoenix* 18 (1964) 137–56.

preached the virtues of *constantia* and *aequabilitas*, and satirists mocked men of excessive changeability. As examples one need only mention Juvenal's lines on the immigrant Greek (*Sat.* 3.74–108) and Horace's thumbnail sketch of Tigellius (*Sat.* 1.3.1–19)[43] which was later elaborated by Dryden in his portrait of Zimri:

> A man so various, that he seemed to be
> Not one, but all mankind's epitome.
> Stiff in opinions, always in the wrong,
> Was everything by starts, and nothing long;
> But in the course of one revolving moon,
> Was chemist, fiddler, statesman and buffoon.

After complexity, the divided mind. Because of their imperial achievement the Romans have gone down in history as an exceptionally confident and purposeful nation. They were nonetheless familiar with inner conflict. Seneca's Medea is torn between maternal affection and the desire for revenge (937–9):

> quid, anime, titubas? ora quid lacrimae rigant
> uariamque nunc huc ira, nunc illuc amor
> diducit?

> *Why does my mind falter? Why do tears stream down my face?*
> *And why do I vacillate, torn now this way by anger, now that by*
> *love?*

The same situation was almost certainly elaborated by Ovid in his version of the play, and there is no reason to doubt that it went back to Ennius, who had himself taken it over from Euripides. In Rome the *controuersiae* of the rhetorical schools greatly influenced the development of these internal debates, but men had long been only too familiar with such dilemmas as part of their real experience. As the civil war drew near Cicero recorded his agonized indecision in his letters. When rejected by Lesbia, Catullus condensed his ambivalent feelings into the famous epigram *odi et amo*. We have already referred to the pathological indecisiveness of Tiberius. Different again is the type of restlessness described by Lucretius in connection with the man who lacks philosophical stability – dashing off to his country house and then falling

---

[43] Horace's passage influenced Diderot. See E. R. Curtius, *European Literature and the Latin Middle Ages*, trans. W. Trask (New York 1953, Harper Torchbook 1963) 577–83. The fullest description of the chameleon type is given by Plutarch in *How to tell a Flatterer from a Friend*, 51c–54b.

asleep from boredom or else starting out again for town (*DRN* 3.1068–9):

> hoc se quisque modo fugit, at quem scilicet, ut fit,
> effugere haud potis est, ingratis haeret et odit

> *In this way everyone runs away from himself, and yet remains reluctantly and resentfully bound to that person whom, of course, he can't escape.*

There were two recognized aids to self-awareness – a candid friend and the habit of introspection.[44] Horace mentions both together: *liber amicus, consilium proprium* (*Sat.* 1.4.132–3), but for our purpose the second is the more important. Persius proclaims that introspection is all too rare: *ut nemo in sese temptat descendere, nemo* (4.23). In fact the habit was clearly quite common. There are countless references, some of which have been mentioned earlier. But it is Seneca who speaks of the matter most fully:

> "The awareness of sin is the beginning of well-being – *initium est salutis notitia peccati*. I think that saying of Epicurus' is quite admirable. For a man unconscious of sin doesn't wish to be set right. You must catch yourself out before you can change for the better...As far as you can, prove yourself guilty, look into yourself. Act the part first of counsel for the prosecution, then that of judge, and finally that of advocate. Be severe with yourself from time to time.' (*Epist.* 28.9–10)

The same message is found in a long section of the *De Ira* (3.36), which may be condensed as follows: The *animus* should be summoned to give an account of itself at the end of every day. Sextius used to do this. Before falling asleep he would interrogate himself: 'What bad habit have you cured today? What temptation have you resisted? In what respect are you a better man?' He slept more soundly as a result. I follow the same practice myself, going over the whole day and examining my actions with complete honesty: *nihil mihi ipsi abscondo, nihil transeo.*

So far, then, we have managed to find Roman parallels to most of the phenomena mentioned by Trilling, in particular the individual with his changes, diversity, conflicts, and self-awareness. Therefore, whatever developments may have taken place in seventeenth-century England,

---

44 For the candid friend see Cicero, *De Off.* 1.91, and Horace, *Epod.* 11.25–6. Other references will be found in A. Michels, *CP 39* (1944) 173–7. For introspection cf. Epictetus iii.23.37.

one can hardly go so far as to say that a new dimension was added to human nature. But if the Roman self was not fundamentally different from our own, one has to admit that it was not at all as fully explored in literature. The period between the fourth century B.C. in Greece and the second century A.D. in Rome produced a mass of biographical material, written with various intentions and from various points of view. But (even allowing for the vast amount that has disappeared) it seems safe to conclude that no ancient biographer tried to trace the development of his subject's personality by showing from the inside, as it were, his feelings, struggles, doubts, and decisions. More relevant still is the fact that no introspective *autobiographies* were written before the *Confessions* of St Augustine (*c.* A.D. 400). There were, of course, other kinds of autobiography – not only formal studies, but also letters, poems, and large volumes of memoirs (of which Sulla, for instance, wrote twenty-two books). But while these works often contained factual information about the writer's family and upbringing and sometimes outlined his philosophy of life, their main purpose was to record the part which the senator, general, or emperor had played in the events of his day, and to present that account in such a way as to justify and glorify what he had done. The narrative was therefore both external and tendentious.[45]

The germ of introspective autobiography was present in Seneca. If only he had *told* us what bad habits he was trying to cure and what temptations he had resisted or failed to resist, he would have travelled far on the road to Rousseau. The same is true of Marcus Aurelius. His *Meditations* are full of worthy reflections and good resolutions, but they tell us very little about the drama of his inner life. Some progress, perhaps, was made by that prince of hypochondriacs, Aelius Aristides; he certainly had the right degree of self-absorption and his symptoms were a great deal more appalling than any of the feeble peccadilloes of St Augustine.[46] And yet the crucial step was never taken. The question *why* St Augustine's autobiography was different can hardly have a simple answer. One might start from the fact that confession implied guilt, and that Augustine's sense of guilt was closely related to the Christian religion with its demanding morality and its awesome father-

---

45 A lot of material (some of it very marginal) was collected by G. Misch in *A History of Autobiography in Antiquity* (Eng. trans. London 1950). See the discussions and bibliographies in T. A. Dorey (ed.) *Latin Biography* (London 1967) and A. Momigliano, *The Development of Greek Biography* (Harvard 1971).

46 See C. A. Behr, *Aelius Aristides and the Sacred Tales* (Amsterdam 1968). Aristides kept notes of his dreams and symptoms in a diary.

god. When a Stoic or Epicurean examined his soul he never did so in a spirit of such remorse, and although he might ask a friend's advice on how to deal with a moral weakness (as Serenus is supposed to do in Seneca's *De Tranquillitate* 1), he would not think it either necessary or gentlemanly to make a public confession. Even those oriental religions that did go in for confession and repentance, like that of Isis or the Magna Mater or the Dea Syria, never produced anything comparable to the work of Augustine.[47] When Lucius in Book 11 of *The Golden Ass* regains his human shape, it is seen as a deliverance from misery and danger and bad luck, not from sin.[48] The only reproach – and that a mild one – comes from the priest of Isis, who says in section 15: 'In the slippery time of youthful vigour you stooped to the pleasures of a slave and got a sorry reward for your ill-starred curiosity.' But Augustine's *Confessions* are much more than confessions. They are a glorification of God and a testimony to his love and power. It is because Augustine has experienced divine grace that he is led to reflect on the transformation which has come about in his own soul. 'How can it be that God, in his infinite majesty, should have taken thought for *my* salvation?' This reminds us of the singular and imponderable element in the whole question. It may be that the sentiment just quoted would have been unlikely before the advent of Christianity, but in A.D. 400 there were many men who had received a rhetorical education and who had undergone various troubles before finding Christ. Yet they did not write spiritual autobiographies. St Augustine was a very extraordinary individual.

While it must be conceded, then, that classical writers did not produce inward-looking autobiographies, this does not make them any the less sincere. For insincerity, as we have stressed all along, involves the intent to deceive. Conversely, it seems that even the most histrionic self-exposure doesn't always convey an impression of total frankness. Those who have read Henri Peyre's excellent survey of sincerity in French literature will no doubt have noticed that however shamelessly a writer uncovers his own meanness and depravity there is always someone to complain that he has presented too favourable a picture.[49] For Peyre himself St Augustine's style 'smacks of pathetic appeal to emotion rather than of naked analytical sincerity' (18). In Montaigne

[47] See R. Pettazzoni, *Harvard Theological Review* 30 (137) 1–14.
[48] The terms used are *aerumnae, casus, pericula, labores,* and *Fortunae tempestates*; the sections are 2, 4, 12, 15, 17, and 19 of *The Golden Ass,* book 11.
[49] H. Peyre, *Literature and Sincerity* (New Haven and London 1963).

we find passages like the following, which has a significant reference to Persius:

> 'Chascun regarde devant soy: moy, je regarde dedans moy; je n'ay affair qu'à moy, je me considere sans cesse, je me contreroolle, je me gouste. Les aultres vont toujours ailleurs, s'ils y pensent bien, ils vont toujours avant; *nemo in sese tentat descendere*: moy, je me roule en moy mesme.' (2.17)

Yet Pascal accused Montaigne of omitting all that might have harmed him in the eyes of posterity, and Rousseau called him 'a falsely sincere man' who confessed only to amiable faults.[50] Michelet in his turn boasted that his diary was written 'with a sincerity which went infinitely farther than that of Rousseau',[51] and much later Valéry asserted that Pascal wasn't really sincere, because his style was so carefully contrived.[52] Gide strove to emulate Montaigne and Rousseau, but Claudel called his journal 'a monument of insincerity',[53] and Cocteau said he always confessed small things to avoid confessing big ones.[54] The truth seems to be that it is simple, monochrome people who come closest to sincerity, and they as a rule are not given to self-examination – they have other things to do. The more complex introvert may with fearless candour strip away layer after layer of falseness, and in the end, like a man peeling an onion, be left with nothing but his tears.

We must now consider, very briefly, how at the beginning of this century a change came over the critical climate in England and America which eventually affected our way of looking at Roman poetry. In a period when poetry was discussed so much in terms of feeling it seemed that the critic's job was to respond as fully as he could and then convey that response to his readers. But if one was involved in an emotional relationship with the poet, it was essential that the emotions in question should be genuine. One could not be expected to weep or exult or tremble without the conviction that the poet himself had been even more intensely moved. Hence the importance of sincerity.[55] But with the waning of romanticism that importance began to diminish. Writers became more interested in the contradictions that might exist within a

---

[50] Peyre 40–1. [51] Peyre 226. [52] Peyre 267.
[53] Peyre 300. [54] Peyre 300.
[55] 'Is Byron's poetry great poetry? Is it genuine poetry? Does it ring true? Is it *sincere*? Yes, there we have – for all poetry, greater or less – the critical word – *sincerity*' Quiller-Couch, *Studies in Literature*, 7. 'Dante's World of Souls! It is at bottom the *sincerest* of all Poems; sincerity, here too, we find to be the measure of worth' Carlyle, *On Heroes and Hero-worship*, lecture 3, 113. 'Sincere work is good work, be it never so humble' G. H. Lewes, *Principles of Success in Literature*, 86.

personality. *Dr Jekyll and Mr Hyde* appeared in 1885, *The Picture of Dorian Gray* in 1890, and *The Happy Hypocrite* in 1896. The precept of Polonius was forgotten and affectation became the order of the day. 'A little sincerity is a dangerous thing', said Oscar Wilde, 'and a great deal of it is absolutely fatal.'[56] Elsewhere he proclaimed that 'the first duty in life is to assume a pose; what the second is no one yet has found out'.[57]

Wilde was one of several among Yeats's friends who adopted pseudonyms. Yeats himself from this time on was much concerned with the problem of identity. An early example is the poem entitled *The Mask*, in which a girl says:

> Put off that mask of burning gold
> with emerald eyes.

The poet finally evades her request, saying:

> O no, my dear, let all that be;
> what matter, so there be but fire
> in you, in me?

This looks forward to the volume entitled *Per Amica Silentia Lunae*, published in 1917, in which Yeats develops his theory of self and anti-self, each of which wears a mask. A year earlier, in *A Portrait of the Artist*, Joyce wrote: 'The personality of the artist...finally refines itself out of existence, impersonalizes itself so to speak...The artist, like the God of creation, remains within or behind or beyond or above his handiwork, invisible, refined out of existence, indifferent, paring his fingernails.'[58] Yeats, Joyce, and Pound (whose *Personae* appeared in 1909) prepared the way for Eliot's statement in 1919: 'The progress of an artist is a continual self-sacrifice, a continual extinction of personality.'[59] This was a far cry from romantic views of the poet, but Eliot sternly insisted that 'there may be a good deal to be said for Romanticism in life; there is no place for it in letters'.[60] Not everyone, of course, heeded these pronouncements, but in the New Criticism which gathered momentum in the thirties and forties and remained vigorous up to recent times the experience, feelings, and personality of the poet ceased to be the focus of attention. A stream of essays and

---

[56] Wilde, 'The critic as artist', Everyman edition 51.
[57] *The Artist as Critic: Critical Writings of Oscar Wilde*, ed. R. Ellmann (London 1970) 433.
[58] Joyce, *A Portrait of the Artist as a Young Man*, chap. 5 (middle).
[59] Eliot, *The Sacred Wood* (London 1932) 53.
[60] Eliot, *The Sacred Wood*, 32.

books warned us to beware of the personal heresy, the biographical fashion, and the intentional fallacy, and to concentrate on tone, diction, and the structural relationships within the poem itself. Many of those who retained an interest in biography became more cautious, choosing titles like 'The Mask of Pope', 'The Masks of Swift', 'Yeats: the Man and the Masks', and 'A. E. Housman: Man behind a Mask'.

It is hard to say when the persona or mask first made its appearance in the criticism of Latin poetry, but certainly a significant moment was the appearance of Maynard Mack's essay 'The Muse of Satire' in *The Yale Review* of 1951. Mack there maintained that there were three voices in Pope's formal satires: the *uir bonus*, the *ingénu*, and the heroic defender of the public interest. The *uir bonus* is a good man who has been forced into writing satire – a situation illustrated by Juvenal's *difficile est saturam non scribere* (*Sat.* 1.30). Mack went on to say that the figure of Umbricius in Juvenal's third satire also represented that persona. By talking about personae Mack wished to divert our attention from Juvenal's life and character (where Gilbert Highet had focused it in *TAPA* 68, 1937) and to make us concentrate on the satires as independent entities. Other Yale scholars adopted a similar approach. In 1950 A. W. Allen had already published his article on 'Sincerity and the Roman Elegists' in which he sought to discourage speculation about Propertius' love-life;[61] in 1959 A. Kernan elaborated the doctrine of the persona in his study of English renaissance satire *The Cankered Muse*, and in the sixties W. S. Anderson applied the theory to Juvenal and Horace.[62]

The concept of the persona is not, of course, a modern invention. Some examples of its use in Roman times will be considered shortly. But to remind us that it was employed in England before the eighteen-nineties here is an observation made by Dr Johnson in 1752: 'A mask, says Castiglione, confers a right of acting and speaking with less restraint, even when the wearer happens to be known.'[63] Dr Johnson's remark is interesting because it mentions a *positive* advantage which a writer may hope to derive from his persona. Later Wilde was to say with a typical paradox: 'A man is least himself when he talks in his

---

61 A. W. Allen, *CP* 45 (1950) 145–60.
62 W. S. Anderson, *YCS* 17 (1961) 26; *Univ. of California Publ. in Classical Philology* 19 (1964) 127ff.; and the chapter on Horace in *Critical Essays on Roman Literature*, ed. J. P. Sullivan (London 1963).
63 This and other interesting passages are mentioned by H. D. Weinbrot in the symposium entitled 'The concept of the persona in satire', *Satire Newsletter* 3 (1966) 146. In the same number (p. 134) A. H. Scouten points out that many personae figured in the periodical literature of the eighteenth century.

own person. Give him a mask and he will tell you the truth.'[64] It was always clear that a persona enabled the writer to try out various roles without necessarily making any serious or final commitment. Yeats went further: 'As I see it Hamlet and King Lear educated Shakespeare, and I have no doubt that in the process of that education he found out that he was an altogether different man to what he thought himself, and had altogether different beliefs.'[65] The mask may also be of assistance to the reader. Apart from directing him to the work itself, which should be his main concern, it saves him from drawing the more naive kinds of personal inference, and it helps him to remember that the creative process is inaccessible and that talent (not to speak of genius) can never be explained in biographical terms.

Nevertheless, like every other doctrine, the doctrine of the persona does not absolve us from using our intelligence. For we may fail to apply the doctrine when it's appropriate, and insist on applying it when it's not. In the first type of error playwrights and novelists are identi-fied with their characters; actors are confused with their roles; and poets are assumed to live exactly as they write. Illustrations are easy to collect. In the biographer Chamaeleon we find the allegation that Aeschylus brought drunken characters into his satyr-plays because he was drunk when he wrote them; Satyrus imputes several disagreeable qualities to Euripides on the principle οἷα μὲν ποιεῖ λέγειν τοῖός ἐστιν— 'the man resembles his characters'.[66] The habit persists. In the sixth chapter of *Lucky Jim* the hero, who is suffering from a hangover amongst other things, recognizes a snatch of song coming from the bathroom as 'some skein of untiring facetiousness by filthy Mozart'. This proved to some anti-Dixon readers that the author was a philistine of the coarsest kind. The creator of the TV character Alf Garnett complains that he is constantly criticized for holding illiberal and reactionary opinions. Actors have always had the same problem. After one of the earliest performances in theatrical history Solon went backstage and remonstrated with Thespis (who had been acting in his own play) for telling a lot of lies in front of the people.[67] Our con-temporaries smile at those American pioneers who used to riddle the

---

[64] Wilde, 'The artist as critic', Everyman edition 48.
[65] Yeats, in a letter to O'Casey, quoted by R. Ellmann, *The Identity of Yeats* (Faber paperback 1968) 42.
[66] See A. Podlecki, *Phoenix* 23 (1969) 123, 124 n. 77, 126, 130. Quintilian (x.1.100) says: 'It is a pity that [Afranius] spoiled his plots by intro-ducing nasty pederastic love-affairs, thus revealing his own character.'
[67] Plutarch, *Solon* 29.5. This and other passages are quoted by C. Garton in *Personal Aspects of the Roman Theatre* (Toronto 1972) chap. 1. Much of that chapter bears directly on our topic.

screen with bullets when the villain seemed likely to get away. But even as I write, some people in England are preparing to order their Christmas turkeys from Dan Archer, a fiction of radio who has become larger than life. As for poets, it is sometimes urged that Homer must have known Troy, otherwise he could not have described the topography in such detail. Over the years a bewildering variety of experience has been foisted onto Shakespeare. It was Ellen Terry, I believe, who reduced the method to absurdity by pointing out that by the same reasoning the great playwright must have been a woman. Today, however, such aberrations are uncommon, and it is more useful to concentrate on the other type of error mentioned above, i.e. that of applying the doctrine of the persona in a dogmatic way where it is not required.

First, in traditional and supra-personal genres the idea of the mask can be discarded altogether; nor is it of much service in the study of narrative or straightforward exposition. In drama, as we have seen, it does have a function, but we are not justified in using it to argue that the outlook of a playwright must always be unknowable. In Greek drama, for example, where two writers sometimes employed the same theatre, the same plots, and possibly even the same actors, there were still significant differences between the plays, and these differences (in characterization, handling of myth, use of chorus etc.) can reasonably be interpreted as reflecting divergent points of view. In this general sense the playwright may be said to sign his masks.

Actors' personalities, too, are not invariably out of reach. It is true that some performers have an exceptionally wide range (Guinness and Sellers are obvious examples in modern times); but such people are usually said to have neutral or fluid or chameleon-like personalities, and they often confirm this themselves. At a different point on the scale we encounter the actor who repeatedly wins success in certain *kinds* of role (one thinks of men like Wolfit and Richardson); we then say that such roles are congenial; they suit him. Why, to use Cicero's example, did Rupilius always play in *Antiopa* and Aesopus avoid *Ajax*? Why has Gielgud succeeded brilliantly in Hamlet and Prospero, but not in Othello? There must be some relation, however obscure, between an actor's technical range and his personality.

This leads to another age-old question.

> 'Should the actor try to reproduce within himself the emotions that he is supposed to represent on the stage, expecting the proper gestures and expressions to proceed naturally from

the central emotion? Or should he, on the contrary, remain cool and objective, and master a variety of physical techniques in the hope of simulating an emotion that he does not feel?'[68]

That is how a modern scholar neatly summarizes the problem. But he is talking about a controversy which was going on in Germany between 1750 and 1770. It was not confined to Germany. One side of the case was put most memorably by Diderot in his *Paradoxe sur le comédien*.[69] The paradox, as Diderot saw it, was that to move the audience the actor must remain unmoved. Success was a matter of artistic technique: 'Actors impress the public not when they are furious, but when they play fury well.' Diderot summed up his position thus: 'What, then, is a great actor? A man who, having learnt the words set down for him by the author, fools you thoroughly, whether in tragedy or comedy.'

In antiquity a similar view was held by the Stoics. To them anger was evil, and therefore the 'angry' orator or actor had to be excused on the grounds that he wasn't really angry at all; he was only pretending.

> 'Do you think I am angry when I make a somewhat bitter and passionate speech in court? Or again, when the case is over and done, and I am writing the speech down, am I angry as I write: "Will someone pay attention to this? Clap him in irons!" Do you think Aesopus was ever angry when he acted this or Accius when he wrote it?'

So writes Cicero in his *Tusculan Disputations* (4.55), quoting some words of Accius. There is a similar discussion in Seneca's *De Ira* (2.17), which Diderot may well have known, especially in view of the following: *histriones in pronuntiando non irati populum mouent, sed iratum bene agentes* – 'an actor stirs the audience by his utterance not when he is angry but when he acts an angry man well'.[70] On this view sincerity is of no importance; the mask is everything.

But the other view makes the distinction between mask and sincerity difficult to maintain. In 1880 the critic William Archer sent a long questionnaire to the foremost actors and actresses of his day, inviting them to describe their psychological approach to a part and their

---

[68] T. Ziolkowski, *Germanic Review* 40 (1965) 265.

[69] Diderot's essay and the rejoinder by William Archer, 'Masks or faces', were printed together by Hill and Wang (New York 1957), with an introduction by Lee Strasberg, who has been closely associated with 'method acting' in our own time.

[70] In ordinary contexts, however, Seneca was quite willing to talk of actors and orators being carried away by uncontrollable emotion – e.g. *Epist.* 40.8.

emotional condition in the course of a performance. Many interesting replies came in, but the general conclusion was (very crudely) that while the actor must have an accomplished technique and retain a rational control over his performance he would be most effective when he reproduced in himself the primary emotions of grief, joy, rage, terror, and shame.[71] In antiquity this view went back to Aristotle and his followers, who believed that emotions were natural and useful. Antonius in Cicero's *De Oratore* (2.193) states his belief that actors feel the emotions they portray; and explicit evidence is provided by Quintilian (VI.2.35) when he says he has often seen actors take off their masks after some especially moving performance and leave the theatre still in tears. The same theory was applied to dramatists. 'Given an equal talent', says Aristotle, 'those who are themselves emotionally affected are the most convincing. A man who is distraught conveys distress and someone who is angry conveys rage most realistically.'[72] Aristotle is again echoed by Antonius in Cicero's *De Oratore* (2.193–4). But the most famous formulation of the idea is given by Horace (*AP* 102–3): *si uis me flere dolendum est primum ipsi tibi* – 'if you want me to weep you must first feel grief yourself'. Horace is here addressing the playwright, though indirectly, through his characters.

Since, however, Roman critics are normally concerned with oratory more than drama, the theory is most fully presented in connection with lawyers. The two types of *actor* had, of course, much in common, but Cicero and Quintilian both remark that the advocate was more directly open to emotion. First of all he was involved in a real-life situation; as Crassus says (*De Orat.* 3.214), the advocate enacts reality, the player merely imitates it. Secondly, the advocate speaks his own lines. Thus Antonius claims that in a given case his emotion was greater than any actor's because he was not performing the role of someone else but was taking responsibility for his own – *neque actor essem alienae personae, sed auctor meae* (*De Orat.* 2.194). Cicero's most objective statement on the matter is probably given in *De Orat.* 3.215. There he says that in principle authenticity (*ueritas*) is superior to imitation (*imitatio*) but that, whether one is genuinely moved or not, one needs a proper

71 W. Archer, 'Masks or faces'.
72 Aristotle, *Poetics* 1455a. Cf. Euripides, *Suppl.* 180ff. Aristotle also says the dramatist should act out the gestures of the character with whom he is working. In his note on the passage D. W. Lucas cites testimony concerning Ibsen, Dickens, and Trollope. A similar idea was adumbrated by Aristophanes, who made Euripides dress in rags when writing about ragged heroes (*Acharn.* 412ff.), and portrayed Agathon composing a woman's role in women's clothes (*Thesm.* 148ff.).

technique of gesture, facial expression, and voice.[73] Elsewhere he comes down more heavily in favour of real emotion. In the *Orator* (130) he maintains that his own mastery of the emotional peroration is due not to any natural gift (*ingenium*) but to genuine sadness (*dolor*). This quality is later described (132) as 'a great power of the soul which inflames me until I am beside myself'. In *De Orat.* 2.189 Antonius, who expresses Cicero's own opinions, denies that there is any need to feign emotion; he himself always sincerely felt what he was saying. The emotion was not always spontaneous, however, for he goes on to say that it is produced by general thoughts (*sententiae*) and commonplaces (*loci*) which arise from the case and are incorporated in the advocate's speech. These thoughts, combined with the appropriate diction and delivery, conjure up the emotion, which the speaker conveys to the audience.

The most illuminating account of the process is found in Quintilian VI.2.26–36, which I will paraphrase for the sake of brevity: the essential requirement for causing emotion in others is to feel it oneself; we must attune our *animus* to grief or anger or whatever the appropriate feeling may be. Often recently bereaved people speak with unaccustomed eloquence and angry men are fluent because of a power which comes from the heart (*uis mentis*) and because of their sincerity of character (*ueritas ipsa morum*). We evoke emotion in ourselves and others by using our imagination, by visualizing the dreadful action or situation that we wish to describe.[74] To awaken pity 'we must believe that the sufferings which we are deploring have happened to *us*; we must convince our own minds that this is so. We must *be* those people about whose grievous, undeserved, and bitter sufferings we are protesting; we mustn't treat the matter as if it were someone else's concern, but rather take that sorrow temporarily on ourselves.' Quintilian himself was often so moved that he was overcome with tears, turned pale, and felt a grief which was just like the real thing.[75] This excellent account of empathy puts us in mind of a famous passage of Wordsworth: 'It will be the wish of the poet to bring his feelings near to those of the persons whose feelings he describes, nay for short spaces of time perhaps to let himself slip into an entire delusion, and even confound and identify his own feelings with theirs.'[76]

These instances are enough to show that some playwrights, actors, advocates, and poets *are* involved, if only by empathy, in the emotions

---

[73] Cf. *Tusc. Disp.* 4.43.   [74] Cf. Longinus 15.
[75] Cf. Quintilian XII.1.29.
[76] Wordsworth, 'Preface to the Lyrical Ballads', ed. R. L. Brett and A. R. Jones (London 1963) 250.

they present. In such cases the idea of an unmoved artist ingeniously manipulating various personae is inadequate. One may add that even those who have stated the theory of masks most forcefully are not always as inscrutable as they purport to be. As a recent critic has remarked, 'with the years, the tradition of Joyce's impersonality has become harder and harder to sustain'.[77] But if the idea of the impersonal poet or artist is not universally valid, neither is its corollary, i.e. the idea of the dutifully agnostic reader. Let us start at the most basic level, outside literature altogether, and ask: 'Can anything be inferred about a man from the way he speaks?' Clearly the answer is yes. Leaving aside matters of diction and accent, if the man is quick, lucid, and acute in debate, we say he has that sort of mind; if he is slow, stumbling, and confused, we say he has the opposite sort. Someone who is amusing or tactless in what he says is thought of as being this or that kind of man. Again, acting and writing are not the only areas in which people assume roles. Life itself is the oldest theatre.[78] And yet we all know a few of the actors tolerably well.

When we turn from everyday speech to writing the range of possible inference is reduced, because literature is a less immediate and more complex mode of communication. Yet a person may still be judged witty, learned, subtle, or profound on the basis of his writings. (One thinks of Goldsmith, who 'wrote like an angel and talked like poor Poll'.) We can often go further and make quite confident statements about his interests and beliefs. Who would deny that Ovid was interested in girls? And who would be silly enough to suggest after reading Lucretius' impassioned praise of Epicurus that the poet was really a Stoic all the time? A writer's social behaviour and actual events in his life represent a different category. When Ovid says (*Trist.* 2.353–4):

crede mihi; distant mores a carmine nostro:
uita uerecunda est, Musa iocosa mea

Believe me – my habits are unlike my poem. My life is respectable; it's my Muse that enjoys her fun,

we may be sceptical (for is this not the man who had written: *usus*

[77] J. Gross, *Joyce* (London 1971) 16.
[78] For this commonplace see, e.g., D.L. 2.66 (Aristippus); 7.160 (Ariston); Teles p. 5 (Bion); Menander (Körte 153); Cicero, *De Off.* 1.114; Epictetus, *Enchir.* 17; Suetonius, *Aug.* 99; Seneca, *Epist.* 77.20. For a readable modern account of social roles see E. Goffman, *The Presentation of the Self in Everyday Life* (London 1969).

opus mouet hoc: uati parete perito – 'it is experience that inspires this work; obey the expert bard'?). But we cannot settle the matter without external biographical evidence. The same applies to similar assertions by Martial, Apuleius, and Ausonius.[79] Other protests leave room for qualification. For example, when Catullus replies to the criticism of some homosexual poems by saying (16.5–6):

> castum esse decet pium poetam
> ipsum, uersiculis nihil necesse est

> *it befits a devoted poet to be pure himself; there's no need for his verses to be the same,*

he seems to be implying that the poems in question were totally distinct from his own behaviour *and thoughts*. Again, when Hadrian addresses a dead poet in the words:

> lasciuus uersu, mente pudicus eras[80]

> *you were wanton in your verses but pure in mind,*

we are aware of an incongruity. Granted *mens* can mean something like 'outlook' or even 'disposition', but it cannot here be wholly separate from the attitude of mind in which the poems were written, and therefore it ought not to be contrasted with *uersus*. Finally a Greek example: after writing a large collection of pederastic epigrams, Strato adds (*Greek Anthology* 12.258):

> 'Perhaps in future years someone listening to these trifles of mine may think that all the heart-aches of love were my own. In fact I keep writing various pieces for various lovers of boys, because some god has given me this gift.'

One cannot therefore be *sure* that Strato was a practising homosexual, but he certainly found the subject engrossing, and that is a legitimate, if not a very important, biographical inference.

---

[79] Martial 1.4.8: *lasciua est nobis pagina, uita proba* ('my page is wanton, my life is pure'); Apuleius, *Apol.* 11: *quasi ullum specimen morum sit uorsibus ludere* ('as if writing frivolous poems provided any evidence of one's moral behaviour'); Ausonius, *Cento* 130: *ne fortasse meos mores spectent de carmine* ('don't let them treat my poem as a mirror of my conduct'). It is interesting that Apuleius identifies Corydon in Virgil's second eclogue with Virgil himself and Alexis with a slave-boy of Asinius Pollio's. This is probably an instance of the very fallacy of which he complains – though Apuleius may have believed he was recording an authentic biographical tradition.

[80] The line is quoted by Apuleius, *Apol.* 11.

If we want more specific information we have to be careful, for a great deal depends on the poet's genre. A sober, and normally reliable, critic of the last century told us some quite interesting details about Propertius' physique: 'His extreme paleness and the slightness of his figure were signs of a constitution unfitting or at least disinclining him for any of the more manly amusements of youth.'[81] Our concern for the delicate lad is relieved when we discover that all this is based on a single couplet (1.5.21–2):

> nec iam pallorem totiens mirabere nostrum,
> aut cur sim toto corpore nullus ego

> *then you won't be so often surprised at my pallor or wonder why I have wasted utterly away.*

An entirely conventional picture of the poet in love – haggard and woebegone. If the lover in Roman elegy wanted his devotion to be taken seriously, he simply couldn't afford to enjoy robust health.

But consider these lines from Horace (*Epist.* 1.20.24–8):

> Tell them I was shorter than average, grey before my time, fond of the sunshine, quick-tempered but easily mollified. And if anyone wants to know my age, I completed my forty-fourth year when Lollius drew Lepidus for his colleague in the consulship.'

Those details are *not* conventional. They come at the end of a major collection and are meant to tell readers in the years ahead what the poet was like. Of all ancient poets Horace shows most clearly the limitations of the persona-theory – at least in its more dogmatic form.[82] And so I will conclude this chapter by arguing that with him there is sometimes no point in assuming the presence of a mask, that at other times a mask is too crude a concept to assist our appreciation of a poem, and that when Horace does use personae (as he undoubtedly does) these do not necessarily prevent us from drawing valid conclusions about his views and character.

Let us start with *Sat.* 1.10. There Horace criticizes Lucilius on the grounds that his humour was too broad, his style too diffuse, and his language too often mixed with Greek. Now is Horace wearing a mask

---

81 W. Y. Sellar, *The Roman Poets of the Augustan Age* (Horace and the Elegiac Poets) 281.

82 Since this chapter was written G. Highet has published a lucid and candid paper on the subject in *Hermes* 102 (1974) 321–37. We are largely in agreement over Horace, though in other areas Highet makes fewer concessions to the persona-theory than I have done here.

here, and if so what kind is it? I must admit I can see no mask at all. For what are the possibilities? Either Horace believed what he said, or he believed something else, or he didn't know or care. The obvious way to check this is to enquire what Horace actually did in his own work. It then becomes clear that in all these respects Horace's satires *were* more refined (and also more limited) than his predecessor's.

But perhaps that poem is a special case. So let us take the previous one, which describes Horace's encounter with the pest on the Sacred Way. Leaving aside the question of the incident's authenticity, consider simply the way in which Horace presents himself. On the one hand he is a member of Maecenas' circle, staving off the comical attempts of an outsider to break in. By drawing attention to his privileged position he is therefore flattering himself and, indirectly, his friends. On the other hand it is the pest who holds the initiative throughout. At every point Horace is cowed or outmanoeuvred, and he is saved in the end only by an act of divine intervention. Moreover, although he affirms his membership of the group, he readily admits that others within it are richer and more important than he is. And although he makes fun of Maecenas, the humour is clearly based on respect. That is the kind of ironical, amusing figure who appears in the poem. But how is that figure different from the man who was actually reciting the poem to those very people?

A similar point can be made in regard to *Sat.* 1.6, a poem which presents a rather complex attitude to political success. It starts by maintaining that positions of power should go to able and reliable men rather than to patrician numskulls; but it then goes off on a different tack, explaining at greater length why the poet refuses to take part in the scramble for office. Now if we had evidence that as he wrote this Horace was standing for the quaestorship, we would have to assume that for some reason he was wearing a mask. But as the attitude taken in the poem is entirely in harmony with what we know of the poet's life-style, there seems to be no point in talking about masks. It is true that Horace appears mainly as a respectful client, a devoted son, and a civilized idler. But those were real aspects of his character.

The metaphor of the mask usually suggests that a person's face has been concealed in order to produce a particular effect or illusion. When Lucretius says (*DRN* 3.58) *eripitur persona, manet res* ('the mask is torn off, the truth left exposed') and when Seneca says (*Epist.* 24.13): *non hominibus tantum sed rebus persona demenda est et reddenda facies sua* ('not just men but also things should have their mask removed and their own face restored') they are talking as if the face were a single static entity. But a face can change expression as a voice changes tone; whereas a mask is rigid. Take, for instance, an ode like II.1 (*motum ex Metello*). It begins as a private poem addressed to a personal acquaintance. Horace is looking forward to the appearance of Pollio's history of the civil war; it is a difficult and delicate subject, but the narrative is bound to be exciting:

> 'Even now you are deafening our ears with the threatening bray of trumpets, now the bugles blare, now the flash of weapons terrifies the panicking horses and the horsemen's faces.'

But with the mention of Cato's name in stanza six the ode moves into a minor key; the thought spreads out from Pollio's history into a general lament on the civil wars:

> 'What pool or river is unaware of our dismal war? What sea has not been stained with Daunian slaughter? What shore is unpolluted by our blood?'

Then with a jerk Horace recovers himself and adds a more light-hearted conclusion:

> 'But don't leave gaiety behind, you impertinent Muse, taking up once more the business of the Cean dirge. Join me in some grotto blessed by Venus, and try to find a tune with a lighter mood.'

The persona is hardly flexible enough to do justice to that kind of changing tone, which is a common feature of both the lyrics and the *sermones*.

All this does not mean that Horace never employed personae. He did; and we must consider a few examples. In doing so we shall ignore such figures as Priapus (*Sat.* I.8), Ulysses (*Sat.* II.5), and Nasidienus (*Sat.* II.8), and select a few which have some connection with the poet himself. In *Sat.* II.4 'Horace' is an eager but inexpert student of gastronomy. The persona functions as an ironic foil to the bumptious and encyclopedic Catius, who has just been attending a lecture on the subject. Yet Horace, who after all wrote the part of Catius, is clearly knowledgeable about the conversation of epicures, and as one who dined with Maecenas and other notabilities he must have had a fair amount of experience in food and wine.

In *Sat.* II.2 the subject is approached from the other end, and in a more straightforward way. Ofellus, a hardy peasant, attacks the gluttony and extravagance of the rich. We are told that he himself, although enjoying an occasional treat, kept to a very simple diet and yet succeeded in living a contented life. Now Ofellus is undoubtedly the mouthpiece of Horace in so far as he attacks abuses which the poet disapproved of. It is also true that in four-fifths of the poem his thought is presented in a manner quite unlike that of a peasant – he has a detailed knowledge of high life and his argument is neat and orderly with several literary allusions. His views are not even quoted directly; they come to us through Horace's mind and are processed accordingly. For this reason there is some difficulty in detaching the character from his creator. Yet he does emerge a little more clearly at the end, when he is allowed to speak for himself. This closing section, in which Ofellus describes his own life as a peasant, combined with the poet's opening disavowal (2–3), should prevent us from trying to identify him completely with Horace. Why then did Horace use the character? Presumably because he felt that he himself was not in a position to lecture his audience in this forthright unsophisticated manner. The points made against modishness, gluttony, and extravagance were sound. If people were inclined to smile at the simple fervour of the presentation, Horace could always say *non meus hic sermo est*.

The same sort of point can be made in connection with the country mouse in *Sat.* II.6. In as much as the fable praises contentment and simplicity above worry and wealth we may be sure that Horace endorsed it. But we cannot equate the rough peasant mouse with the cultivated poet, who lived in a comfortable house run by eight servants. And no one *asks* us to make such an equation, because the fable is told by a local character called Cervius whom Horace has invited round for the evening. Quite early in his career Horace played a joke on those who were too careless to notice such distinctions. He wrote a beautiful lyric of over sixty lines in praise of country life: how happy the farmer is, grafting his pears, shearing his sheep, and coming home in the evening to a fine hardy peasant wife. At the very end he added:

> 'That's what Alfius the money-lender said, just on the point of becoming a countryman. Then he called in all his cash on the thirteenth and set about lending it again on the first of the month.' (*Epod.* 2)

These cases, which are by no means untypical, show that when Horace employs a persona he doesn't automatically prevent us from learning about himself. In fact one might argue that it's *because* we have a grasp of biographical reality that we can talk with some confidence about poetic fiction. At any rate one helps to define the other.

As we read through Horace's work we gradually build up a picture of his concerns and attitudes. The difficulties usually occur with passages that are not characteristic, e.g. the cynical view of sex in the last fifty lines of *Sat.* i.2, the denunciation of human inventiveness in *Odes* i.3, the claim to Dionysiac inspiration in *Odes* ii.19, the censure of Crassus, army in *Odes* iii.5, or the exultation over the slaughter of the Alpine tribes in *Odes* iv.14. We may want to suggest explanations for these features by saying that one passage is entirely sincere but represents just a temporary mood or phase; that another, though genuine enough in a superficial way, does not reflect the poet's deeper and more constant feelings; that in another case Horace's official role does not suit his real character or he is not at ease with his persona. These explanations are fundamentally of the same type, and they are all unsatisfactory, partly because they cannot be proved or disproved, and partly because they are in principle unreliable. Thus we may suspect that in singing the praises of Drusus and Tiberius in *Odes* iv.14 Horace was responding (willingly) to the promptings of Augustus rather than expressing his own enthusiasm. Yet this can never be established, and one cannot assert it with any great confidence, because a great deal of imperfect writing is produced by perfectly sincere people. One has only to think of all those *in memoriam* notices that testify to genuine grief in verses of ludicrous banality. It is wiser, then, simply to ask whether the unusual feature impairs the poem as a whole. If it doesn't (and in i.3 and ii.19 it surely doesn't), then we note the piece is untypical and leave it at that. If it does (as in iii.5 and iv.14), then we have to admit it. It would be a very undiscriminating critic who tried to make out that Horace's odes were uniformly excellent.

To sum up. In literary criticism sincerity has a rather limited function. It is directly relevant only in those genres where the author makes some kind of personal declaration. (No one asks whether Homer was sincere.) And it is properly concerned with opinions, thoughts, and feelings rather than acts or events. The concept is of no assistance in the appreciation of form or structure; nor is it a reliable criterion of value. In the course of the romantic movement people lost sight of these limitations; they exaggerated the importance of sincerity and tried to use it in areas where it didn't apply. And so when the movement slackened in the eighteen-nineties and new forces began to assert themselves sincerity was an early casualty. What took its place was the persona. Where the doctrine of sincerity had expressed belief or disbelief in the writer's commitment to his words, the doctrine of the mask affirmed a strict agnosticism. But in other ways the two ideas had much in common. For, like sincerity, the persona was limited in the main to the more private genres and to questions of thought, feeling, and attitude; like sincerity, it had nothing to say about structure or value; and we are now becoming aware that the persona too has been over-used. Yet persona and sincerity represent two perennial concerns which are almost as inseparable as concave and convex, and this is where their importance lies. While one, by restraining our curiosity about the poet, directs us to the artifact itself, the other reminds us that the poet is, after all, a man speaking to men. Both ideas were familiar to the ancients, and this leads us to another area in which equilibrium is vital. While scholars strive to find out all they can about the distinctive features of Greek and Roman social organization, ritual, technology, and the rest, we mustn't forget that in most essential respects those people were like us. In particular, when we read the major authors of the two centuries between, say, 70 B.C. and A.D. 130, we find them a great deal *less* remote than hundreds of millions of our contemporaries. If we lose sight of that kinship, we diminish ourselves.

7

TRANSLATION

Unlike imitators, all translators aspire to faithfulness. But, as we know, this unity of purpose is largely nominal. One sets out to affect his readers in the same way as the original writer affected his; another strives to produce the sort of poem that the ancient author would have given us had he been born an Englishman; a third resists the spirit of his own age to avoid being ephemeral, while a fourth aims to turn out a contemporary work capable of standing on its own feet. And what kind of reader should the translator have in mind? The general reader who can compare the work only with other translations, or the man who has enough Latin or Greek to make some judgement of the version's accuracy, or the scholar who is assumed (sometimes wrongly) to be an expert? In discussing such matters some translators remind us that the letter killeth while the spirit giveth life; others with equal sincerity point out that if the letter is ignored the spirit will probably be sacrificed as well.

All these aims are to some degree nebulous, and a couple at least are absurd in principle. Yet they do serve as guides to the translator, helping him to decide what he wants to do. What he achieves is another matter. One doesn't have to read many versions to see that there is nearly always a gap, and sometimes a chasm, between intention and performance. Like Cynara's lover, the translator only succeeds in being faithful 'in his fashion'. Nor is this surprising. For, to take only the last point of the previous paragraph, letter and spirit represent a very crude dichotomy. A Latin poem, like any other, is of a certain length; it is written in a metre which conditions its pace and movement; the words are chosen and combined so as to occur in a particular order and to carry particular sounds, images and associations; the thought may be simple or complex, the tone straightforward or subtle, continuous or changing; and the poem's meaning will be related in some way to the experience of a people at a particular point in their history. Obviously all these factors cannot be fully appreciated, much less embodied in a translation. The problems will also vary enormously between one poet and another – Homer and Martial may be taken to represent opposite poles. The most any version can do is to reflect with the minimum of distortion what the translator, consciously or otherwise, thinks important. The result is then a commentary on him as much as on the original. To elaborate on these points would take us into the fascinating jungle of translation theory. Our present purpose is different, namely to use translations from different periods as aids towards apprehending the qualities of three Latin poems. But as comparison works both ways this will also involve some comment on the translations. We begin with a famous epigram:

Catullus 85

Odi et amo. quare id faciam, fortasse requiris.
   nescio, sed fieri sentio et excrucior.

An early version, and one of the more successful, is contained in *The Adventures of Catullus and the History of his Amours with Lesbia* by several hands, 'done from the French' in 1707:

I hate and love; perhaps you'll ask me why?
I know not, but 'tis so, and I in torments lie.

That is short, simple, and compressed. The omissions, which are very few (though important), will be taken up in connection with other attempts. At the moment we need only note two points. First, the one piece of padding – 'in torments lie' for *excrucior* – is due to the exigencies of rhyme. Most readers would agree, I think, that an epigrammatic couplet does call for rhyme; but what if the translator cannot find the appropriate words? Should he make do with something inferior or abandon rhyme altogether? In this case one feels that the phrase which produces the rhyme is just good enough, though it does weaken the poem at the very point where it should be strongest. Secondly, the relative length of the two lines has been altered. How seriously this impairs Catullus' emphasis is open to debate, but it does bring out an interesting feature of the original, namely that the pentameter is in some way denser than the hexameter. Perhaps it is just more intractable in English – as any translator of the epigram will admit – but I suspect there is also an intrinsic difference in the Latin.

Fortasse does indeed contribute to the sound, and it provides an effectively casual nuance which no one would want to sacrifice; yet it could be removed without wrecking the basic sense. That is not true of any word in the pentameter.

I now print a version attributed by Postgate to Thomas Moore,[1] though I have not been able to find it in any collection of Moore's poems:

> I love thee and hate thee, but if I can tell
> the cause of my love and my hate may I die!
> I feel it alas! I can feel it too well,
> that I love thee and hate thee, but cannot tell why.

Whereas the previous version contained only twenty-two syllables, this has forty-five. It should therefore include all the basic sense without relying too heavily on monosyllables. But in fact it is composed almost entirely of monosyllables, and the extra words are wasted on repetitions. Apart from these flaws, the waltzing amphibrachs ruin any hope of authenticity; and there is one final disadvantage, for which Moore can hardly be held responsible, namely that behind his translation we sense the presence of a phantom figure – the ghost of Dr Fell.

A more successful quatrain was written by James Cranstoun in 1867:

> I hate and love. Why do I so?
> Perhaps you ask. I can't explain.
> The bitter fact I only know,
> And torture racks my brain.

As well as being closer than Moore's effort, this cleverly produces something analogous to the elegiac couplet in that the first two lines together contain eight stresses whereas the second two have only seven. In another way, however, the proportions of the original have been changed. 'I can't explain' (*nescio*) has been transferred from the beginning of Catullus' pentameter to the end of Cranstoun's second line. This makes the pentameter easier to deal with and distributes the weight more evenly over the quatrain. The rhythmical corollary is that Cranstoun's first two lines tend to fall into iambic pairs, and the whole piece is divided ‿‿‾ ‿‿‿ ‿‿‾ ‿‿‿ ‿‿‿‿‿ ‿‿‿‾. Such evenness, however, is not in the original, which falls into four main sense-units containing 4, 11, 3, and 11 syllables respectively.

With Sir Richard Burton's translation (1894) we are back again

---

1 J. P. Postgate, *Translation and Translations* (London 1922) 78.

with the couplet. In the foreword, which was written to accompany an earlier work, Burton says: 'These pages hold in view one object sole and simple, namely to prove that a translation, metrical and literal, may be true and may be trustworthy.' Bold words. A later passage deepens our misgivings: 'The translator of original mind, who notes the innumerable shades of tone, manner, and complexion, will not neglect the frequent opportunities of enriching his mother-tongue with novel and alien ornaments which shall justly be accounted barbarisms until finally naturalized and adopted.' That is the spirit of the great explorer, though in his version of no. 85 it was not a penchant for neologisms that brought him to grief. Perhaps it was hastiness. According to his wife his notes were made in a rather curious way. 'He used to bring his Latin Catullus down to *table d'hôte* with him, and he used to come and sit by me, but the moment he got a person on the other side who did not interest him, he used to whisper to me "Talk that I may do my Catullus", and between the courses he wrote what I now give you.' Yet Lady Burton insists that Sir Richard's second thoughts were unreliable. '[He] would go on weakening his first copy by improvements and then appeal to me to say which was the best.' So perhaps it was just wrong-headed archaizing that led to this eccentric version:

> Hate I, and love I. Haps thou'lt ask me wherefore I do so.
> Wot I not, yet so I do feeling a torture of pain.

In point of accuracy most verse translations are inferior to the prose of F. W. Cornish in the Loeb volume (1913):

> I hate and love. Why I do so, perhaps you ask. I know not, but
> I feel it, and I am in torment.

That is a good guide to the Latin, and a prose version has scarcely any other justification. But when one is not restricted by metre there seems no point in changing the normal word order. 'Why I do so' is nearly right, but Catullus' *id* helps to establish the idea that the two feelings are contemporaneous and form, as it were, a single experience. 'I feel it' is inadequate, for it leaves out the important *fieri*, which asserts that the phenomenon is caused by something outside the poet's will: 'Perhaps you ask why I do it. I don't know, but I feel it happening.' Finally, even if all these points were set aside, the *tension* of the original, which is largely a function of metre, has been lost.

Returning to verse translations, we have the attempt by K. P. Harrington:[2]

---

[2] K. P. Harrington, *Catullus and his Influence* (London n.d.) 37.

I love and I hate! You ask how I can do it?
I know not, but feel it: in torment I rue it.

Like Moore, Harrington begins with love, but in Catullus our first impression is one of hatred. The rhythm is also unsatisfactory. As in Moore's version, the triple time has a trivializing effect, and in the first line we are almost obliged to stress 'how' rather than 'ask'. Harrington's couplet is instructive, however, in showing that there is no suitable rhyme for 'do it' and that in any case a feminine rhyme is too weak for the context. So if one insists on literal accuracy the natural word order may have to be inverted.

In 1939 E. A. Havelock published his influential book on Catullus, which contained several very accomplished versions.[3] He has this to say about *odi et amo*: 'These are the words of barest prose, and placed in prose order. The couplet indeed is scarcely poetry in the usual sense of that word...Its poetic power, if it has one, consists in defying the arts of poetry.' I do not want to comment on that judgement at the moment, except to say that the arts of poetry have to be rather narrowly defined if the epigram is to be excluded. Our immediate concern is with Havelock's version, which runs like this:

I loathe her and I love her. 'Can I show
How both should be?'
I loathe and love, and nothing else I know
But agony.

As this is called an imitation rather than a translation it does not claim to keep very close to the original. Yet it is interesting to see what has been preserved and what let go. Havelock has fastened above all on the conflict of emotions. To bring this out he has repeated the substance of his first sentence at the cost of omitting other features of the poem. The smooth sound betokens an ear sensitive to musical phrasing – and that is a valuable asset for someone writing on Catullus' lyric genius. But this is an epigram, and 'singability' is not the first requirement. So perhaps loathe/love should not have been chosen in preference to the ordinary antithesis of hate/love. There is, after all, no similar auditory relationship between *odi* and *amo*. Again, it is doubtful if the verbs should have been given an object. Granted, Lesbia is the person concerned, but she is not in the Latin, and to introduce her has the effect of diminishing the poet's self-absorption.

We then come to 'Can I show how both should be?' Here too the

---

[3] E. A. Havelock, *The Lyric Genius of Catullus* (Oxford 1939) 59.

original has been made into something more poetic. The rational, commonsense, quality of the question has been lost, and as a result the background of *ordinariness* (dull but practical), with which the poet's own experience is so poignantly contrasted, disappears. All this seems to indicate that, perhaps half consciously, Havelock set out to give the epigram a more lyrical colouring. His own version could certainly not be called prosaic. Finally, if 'I loathe and love' is to function as a repetition, adding weight and emphasis to the first line, ought it not to have the same syntax and prosody? As it is, the object has been dropped and the stress has been removed from 'and'. Nevertheless, Havelock's imitation is recognizably a poem, and that separates it from a great many competitors.

Although Havelock's book appeared in 1939, some of the pieces had been written earlier, and so his rendering of *odi et amo* probably belongs to much the same period as Horace Gregory's:[4]

> I hate and love.
>   And if you ask me why,
> I have no answer, but I discern,
> can feel, my senses rooted in eternal torture.

This is the first of our samples to move away from strict verse-forms, yet it has a degree of regularity in that each line carries one stress more than its predecessor. The writer seems to have acknowledged the greater weight of Catullus' pentameter and to have adjusted his form accordingly. No doubt he also intended 'dis*cern*' and 'e*ter*nal' (like '*I* hate' and '*I* have') to serve as auditory links. But apart from sound, 'discern' and 'eternal' have no business in the poem – not even on the principle of compensation; and the metaphor in the last line is hardly precise enough to render Catullus' meaning. No one would deny, however, that Gregory had made a serious attempt to reproduce Catullus' epigram in an intelligible form.

The same can hardly be said of Louis Zukofsky:[5]

> O th'hate I move love. Quarry it fact I am, for that's so re
>   queries.
> Nescience, say th'fiery scent I owe whets crookeder.

The theory behind this rendering is expressed as follows:

> This translation of Catullus follows
> the sound, rhythm, and syntax of his

---

[4] Horace Gregory, *The Poems of Catullus* (London 1956; first ed. 1931).
[5] C. and L. Zukofsky, *Catullus* (London 1969).

Latin – tries, as is said, to breathe
the 'literal' meaning with him.

A short inspection will show, however, that the translation of no. 85 only occasionally follows the sound and rhythm, and never the syntax. As for the 'literal' meaning, we may concede that a fairly high proportion of Catullus' letters are there, though not always in the same order. It is hard to know when Zukofsky thought of this idea. In *All the collected short poems 1923–1958* (p. 97) there is a perfectly intelligible version of Catullus no. 8 (*miser Catulle*). Perhaps as time went on Zukofsky became more and more concerned with those elements of a poem which do not convey information. In Poem 14 from *Anew* (published in '*A*' *13–21*, 1969) he writes:

> If number, measure and weighing
> Be taken away from any art,
> That which remains will not be much.

Excellent – one only wishes this ancient discovery had been more widely known in the last fifty years. But most readers of poetry, past and present, have taken the view that a poem is made up of number, measure, and weighing plus (not minus) sense. And therefore they would expect a translation of *odi et amo* to resemble neither on the one hand an excerpt from the railway timetable nor on the other a dream from the protracted slumbers of H. C. Earwicker.

We return to some more traditional versions. One, quoted by Postgate, is by a Mrs Krause:[6]

> I hate yet love. You ask how this can be.
> I only know its truth and agony.

That is undoubtedly neat, but the metrical form cannot be expected to contain much more than half the original. Catullus has thirty-two syllables, of which three are elided; Mrs. Krause has only twenty. The contrasts *faciam | fieri* and *nescio | sentio* have gone, and the proportions of Catullus' pentameter have been drastically altered. In the original, *nescio* (the failure of the intellect) takes up only one foot; the rest of the line is devoted to the heart's anguish. In the translation the two separate views have been conflated into one.

While using the same rhymes, Gilbert Highet avoided several of these pitfalls:[7]

---

[6] J. P. Postgate, *Translation and Translations* 78.

[7] Gilbert Highet, *Poets in a Landscape* (London 1957; Pelican 1959) 33.

> I hate and love. You ask, perhaps, how that can be?
> I know not, but I feel the agony.

'I hate and love' is better than 'I hate yet love', for in Catullus the two emotions are simply presented as co-existing. The paradox is not underlined; it inheres in the situation itself. Highet has wisely added an extra foot to the first line, which leaves room for Catullus' *fortasse*. And in the second line he has managed to keep the contrast between knowing and feeling. On the whole this is the most successful rendering I have seen. But Highet himself would readily admit that a few problems remained. The personal and positive action of *faciam* has been replaced by a vaguer expression, and the other contrasting word *fieri* has been omitted. 'I feel the agony' is slightly more artificial than *excrucior*, and also less exact in that the Latin verb looks back to *odi et amo* and sums up the poet's inner division: 'I am being pulled apart.' Finally there is the difficulty of rendering *nescio*. The word is maddeningly economical, carrying only a single stress. In an earlier period 'I know not' would have served well enough; in the twentieth century the inversion sounds a little too mannered. Yet any alternative, such as 'I don't know' or 'God knows', inevitably takes two stresses. The only way round this is to lengthen the line, e.g. as follows:

> I hate and love. Why I do it perhaps you wonder.
> I don't know, but I feel it, and it's tearing me asunder.

Since 'me' is unemphatic, the second line has still fewer stresses than the first, though it has three more syllables. One could argue, I think, that 'don't' and 'it's' are now inoffensive. (Certainly numerous examples could be quoted from reputable contemporaries.) And they could be taken as corresponding in some way to Catullus' elisions. Still, the second line is a bit too long, and we have also lost *fieri*. However, I can think of nothing better and pass the challenge over to the reader.

Horace, *Odes* IV.7

The first dated edition of Horace was produced by Antonius Zarotus of Milan in 1474. The editio princeps, however, probably appeared three years earlier. It, too, was once thought to have come from Milan, but Dibdin argued strongly for Venice,[8] and the British Museum has accepted this, attributing the edition to the Printer of Basilius. The first page of the *Odes*, *Satires*, *Ars Poetica*, and *Epistles* is in each case

---

[8] *Bibliotheca Spenceriana* II.64ff.

illuminated with gold and colours, and the first letter of every poem is similarly treated. The type, however, is not of high quality and there are numerous howlers in the text. In the present ode, for example, it gives *cum nimphis genibusque sororibus, frigora nitescunt,* and *praeter aeneas,* in addition to the false but intelligible reading *crastina uitae.* Over twenty editions appeared in Italy between this and 1500. As the renaissance moved across Europe, an edition was published in Paris in 1498 and twenty more followed before 1550. The first London edition of the works was that of William Norton in 1574, but apparently no translation was available until 1621, when a small selection of odes (not including IV.7) was translated by J. Ashmore. The earliest version of IV.7, as far as I know, was that of Sir Thomas Hawkins (1631).[9] I print it here, after the text, not merely *causa antiquitatis* but because of its agreeable fluency.

> Diffugere niues, redeunt iam gramina campis
> arboribusque comae;
> mutat terra uices, et decrescentia ripas
> flumina praetereunt;
> Gratia cum Nymphis geminisque sororibus audet   5
> ducere nuda choros.
> immortalia ne speres, monet annus et almum
> quae rapit hora diem:
> frigora mitescunt Zephyris, uer proterit aestas
> interitura simul   10
> pomifer Autumnus fruges effuderit, et mox
> bruma recurrit iners.
> damna tamen celeres reparant caelestia lunae:
> nos ubi decidimus
> quo pater Aeneas, quo Tullus diues et Ancus,   15
> puluis et umbra sumus.
> quis scit an adiciant hodiernae crastina summae
> tempora di superi?
> cuncta manus auidas fugient heredis, amico
> quae dederis animo.   20
> cum semel occideris et de te splendida Minos
> fecerit arbitria,
> non, Torquate, genus, non te facundia, non te
> restituet pietas;

---

[9] *Odes of Horace,* the best of lyric poets, contayning much morallity and sweetnesse (London 1631).

infernis neque enim tenebris Diana pudicum 25
    liberat Hippolytum,
nec Lethaea ualet Theseus abrumpere caro
    uincula Pirithoo.

Now snowes are quite dissolv'd, fresh grasse we see
To fields return'd, and leaves to every tree.
The earth with various change each season rankes,
And falling rivers glide within their bankes.
Aglaia naked dares upon the ground 5
With nimphes and her two sisters dance a-round.
Hope not in mortall things, the year doth say,
So warnes the hour that circumvolves the day.
Soft Westerne windes on Winter mildnesse bring,
Soone-wither'd Summer weareth out the Spring, 10
Then mellow Autume powres his fruits amaine,
And instantly dull Winter turnes againe.
Yet speedy Moones these heav'nly harmes restore,
But when we hence depart, where, gone before,
Rich Tullus, good Aeneas, Ancus stay, 15
We are but dust; like shadowes passe away.
Who knoweth whether the caelestiall powers
Will add to this dayes summe tomorrow's howers?
Your greedy heire in nothing shall have part
Of what you (living) gave with bounteous heart. 20
But when you once are dead, and powers divine
To you an equall sentence shall assign,
Nor bloud (Torquatus) then, nor fluent vaine,
Nor piety can life restore againe;
For neither chaste Hippolitus was free 25
By Dian set from hell's obscurity;
Nor for his deare Pyrithöus the paines
Of Theseus could dissolve Lethean chaines.

    The royalist diplomat Sir Richard Fanshawe published his translation of the *Odes* in 1652. Like Hawkins', his version of iv.7 rhymes AA, BB, CC etc., but it makes a bold attempt to follow Horace's alternation of long and short lines:

    The snows are thaw'd, now grass new cloaths the earth,
        And trees new hair thrust forth.
    The season's chang'd, and brooks late swoln with rain
        Their proper banks contain.

Neither Fanshawe nor anyone else, however, can convey the subtlety of Horace's trimeters. No spondees are admitted, and the dactyls often corroborate the idea of lightness or speed, as in *flumina praetereunt, quae rapit hora diem,* and *bruma recurrit iners.* (One remarks how frequently the trimeter contains some part of the verb.) The effect is partly one of repetition, in that the trimeters answer (more lightly) the first part of the hexameters, but also one of recovery, as in the rhythm of rowing or hauling up a boat.

A slightly different scheme again was employed by Thomas Creech, who brought out his translation in 1684, with a dedicatory epistle to Dryden:

> The snows are gone, and grass returns again,
>   New leaves adorn the widow trees,
> The unswoln streams their narrow banks contain,
>   And softly roul to quiet seas.

Creech was always better known for his translation of Lucretius. (And indeed when the poor man committed suicide some viewed it as a final attempt to remain faithful to his original.) The version of Horace was done when he was less than twenty-five years old; yet it must have satisfied the expectations of the period, for it went through six editions and was superseded only by that of Philip Francis in 1743.

Francis, the son of a Dublin rector, may claim to have been the most successful of all Horace's translators, in that his version remained in favour for over a hundred years. 'The lyrical part of Horace', wrote Dr Johnson, 'never can be properly translated; so much of the excellence is in the numbers and the expression. Francis has done it the best. I'll take his, five out of six, against them all.' Here it is:

> The snow dissolves, the field its verdure spreads,
> The trees high wave in air their leafy heads;
> Earth feels the change; the rivers calm subside,
> And smooth along their banks decreasing glide;
> The elder Grace, with her fair sister-train,   5
> In naked beauty dances o'er the plain.
> The circling hours that swiftly wing their way,
> And in their flight consume the smiling day –
> Those circling hours, and all the various year,
> Convince us nothing is immortal here.   10
>
> In vernal gales cold winter melts away;
> Soon wastes the spring in summer's burning ray;

Yet summer dies in autumn's fruitful reign,
And slow-pac'd winter soon returns again.
The moon renews her orb with growing light;   15
But when we sink into the depths of night,
Where all the good, the rich, the brave are laid,
Our best remains are ashes and a shade.

Who knows that Heaven, with ever-bounteous power,
Shall add tomorrow to the present hour?   20
The wealth you give to pleasure and delight,
Far from thy ravening heir shall speed its flight;
But soon as Minos, thron'd in awful state,
Shall o'er thee speak the solemn words of Fate,
Nor virtue, birth, nor eloquence divine,   25
Shall bid the grave its destin'd prey resign:
Nor chaste Diana from infernal night
Could bring her modest favourite back to light;
And hell-descending Theseus strove in vain
To break his amorous friend's Lethean chain.   30

A rhyming version that seeks to accommodate most of the meaning is
bound to be longer than the original. So it is no surprise that Francis,
although writing pentameters throughout, should still have two lines
more than Horace.

Johnson's own translation begins:

The snow dissolv'd no more is seen,
The fields and woods, behold, are green,
The changing year renews the plain,
The rivers know their banks again.

The translation as a whole is not quite so monotonous as this, though
the first seven lines all begin with the definite article. But most readers
would agree that the rhyming tetrameters produced too small and neat
an effect – Horace's longer line was, after all, basically the metre of
Ennius and Virgil. So here, for once, we are bound to find Dr Johnson
deficient in weight.

In the latter part of the nineteenth century several translations
appeared, including those of John Conington, Theodore Martin, Lord
Lytton, W. E. Gladstone and A. E. Housman. Their approach, which
may be termed traditional in as much as it involved regular foot-pat-
terns (e.g. 5:2 or 5:3 for the long and short lines) and strict rhyme-
schemes (AB, AB or AA, BB), has been continued in this century by Sir

William Marris, Hugh MacNaghten, Edward Marsh, and Lord Dunsany.[10] A different procedure was adopted by A. H. Clough, who unlike his Victorian contemporaries, abandoned rhyme and tried to reproduce Horace's quantities by means of stress. He has been followed in modern times by Leishman (1956), who defended the practice in his introduction, by Michie (1964), and to some extent by Clancy (1960).[11] Of these three, Clough allows the largest number of inversions, Clancy the fewest. But the main difference, as one would expect, is in diction. Here too, Leishman and Michie hold an intermediate position. For while Clough freely used forms like 'relaxeth', 'e'en now', and 'morn', which are now archaic, Clancy (in addition to his looser syntax) occasionally employs modern colloquialisms: his Grace 'takes her chances' (*audet*), his heir is 'sticky-fingered' (*manus auidas*), and he speaks of 'tomorrow's bonus of hours' (*crastina tempora*). In this respect Clancy looks forward to some of the more recent translators mentioned below.

The larger question of the hexameter's viability in English has often been debated. No doubt it is partly a subjective matter. Some readers *prefer* a translation to retain a slightly foreign flavour, and the many admirers of Rolfe Humphries' Ovid clearly find his metre no obstacle.[12] Translations apart, one can point to works like *Evangeline* and *The Bothie*, which had a high reputation in their day. And in modern times a beautiful poem like Betjeman's elegy *In Memory of Basil, Marquess of Dufferin and Ava* should discourage us from dogmatizing too heavily.[13] Nevertheless, to most English poets the hexameter has never sounded right, possibly because of 'the tyranny of stress in English, its very different syllabation, its glut of consonants, and the preponderance of monosyllables'.[14] It is also worth remembering that the Latin hexameter acknowledged both quantity *and* stress. So Horace's reader (however he pronounced the lines) was aware of *níues*, *rédeunt*, and *cómae*, as well as of *nĭuēs*, *rĕdĕūnt*, and *cŏmāe*. This double effect is impossible in English, and so when Clough writes:

> Fleeted and fled have the snows, to the field do the grasses
> return, as
> Unto the tree do the leaves;

---

[10] W. S. Marris (Oxford 1912); H. MacNaghten (Cambridge 1926);
E. Marsh (London 1941); Lord Dunsany (London 1947).

[11] J. B. Leishman, *Translating Horace* (Oxford 1956); J. Michie, *The Odes of Horace* (London 1964); J. P. Clancy, *The Odes and Epodes of Horace* (University of Chicago 1960).

[12] Rolfe Humphries, *Ovid, the Art of Love* (Indiana 1957) 105ff.

[13] *John Betjeman's Collected Poems* (London 1958) 138ff.

[14] J. P. Postgate, *Translation and Translations* (n. 1 above) 86.

> Earth thro' a change doth pass, her rivers smaller in volume
> Under the banks flow along

a rhythmic dimension has been lost.

Finally, in the last few years three versions have appeared in the periodical *Arion*. Of these Jay's (1974) is the most traditional in form, consisting of a five-stress followed by a three-stress line; the shorter lines are also linked by half rhymes, e.g. choir/hour, interred/inert, ours/heirs. Braun's version (1970), which contains some arresting imagery, is arranged in unrhymed quatrains usually with five stresses on the longer line and three on the shorter. McCulloch's (1970) is in free verse, but it partly makes up for the loss of rhythmic regularity by verbal inventiveness.

In 1930, speaking of the numerous versions of Horace's *Odes* in the British Museum, Pound said: 'You could probably make a fairly accurate graph of the development and changes of fashion in English verse style without using anything save this mass of translation.'[15] I wonder. In recent experience, at any rate, there has been a long time-lag between the poetic pioneers and the translators of Horace. As far as I know, the influence of Pound himself was negligible, at least until the 1960s. And in any given decade there may be several translators at work, each using a different strategy and idiom. The problems, however, remain very much the same; and we must now turn from this short and very general survey to consider what they are.

1. *Sense*. The initial *diffugere* is simple. Whether we acknowledge the prefix doesn't greatly matter, though 'in all directions' (Braun) gives a rather unnecessary emphasis and takes up valuable space. But strictly speaking *redeunt*, *mutat*, and *praetereunt* all describe a process, and therefore the correct English is 'are returning', 'is changing' etc. This is ignored by all the versions I have seen, except those of Dunsany and Leishman, and even they are not wholly consistent. Presumably the continuous tenses involve too many syllables, even for a rendering in free verse. The sound is perhaps another objection. At v. 3, seemingly for the first time on record, Horace uses *uices* as the object of a verb, and surprisingly the verb is *mutat*. The pleonasm is well rendered by Hawkins, but the earliest imitator of iv.7 – viz the author of the *Laus Pisonis* – wrote *ipsa uices natura subit* (145) – 'earth herself *undergoes* changes', and that is the sense given by most of Horace's translators.

The only real difficulty of interpretation (and it is a minor one)

---

15 Pound was writing in *Criterion* 9 (1929–30). The essay is reprinted in *Arion* 9 (1970) 178–87.

comes in v. 13. What is meant by *damna caelestia*? Commentators and translators are about equally divided. The simpler explanation is to say that the moon in her successive appearances (hence the plural) recoups the losses which she suffers in the sky, whereas once we vanish below the earth we never rise again. The other suggestion establishes a closer connection with the previous lines. Horace has just described the decay of the year as it moves through autumn to midwinter. Therefore when he says *damna tamen* he ought to be referring directly to that process. The *damna* are *caelestia* because each season has its own constellations, which set as the season passes. The sense, therefore, would be 'the moons (i.e. the months) quickly bring back the things which the sky loses (i.e. the constellations)'. In other words the *damna* are the losses suffered by the sky, not by the moon.[16] Those who, like myself, incline to the second theory can claim the authority of Housman. But since the truth is in doubt this is clearly not the kind of point on which a translation can be judged.

In other cases the truth is not in doubt, but accuracy is avoided for reasons of moral sensitivity. For *nuda* (6) Merivale in 1806 wrote 'in light attire'. Clearly he was ahead of his time. One likes to think he was the first man to put a skirt around the legs of his drawing-room sofa. A more serious point occurs at vv. 19–20, where many have balked at *amico animo*. Hawkins (above) rendered it as an ablative. So too Gladstone: 'Give! all thou giv'st with open hand away | escapes thy greedy heir.' Johnson put 'What with your friend you nobly share | at least you rescue from your heir.' Creech saw the meaning but couldn't quite bring himself to translate it: 'Whate'er is for thy greedy heir design'd | will slip his hands and fly away' (one wonders how). Fanshawe omitted the couplet altogether,[17] and in fact a well-known modern scholar has argued that the lines are spurious.[18] But surgery is a drastic remedy. Retaining the text, we must take *animo* as dative and explain the lines as providing the traditional advice always found in odes of this kind – viz 'enjoy life to the full'. But even though we bear in mind other expressions like *genio indulgere* and ψυχῇ χαρίζεσθαι, and remind ourselves that generosity to one's *animus* entailed generosity to one's friends, we may still feel that the intrusion of the greedy heir, a figure from satire and comedy, is something of a blemish.

16 See D. A. Kidd, *CR* 62 (1948) 13.
17 Fanshawe's version is printed in *Horace*, rendered in English and paraphrased by several persons, second ed. (London 1671) with a preface by A. Brome.
18 C. Becker, *Das Spätwerk des Horaz* (Göttingen 1963) 152ff.

2. *Additions.* Most additions are due to the demands of rhyme. Thus when Creech ends his first stanza with 'the unswoln streams their narrow banks contain, | And softly roul to quiet seas' the last line is all his own. It is, in fact, a beautiful line, and one can only regret the grammatical confusion which makes the accusative 'Streams' into the subject of 'roul'. A different, and more harmful, kind of addition is represented by Johnson's rendering of vv. 14–16:

> But wretched Man, when once he lies
> Where Priam and his sons are laid,
> Is naught but ashes and a shade.

The substitution of Priam and his sons for Aeneas, Tullus, and Ancus diminishes the Roman element in the poem (which is one of the features that distinguish it from 1.4); and the proportions suffer accordingly.

Sometimes the addition is a matter of association rather than words. There are no serious incongruities in any of the versions I have seen – none of those absurd allusions that turn Robert Graves' *Iliad* into a literary curiosity. But when Michie writes 'Great is the power of Diana', one may be momentarily distracted by the echo of the silversmiths' cry in *Acts* 19.28: 'Great is Diana of the Ephesians.' And if the echo lingers one may get a picture of the many-breasted fertility goddess – a very different figure from the virgin huntress. But this may well be hypercritical. Equally we should perhaps accept the ethos of McCulloch's last verse with its 'hell', 'redeem', 'heaven', and 'resurrect' on the grounds that the Christian associations are meant to enforce the pagan mythology rather than work against it.

3. *Image.* As the central idea is the contrast between the recurrent natural cycle and the non-recurrent human cycle, we should attend to *redeunt* (1), *recurrit* (12), *reparant* (13), and *restituet* (24). This simple point is very often ignored. More difficult is the problem of *decidimus* (14) and *occideris* (21). As the first word is frequently used of leaves, fruit, and flowers, one would like to consider 'fall'. The second is, of course, the regular word for the setting of the sun (*soles occidere et redire possunt*). Perhaps 'go down' is the nearest equivalent. *Comae* (2) also poses a problem in that it means both 'leaves' and 'hair' and so contributes to the quiet personification of nature. Fanshawe courageously chose 'hair'; Francis' 'leafy heads' is a clever compromise. Lytton tried 'locks' and Leishman quite recently put 'tresses'. But the metaphor is not really available at present, and most modern translators, not surprisingly, have settled for something else. Braun has 'wreaths to

trees' and McCulloch, more flamboyantly, 'a coronation of blossoming trees'. Before leaving *comae* we may note that, like *niues* and *gramina*, it is plural. Without offering an explicit military metaphor the number implies that a large host has (temporarily) made off and others have moved in to take its place. This effect is now impossible, because 'snows' and 'grasses' sound affected. Yet another impossibility is to find a phrase with the same connotations as *splendida arbitria* (21–2). Some translators (e.g. Creech and Johnson) omit the adjective. Others, perhaps wisely, sacrifice the secondary idea of brightness to the primary idea of solemnity; hence 'august verdict' (Michie), 'the stern assize and equal judgment' (Housman) and the even longer expansion of Francis (above). But McCulloch's 'blinding judgment' compels admiration; for if we ask *why* the judgement is blinding the answer can only be given in terms of its inexorable finality. The contrast with the surrounding darkness has also been noticed. Daring, however, can sometimes be taken too far. *Almum* (7) is indeed from *alere* 'to nourish', but to talk of the hour 'which tears | the teat of the morning away' (Braun) is too violent a departure from Horace's tone. Yet in translations of Horace crudity is a far less common fault than gentility. In *damna reparant lunae* (13) Horace used a plain expression drawn, like *summae adiciant* (17), from the world of commerce. This gave Creech no trouble – 'The Moon, 'tis true, her Monthly Loss repairs' – and Braun has 'New moons are quick to make good the losses....'. But many translators find the phrase too common, and contrive something more fancy instead, e.g.:

> But oh, whate'er the sky-led seasons mar,
> Moon upon moon rebuilds it with her beams.

So Housman.

4. *Juxtaposition*. Being an inflected language Latin can exploit this device in various ways. In *Odes* IV.7 *Zephyris uer* (9) expresses swift continuity, *hodiernae crastina* (17) suggests addition, *heredis amico* (19) indicates a contrast, and *Diana pudicum* (25) implies affinity. In the first passage Marsh has 'Zephyrs breathe warm on the frost; then Summer treads upon Spring.' Here the two references to spring are separated by winter and summer. Leishman is much closer: 'Chillness yields to the western wind, Spring's victim of Summer.' But 'Spring's victim' is rather inelegant and is apt to be taken initially as a possessive phrase. In the case of *hodiernae crastina* Braun gives the literal effect: 'add tomorrow to today's amount', but the stuttering 'to's' are un-

pleasant. Housman's 'add the morrow to the day' sounds like an evasion of the difficulty, as does Gladstone's 'grant a morrow for today'. Creech, though less close, emerges safely with 'and join to this another day'. As for *Diana pudicum*, Leishman cleverly notes the connection by writing: 'Chaste Diana has failed...to carry | chaster Hippolytus back.' But the Horatian effect cannot be produced without inversion, as in Housman's rendering: 'Night holds Hippolytus the pure of stain, | Diana steads him nothing'.

5. *Sound.* Even when we read the poem aloud we are probably unaware of certain sequences in its music, like *iam gram*ina *camp*is, *duc*ere *nuda*, pro*terit* aestas inter*itu*ra, and *dam*na *tam*en. These sound-groups enhance the ode's incantatory effect without contributing anything to the basic sense. Other groups do contribute, e.g. the long *e*'s in *ne spe-res* convey a sad solemnity, the *u*'s in *fruges effuderit* seem to express the abundance of the crops as they tumble from Autumn's cornucopia, and the sonorities of *non* Torquate genus, *non te* facundia *non te* largely account for the effect of that great tolling line. In such cases the most a translation can do is to supply some kind of analogous impression. Conington's rendering of vv. 23–4 deserves to be quoted:

> Not birth, nor eloquence, nor worth, shall burst
> Torquatus' tomb.

Michie is also admirable:

> No blue blood, no good deeds done, no eloquent pleading
> Ever shall conjure you back.

In the closing quatrain Horace has given us two rhyming couplets. In each case an epithet rhymes with its proper name; it also carries a special force in virtue of its final position. This force is well brought out by Clough: 'Pure tho' he be...Dear as he love him'. The very last words are *uincula Pīrĭthŏō*. That wonderful cadence not merely defeats the skill of this or that translator; it is beyond the resources of our language.

Ovid, *Amores* i.5

> Aestus erat, mediamque dies exegerat horam;
>   adposui medio membra leuanda toro.
> pars adaperta fuit, pars altera clausa fenestrae,
>   quale fere siluae lumen habere solent,

qualia sublucent fugiente crepuscula Phoebo   5
  aut ubi nox abiit nec tamen orta dies.
illa uerecundis lux est praebenda puellis,
  qua timidus latebras speret habere pudor.
ecce, Corinna uenit tunica uelata recincta,
  candida diuidua colla tegente coma,   10
qualiter in thalamos formosa Sameramis isse
  dicitur et multis Lais amata uiris.
deripui tunicam; nec multum rara nocebat,
  pugnabat tunica sed tamen illa tegi;
quae, cum ita pugnaret tamquam quae uincere nollet,   15
  uicta est non aegre proditione sua.
ut stetit ante oculos posito uelamine nostros,
  in toto nusquam corpore menda fuit:
quos umeros, quales uidi tetigique lacertos!
  forma papillarum quam fuit apta premi!   20
quam castigato planus sub pectore uenter!
  quantum et quale latus! quam iuuenale femur!
singula quid referam? nil non laudabile uidi,
  et nudam pressi corpus ad usque meum.
cetera quis nescit? lassi requieuimus ambo.   25
  proueniant medii sic mihi saepe dies.

Here we shall confine ourselves to three admirable versions,[19] taking
them one by one. The first is Marlowe's:

In summers heate, and midtime of the day,
To rest my limbes, uppon a bedde I lay,
One window shut, the other open stood,
Which gave such light as twincles in a wood,
Like twilight glimps at setting of the sunne,   5
Or night being past, and yet not day begunne.
Such light to shamefaste maidens must be showne,
Where they may sport, and seeme to be unknowne.
Then came Corinna in a long loose gowne,
Her white necke hid with tresses hanging downe,   10
Resembling faire Semiramis going to bed,
Or Layis of a thousand lovers sped.
I snatcht her gowne: being thin, the harme was small,
Yet strivde she to be covered therewithall,

---

[19] Rolfe Humphries' version is also very good, but the scope of this section
does not allow a discussion of it.

And striving thus as one that would be cast,   15
Betrayde her selfe, and yeelded at the last.
Starke naked as she stood before mine eie,
Not one wen in her bodie could I spie,
What armes and shoulders did I touch and see,
How apt her breasts were to be prest by me,   20
How smoothe a bellie under her waste sawe I,
How large a legge, and what a lustie thigh!
To leave the rest, all likt me passing well.
I clinged her naked bodie, downe she fell.
Judge you the rest, being tyrde she bad me kisse,   25
Jove send me more such afternoones as this.

Marlowe renders the first line very closely, though he does not step off so briskly as Ovid. In v. 2 there is a slight awkwardness in 'a' bed. Clearly it is the poet's own bed, but Marlowe is reluctant to put 'my,' having just used it with 'limbs'. In Latin, since there is no question about the ownership of the bed or the limbs, the possessive is naturally omitted. About Marlowe's 'window' (3) the modern reader can easily go wrong. I myself once assumed that the poet had been careless; for obviously it would make no difference to the light whether a glass window were open or shut, and certainly the effect would not be like that of sunlight filtering through a forest. But this is unfair, for in the sixteenth century 'window' could be used as the equivalent of 'shutter'. Towards the end of *Tamburlaine* Part 1.5.1 Marlowe himself has 'And shut the windows of the lightsome heavens'. Shakespeare writes 'Shuts up his windows, locks fair daylight out' (*Romeo and Juliet* 1.1.144) and 'Pluck down forms, windows, anything' (*Julius Caesar* 111.2.264); he also uses the word metaphorically in the sense of eyelid (*Romeo and Juliet* 1v.1.100 and *Richard III* v.3.129).[20] Marlowe's line is therefore entirely appropriate.

In v. 7 'must be shown' is not quite accurate. When Ovid says *praebenda* he means that a half light 'must be provided' for shy girls – a phrase which implies that the poet (tactful and experienced) has gone to some trouble to set the stage. 'Seem to be unknown' is also weak. What Ovid means, of course, is that in such a light the nakedness of a girl is not too harshly exposed. That meaning cannot easily be extracted from Marlowe. In a recitation some excitement could be imparted to 'Then came Corinna', but in Ovid the excitement is in the words themselves: *ecce, Corinna uenit*. (One notes the present tense.)

---

[20] See G. Tillotson, *Essays in Criticism and Research* (Cambridge 1942) Appendix 1 (by K. Tillotson).

Marlowe's v. 10 is an attactive line. It omits *diuidua*, but that scarcely matters, for Ovid is only saying (I think) that Corinna has a parting in her hair. Two braids or bunches would not conceal the neck and would be less in harmony with the simile that follows. In v. 13 Marlowe's syntax is not quite clear. In sense 'thin' refers to Corinna's gown, but grammatically it ought to go with 'harm'. The Latin expression involves a slight paradox. One wonders whether Ovid's first intention had been *nec multum rara tegebat* – 'Being thin it didn't conceal much.' He might then have altered the verb to *nocebat* to avoid the repetition with *tegi* (14) and to add an extra touch of cleverness. Marlowe's 'cast' (15) is more specific and lively than Ovid's *uicta*. The modern equivalent would be 'thrown', but the status and ethos of modern wrestling would make it inadvisable. Marlowe's rhymes in vv. 19 and 20 are below his usual standard; for 'touch and see' is an inversion of logic, and 'me' doesn't call for any stress – in fact the word is otiose. 'Down she fell' (24) is put in to supply a rhyme, and it brings with it a rather clumsy idea; for at this point Ovid is supposed to have his arms around the girl, and the *magister amoris* would never have lost his balance at such a vital juncture. The last line is good, though it omits the echo of v. 1 with which Ovid rounds the episode off.

Scholars regard Marlowe's *Elegies* as an early work; this has been made the basis of some adverse criticism. Tucker Brooke said they were 'characterized alike by boyish stiffness of expression, by metrical inexperience and defective scholarship'.[21] Such an unfavourable view is not borne out by the poem which we have just been discussing. And it is heartening to find that more recent writers, like J. B. Stearne,[22] speak about the *Elegies* with greater enthusiasm. They are, for one thing, an achievement of considerable originality. Other Ovidian works had been translated before by Golding (*Metamorphoses*), Turberville (*Heroides*) and Churchyard (*Tristia* I–III), but none of them had used the heroic couplet. This metre made heavy demands on the translator, for it supplied only ten feet where Ovid had taken eleven. But it was clearly a more suitable vehicle for the *Amores* than the lumbering fourteener, and Marlowe's success may be judged by the fact that Drayton, Heywood, Beaumont, Overbury, and Sandys all chose the same medium. The *Elegies* as a whole do contain some errors,[23]

---

[21] Tucker Brooke's edition of Marlowe p. 554.

[22] J. B. Stearne, *Marlowe* (Cambridge 1965).

[23] See F. S. Boas, *Christopher Marlowe* (Oxford 1940) 35. Marlowe's accuracy must, of course, be judged with reference to the text he was using – apparently that printed in Basle in 1568. See M. Maclure in The Revels edition of Marlowe's poems (London 1968) xxxiii.

but they are relatively few, and when the work is set beside other translations from the same period, which were conspicuous for exuberance rather than fidelity,[24] it is seen to be exceptionally close and conscientious. More important still, it is remarkably successful in catching Ovid's tone of sophistication and well bred ease, and in the case of the present poem one scholar goes so far as to say that 'in 1.5 Marlowe rises fully to Ovid's challenge, and there is no incident in Elizabethan love poetry of such lightness and immediacy'.[25]

Another version in couplets was written by a Mr Duke in 1748.[26] It is quite independent of Marlowe and has several very good points; but instead of printing it *in toto* I shall refer to it from time to time in connection with two modern translations. The first of these is contained in L. P. Wilkinson's delightful book *Ovid Recalled* (1955):

It was full noontide on a sultry day;
Taking siesta on my bed I lay;
One shutter closed, the other open stood,
Making a half-light much as in a wood,
Like the dim gloaming at the set of sun,
Or when night's gone but day's not yet begun:–
A light beloved of timorous girls and shy
That seek to veil their maiden modesty.

Sudden, Corinna comes: ungirt her dress:
On either side her neck a braided tress.
E'en so, methinks, into her chamber moved
Semiramis, or Laïs much-beloved.
I snatched the dress, so fine, it half revealed;
Though e'en with this she strove to be concealed;
Yet strove she not as one intent to win:
Easily, self-betrayed, she soon gave in.

So there she stood all naked to my gaze.
In all her body not one fault there was.
What shoulders and what arms I saw, I held,
What dainty nipples asking to be felt,
Beneath the shapely breast what belly smooth,
Hips large and beautiful, the thighs of youth!

---

[24] See C. Whibley in *The Camb. Hist. of Eng. Lit.* vol. 4, chap. 1 and F. O. Matthiessen, *Translation, an Elizabethan Art* (Harvard 1931).

[25] E. Jacobsen, *Translation: a Traditional Craft* (Copenhagen 1958) 186.

[26] Duke's version is printed in *Ovid's Epistles with his Amours*, translated by the most eminent hands (London 1748).

Why single out? No part but stood the test.
Her naked to my naked form I pressed.
All know the sequel. We relaxed in swoon.
O, oft may Fortune grant me such a noon!

It is evident that Wilkinson owes something to Marlowe; the first three couplets even have the same rhymes. But there is nothing in the least discreditable in this. The object, after all, is to produce the best possible translation of Ovid, and there is no reason why one should avoid certain rhymes just because they have been used by someone else; the choice in such matters is often limited. Moreover, apart from those places where Wilkinson has modified Marlowe's phrasing there are many others where he has thought the whole couplet out afresh. To see how independent he really is, one has only to compare Ben Jonson's treatment of *Elegy* 1.15.[27]

Another question arises: 'Is Wilkinson's really a *modern* translation? And can it be quite *genuine* if it isn't written in a contemporary idiom?' First, although rhyme may be unsuitable for the long continuous passages of satire and epic, there is a case for retaining it to render the elegiac couplet – particularly the Ovidian couplet where neatness and point are so essential. If that is granted, then the translator, having accepted the restrictions of the form, is also entitled to claim its licences. He may use inversions, abbreviations, and periphrases within the limits of discretion. But if he does, he must then avoid anachronisms; the twentieth century must be firmly shut out. The result ought to be something analogous to the best kind of reproduction, with all the skill, care, and respect which that term implies. And if anyone catches himself sniffing he may reflect that many a reproduction, whether a building, a cabinet or even a motorcar, will still look good long after our contemporary kitsch has been discarded. In brief, if Wilkinson sees Ovid as something akin to a seventeenth- or eighteenth-century gentleman, surely he has the right to present him as such instead of trying to turn him into a modern swinger.

To come to details. In the opening line Wilkinson reverses the time-words so as to obtain a more natural expression. (It seems that Ovid's order can be kept in English only if we retain the two co-ordinate sentences – 'it was summer, and the time was mid-day'. When the two ideas are combined into a single sentence we tend to put the particular before the general.) 'Sultry' is good and enables the setting

---

[27] Jonson's 'correction' of *Elegy* 1.15 is printed by Maclure in The Revels edition of Marlowe's poems.

to prefigure the episode that follows.[28] Duke allows this idea to get
out of hand:

> 'Twas noon, and I, scorched with the double fire
> Of the hot sun and my more hot desire,
> Stretched on my downy couch at ease was laid,
> Big with expectance of the lovely maid.

In v. 2 Wilkinson abandons Marlowe's literal rendering of *adposui
membra*, thus avoiding the problem of the repeated 'my'. None of the
translators tries to reproduce Ovid's *medio* – rightly, for it provides
only a strained and unwanted link with *mediam* (1), and it adds nothing
to the sense. Wilkinson's 'shutter' (3) is better than Duke's 'curtain',
for the slats contribute to the poem's lighting. In v. 4 Wilkinson is
closer than Marlowe to the original, but one is sorry to lose Marlowe's 'twinkles'. The principle of compensation involves risks, and
some translators will have nothing to do with it, but many would agree
with Rolfe Humphries when he says: 'If there are rare moments when
I think I can improve on [the author] and not violate his spirit, I must
not, out of modesty, refrain, for I shall already have weakened so many
passages that the debt is still all on my side.'[29] In v. 6 Wilkinson has
tidied up Marlowe's syntax and also given a smoother line by altering
the position and meaning of 'yet'.

In v. 10, where Marlowe sacrificed *diuidua*, Wilkinson decided to
forego *candida*. Admittedly the adjective has a rather indeterminate
function in that Corinna's neck is actually concealed by her hair. Yet
it's a pity to lose the word, for in a small way it assists the chiaroscuro
effect of the opening lines. (There is, of course, no colour.) 'E'en so,
methinks' (11) may sound rather too antique, but it is in fact very close
to the Latin *qualiter...dicitur*. And 'into her chamber' has the right
queenly tone for *in thalamos*. (Marlowe's 'going to bed' is rather
prosaic and perfunctory, more suited to a girl in a dressing-gown carrying a mug of Horlicks.) In obtaining this effect, however, Wilkinson
was obliged to omit Ovid's *formosa*. The phrase *multis Lais amata uiris*
(12) is hard. Marlowe, if I am not mistaken, has slightly vulgarized
it,[30] whereas Wilkinson is a shade over-romantic. But both are
superior to Duke:

28 In the *Metamorphoses* the woods at noon would be the setting for a less
agreeable kind of violence.
29 *On Translation*, ed. R. A. Brower (Oxford 1966) 66. The purist's point
of view is represented by D. G. Rossetti: 'Sometimes too a flaw in the
work galls him, and he would fain remove it...but no – it is not in the
bond' (Preface to his translations (London 1886) xv).
30 'Sped' carries the idea of an aim successfully achieved. 'Spread', the

So Lais looked when all the youth of Greece
With adoration did her charms confess.

In v. 25 Wilkinson's 'we relaxed in swoon' is a clear improvement on
Marlowe. For apart from being intrinsically feeble, 'she bade me kiss'
impairs the lovers' unison asserted by *ambo*. Duke is good here:

Thus intranced we lay
Till in each other's arms we died away.
O give me such a noon (ye Gods) to every day!

Finally, Wilkinson's 'noon' (26) echoes his opening 'noontide' in a
way which exactly reproduces Ovid's effect. The whole translation is
brilliant; and it is a measure of Wilkinson's dexterity that one can
rarely tell which of his rhyming words was decided on first.

Equally brilliant in a different way is the version of Guy Lee:[31]

Siesta time in sultry summer.
I lay relaxed on the divan.

One shutter closed, the other ajar,
made sylvan semi-darkness,

a glimmering dusk, as after sunset,
or between night's end and day's beginning –

the half light shy girls need
to hide their hesitation.

At last – Corinna. On the loose in a short dress,
long hair parted and tumbling past the pale neck –

lovely as Lais of the many lovers,
Queen Semiramis gliding in.

I grabbed the dress; it didn't hide much,
but she fought to keep it,

only half-heartedly though.
Victory was easy, a self-betrayal.

There she stood, faultless beauty
in front of me, naked.

reading of 01–2 in Fredson Bowers' numeration is more vulgar still.
That was the reading known to Pound. He also reads 'trellis' for 'tresses'.
Literary Essays ed. T. S. Eliot (London 1954, repr. 1963) 242.
[31] Guy Lee, *Ovid's Amores* (London 1968) 15–16.

Shoulders and arms challenging eyes and fingers.
Nipples firmly demanding attention.

Breasts in high relief above the smooth belly.
Long and slender waist. Thighs of a girl.

Why list perfection?
I hugged her tight.

The rest can be imagined – we fell asleep.
Such afternoons are rare.

In this free verse rendering Lee concentrates on the essential mood and image of each couplet. The result is wonderfully fresh. Ovid steps easily into the middle of the twentieth century – as an intellectual, perhaps, with private means and a good deal of free time. In the situation described here he has left the door of his apartment unlocked and is waiting for Corinna, who has taken the afternoon off.

Consciously or otherwise, Lee avails himself of Wilkinson's 'siesta' and 'sultry', but 'sylvan semi-darkness' is a phrase of real originality. There is also an effective Yeatsian ring about 'glimmering dusk'. But v. 6 illustrates that free verse is not quite so suitable for handling the Augustan antithesis. In this couplet Lee dispenses, as one would expect, with Ovid's personifications *fugiente Phoebo* and *timidus pudor*; the interesting thing is that Wilkinson and Marlowe have done the same. Duke comes closest to Ovid with 'when the sun flies away' (the end of an unpleasantly discordant line) and 'where shame may hope its guilty head to shroud'. The historian of morals will observe the dilution of *pudor* from 'shame' to 'modesty' to 'hesitation'. It is hard to gauge just where Ovid stands. 'Shyness' (an idea also used by Wilkinson and Lee) seems about right. The combination of *pudor* and *uerecundis* implies scruples which, in everybody's interests, have to be respected. But here we encounter an ambiguity; for if Corinna is as demure as all that, what is she doing in a loose diaphanous dress? (Lee's 'on the loose' is clever, but perhaps a bit too explicit.) Verses 7–8 could, of course, have been written tongue in cheek, but it is more likely that they represent a harmless fantasy in which Corinna is thought of as a girl who cannot be wholly taken for granted. If so, then Ovid's fantasy corresponds to Corinna's token resistance. Both are essentially tactical in nature.

Candidus always presents problems. We still talk of a fair skin and a fair complexion, but the useful alternative sense of 'pretty' has become old fashioned. Yet one has doubts about 'pale'. It was a favourite word at the end of the last century, but now it tends to sound a bit anaemic. There can be no similar doubts about the splendid 'tumbling'; it is more voluptuous than Ovid's *tegente*, but who cares? The inversion of vv. 11–12 is also defensible, as the queen provides a more fitting climax than the courtesan. The built-in gloss 'Queen Semiramis' partly makes up for the loss of *in thalamos*, and 'gliding' is admirable. But one may feel that 'lovely...Lais...lovers' is rather too aesthetic an effect for Ovid. In v. 16 the primary meaning of *non aegre* is no doubt 'without difficulty', but one can hardly exclude the secondary connotation 'without reluctance'. So the question of who really wins is left open. (The answer of course is both.) This cannot be conveyed in neat English. Even without the ambiguity translation is difficult. Lee's version involves rather an abrupt change of subject, while Duke requires an extra line:

> So I at last an easy conquest had,
> Whilst my fair combatant herself betrayed.

In v. 18 none of the translators is quite so gentle as Ovid. They all say 'naked', and Marlowe says 'stark naked'. The Latin phrase is *posito uelamine*, which deftly recalls *tunica uelata* (9). Ovid's description of Corinna inspired Duke to add a whole couplet of opulent appreciation:

> What snowy arms did I both see and feel!
> With what rich globes did her soft bosom swell!
> Plump as ripe clusters rose each glowing breast
> Courting the hand and suing to be pressed!

Great stuff, but more reminiscent of Rubens than Ovid. The word *castigato* (21) suggests the elegant shape given by an artist; so Lee's 'high relief' is very apt. In the final couplet Lee felt obliged to sacrifice *lassi*, and he had difficulty in finding a convincing modern equivalent for the optative *proueniant*. But 'rare', with its double function of 'few' and 'precious' is a brave effort.

This brief survey may help to clarify the old question of whether a poet's translator must himself be a poet. We can say at once that being a poet is no *guarantee* of success. A wrong-headed theory of translation (Zukofsky) will vitiate the enterprise from the beginning. So will a basic misunderstanding of the original's ethos – though one can point to exceptional cases like Fitzgerald's Omar Khayyam, where a misleading translation turns out to be an excellent poem in its own right. Again, a translator, in spite of being a poet, may through carelessness or bad luck fail to do justice to either the original or himself. Abraham Cowley (whatever estimate one may have of his work) was undoubtedly a poet. Yet his translation of *odi et amo* was undistinguished, especially in the second half:

> I hate, and yet I love thee too;
> How can that be? I know not how;
> Only that so it is I know;
> And feel with torment that 'tis so.

Finally, if the poet-translator is a writer of marked individuality and narrow range, he may do his best to render the spirit of his author and yet be unable to step off his own shadow. That, surely, is what happened with Housman. *Diffugere niues* appealed to him precisely because its melancholy was deeper and its exhortation fainter than in any other ode. He thought it the finest poem in the language. Yet, although his translation has been greatly admired (and indeed it has some beautiful lines), it does not provide a steady transmission of Horace's tone. The third stanza is perhaps the best; in the others, where Horace is plain Housman tends to be archaic-romantic, as in 'shaws', 'mead', 'unapparalled', 'tongue', 'friend' (as a verb), and 'steads'. As a result the version is not quite Horatian; nor does it represent the best of Housman.[32]

So it is not sufficient to be a poet. But what of non-poets? Are they doomed to failure? If by a 'non-poet' one means a man who has written little or nothing in the way of original verse, then as a general rule the prospects of such a man are not hopeful. Yet he may succeed in certain forms. In an epigram, for instance, he may have one bright idea, and that may be enough to see him through. Elegiac couplets are much harder, for there he must have a *succession* of bright ideas. Worst of all is a major lyric, where the complexity of sound, image, and thought is bound to reveal his deficiencies. In all this, however, we must avoid being trapped by our own terms. If someone produced a really successful translation of, say, Catullus no. 76 (*siqua recordanti*) or Horace III.29 (*Tyrrhena regum*), it would be irrelevant to ask what he had already written. The translation itself would be evidence of his talent. Such achievements, however, are bound to be rare. (We have seen a few examples.) Even for men of great poetic distinction the problems of translation remain formidable. As Dryden himself said: 'He who invents is master of his thoughts and words: he can turn and vary them

[32] Cf. B. Otis, 'Housman and Horace', *Pacific Coast Philology* 2 (1967) 5–24.

as he pleases till he renders them harmonious; but the wretched translator has no such privilege: for, being tied to the thoughts, he must
make what music he can in the expression.'[33] Let us agree, then, that in
return for his pains the translator is entitled to some tolerance, and
even gratitude. But not too much of either.

[33] Dryden, 'Dedication of the Aeneis', *Essays*, ed. Ker vol. 2, 232.

Index of writers, scholars, and translators

INDEX